HISTORY OF ASSAM RIFLES; WITH ILLUSTRATIONS AND MAP

HISTORY OF ASSAM RIFLES; WITH ILLUSTRATIONS AND MAP

By

COLONEL L.W.SHAKESPEAR

GYAN

Published by

Gyan Publishing House
5, Ansari Road
Daryaganj, New Delhi-110002
Phone: 011-47034999, 9811692060
E-mail: books@gyanbooks.com

Distribution Network
gyanbooks.com
India, USA, Canada, UK, Australia, France

ISBN: 978-81-212-0587-0 (HB)

Reprint in India, 2024
First Published, 2017

Printed at: Gyan Press, Delhi.

History of Assam Rifles: With Illustrations and Map
Author: Colonel L. W. Shakespear

HISTORY OF THE ASSAM RIFLES

Head-quarter Companies Naga Hills Military Police Battalion on Parade, 1897.

HISTORY OF THE ASSAM RIFLES

BY

COLONEL L. W. Shakespear
C. B., C. I. E.

WITH ILLUSTRATIONS AND MAP

Cultural Publishing House
18 D, Kamla Nagar, Delhi-110007

FOREWORDS

Colonel Shakespear has asked me to contribute a few words of introduction to his history of the origin and development of the Assam Rifles. I do so with pleasure, as I have still very grateful recollections of the resourceful strength with which this force endowed the Government of the province. The economic growth of Assam has been threatened with a peculiar danger—that of trans-frontier forays. Its two valleys run deeply into mountainous country that is inhabited by tribesmen who are still inspired by the ancient ideas that war is one of the most exhilarating of life's experiences, and its commemoration, in war-dress and war-dances, the most enjoyable of amusements. To possess the head of an alien man, woman or child has been a treasured assurance of success and a necessary passport to good fortune in courtship. Society is organised upon a war footing. "*Mutuo metu separati et montibus*," peoples of the same blood have grouped themselves into clans, isolated so completely from one another as to have developed languages that are mutually unintelligible. To ambuscade an alien village—even its women when drawing water from the stream—to burn its houses and massacre its inhabitants have been regarded as "sporting" enterprises that relieve the monotony of life. Forays into the lowlands have been still more tempting; and, had they not been checked, the development of the tea industry would have been impossible.

The most obvious method of stopping these marauding raids was by retaliatory incursions into tribal territory. For such small expeditions regular troops would have been too elaborate and costly an instrument, and have involved too serious commitments. The punishment that was required could be inflicted most rapidly and economically by a special Police Force led by Civil officers. So originated the Military Police that has developed into the five battalions of Assam Rifles. The knowledge that was acquired in the course of these expeditions naturally stimulated further exploration; and the influence which they begat took shape in such political control over the nearer villages as would protect the weak from being harried by their stronger neighbours. This influence could only be maintained by the occasional visits of British officers—very frequently at the risk of their lives. Holcombe, Butler and Damant were killed in the Naga Hills, Stewart and Browne in the Lushai Hills, Williamson in the Abor country. For the repression of the outbreaks in which they fell, it was necessary to undertake military expeditions in some strength, ending, in the case of the Naga and Lushai Hills, in the annexation of extensive areas of tribal territory. It was fortunate for the Government of the province that, on these emergent occasions, it could rely upon a garrison of regular troops that included three Gurkha regiments; and it was fortunate for the troops that they were assisted by trained police forces with special knowledge of the localities. The annexed territory was garrisoned by localised battalions of Military Police that were constituted and organised on the model of Gurkha regiments. This has, indeed, been the ideal of the Assam Military Police generally. There could not have been a better one.

The definite control which annexation involved relied very greatly upon the establishment of Military Police outposts, and upon tours of inspection, under Military Police escort, which kept the District Officers in touch with the people. To punish offending villages it was occasionally necessary to proceed in arms against them. And it was exceedingly difficult to confine government intervention rigidly within the limits of the annexed territory; for villages inside the boundary line were sometimes raided from the outside. Moreover, our officers could hardly ignore atrocities that were perpetrated just outside their jurisdiction: they could not stand unmoved on their frontier watching villages go up in flames, when by crossing a boundary stream they could stop this cruelty. By promptitude in action and steady pressure peace was gradually established throughout an area that was considerably larger than that originally annexed. Men who had been accustomed to decorate their houses with skulls felt almost content in using pumpkins for this purpose; and so, instead of raiding villages of the open country, they commenced to trade with them. Schools were opened. The tribesmen are by no means lacking in intelligence, and the children could show quite remarkable aptitude in learning arithmetic. The civilising influence of Christian missionaries spread to the interior, and in one district—the Lushai Hills—an astonishingly large proportion of the people have accepted Christianity. Progress was interrupted by the Kuki insurrection of 1917, which required a large Military Police force for its suppression. But this disturbance was due to a special cause—the recruitment of labour for service in the Great War—and there is little reason to suppose that it was a protest against the normal activities of the Government. It is true, no doubt, that, if released from control, some of the tribesmen would revert to their head-hunting. There is a craving for some excitement to relieve the dulness of habitual routine. But war is not the only means of procuring it. Detachments of Military Police in the course of their rounds have been known to drop their official dignity and "let themselves go" in organising games for the entertainment of the people. They are proud of their battalion sports, and in time may be able to bring home to the village braves that one can gain almost as much excitement in football and hockey as by harrying a village and massacring its inhabitants.

The task of pacifying and humanising these primitive hill people would have been impossible had there not been at the command of the Civil Government a trained and armed force which could be employed in small detachments, could be rapidly set in movement and could make shift with a minimum of transport. These have been amongst the distinctive features of the Assam Military Police. The province is very largely indebted to regular troops for its expansion. But the experiences of the Mishmi campaign of 1899 and of the Abor campaign of 1912 have shown that the employment of regular troops for the making of punitive expeditions into the hills may result in a very large expenditure with quite incommensurate results.

The Military Police have now attained a higher status as the Assam Rifles, and have in great measure replaced the military garrison of the province. This leaves the position unchanged, viz. that they are under the orders of the Civil Government, and can be set in action without the formalities and delay that are involved in a recourse to the Military Department of the Government of India. And they will, no doubt, retain the easy mobility which has rendered their services so effective in the past. In 1904 there were threats of disturbance in the State of Manipur. Troubles, which might have had serious developments, were arrested by the prompt arrival of the Naga Hills Military Police: a strong detachment put itself on the march immediately on the receipt of orders and covered a distance of 88 miles in three days—an achievement which received the Viceroy's special commendation. The chief difficulty in the hills is that of transport. In old days men carried their own rations. Coolies are now gathered together for this purpose. But so long as it is realised that demands for transport must be kept at the lowest possible figure, the Assam Rifles will retain their credit for resourceful mobility.

BAMPFYLDE FULLER.

THIS history already has a Foreword written by my former Chief, Sir Bampfylde Fuller, but Colonel Shakespear has asked me to add a word from one who has been long and closely associated with the Assam Rifles. I do this with extreme pleasure, as it enables me to pay two tributes, one to the officers and men of the Assam Rifles, and the other to the author of the history.

Few can have had my opportunities of judging the quality of the Force which I have known throughout my thirty-four years of service. For some five years I held charge in succession of two districts, at the headquarters of each of which was a battalion of Military Police. Both battalions furnished me from time to time with escorts on trans-frontier tours—some peaceful, some warlike. Both were ever ready to meet at the shortest notice any call made on them. Later on, as a Collector and a Commissioner in Eastern Bengal, I had occasion to admire the discipline of the men and the tact and forbearance shown by the officers of detachments sent down to assist in keeping the peace in times of seditious trouble, under conditions outside all experience. Later still I saw the same qualities displayed during the railway strike of 1921 and the promenade of 1922. I witnessed the honourable part played by all the battalions so far as opportunity was afforded them in the Great War—a part which the history sets forth in language eloquent in its simplicity. The Assam Rifles have a fine record of arduous undertakings on the North-eastern Frontier of India, now for the first time made available. The spirit that carried Lieut. Eden and his little band to success in 1855 still animates them, and obstacles as great as those which attended the capture of Kaisha in his mountain stronghold have been surmounted in more recent days with too often none to chronicle the feat.

Colonel Shakespear's book goes far beyond its modest title, for not only does it record the history of the Assam Rifles, but it covers the gradual pacification of Assam since the British Power was first compelled to interfere in its affairs, and closes with a chapter on the ancient ruins of historical interest to be found in various parts of the Province. To him are due in special measure the thanks of the Government for his services, first as Commandant of the Naga Hills Battalion, which in his time was easily the most efficient in the Province, and, secondly, as Deputy-Inspector-General, a post which he was peculiarly well fitted to occupy.

W. J. Reid.

PREFACE

In compiling this history of the five battalions of the Assam Rifles, in one of which I had the honour of serving as Commandant thirty years ago, to be in later years followed by being appointed Deputy-Inspector-General to the Force, I have endeavoured to search all available documents and books from the early days of Assam under British rule onwards for material with which to form it, and have arranged it as far as possible in proper sequence. Sometimes information has been turned up in most unlikely places; for instance, who would have thought that the best account of Col. Hannay's Abor Expedition in 1859 could have come out of the "History of the Indian Navy"? But so it was, and due to the fact that in early days the Indian Navy had a few gunboats on the main rivers, two of which were on the Brahmaputra river at Dibrugarh, and sent a naval contingent with Hannay's force. Again the "History of Indian Railways" (Assam section) gave accounts of Frontier Police escorts to railway survey parties which were not alluded to anywhere else, for prior to about 1899 no such thing as Battalion Records were kept up. Many episodes of the consolidation of British rule east of Bengal have been derived from old musty records and books and are brought out as a connected narrative, trouble having been taken to get as true and complete a history of this little known old Force, without embellishment or drawing on the imagination, in spite of Bacon's statement that "the mixture of a lie doth ever add pleasure."

I am most grateful to the Commandants of the Assam

Rifle Battalions for assistance given me in their extracts from their Battalion Records, and to the Inspector-General of Police for kindly allowing me the use of numerous notes on the internal economy of the Force and other matters, without all of which this history would have been incomplete. My hearty thanks are also given to Col. J. Shakespear, C.M.G., C.I.E., D.S.O., who kindly helped me in a large measure with a great portion dealing with the Lushai Hills, of which he was Superintendent for many years, and to Major A. Dallas Smith, M.C., lately Commandant 4th A.R., who went through most of the work in the rough and assisted with corrections and useful suggestions.

In the earlier years of the province the Frontier Police being one body, they are dealt with as such until the 'sixties, when this body was divided into territorial units, as it were. From then onwards to the Great War separate chapters deal with the life and doings of each individual unit or Military Police Battalion, as they came to be designated on the reorganisation of the Frontier Police and border defence in 1882. From 1914 on the history deals with the Force as a whole, for its activities in this last period embraced detachments from all battalions.

The Assam Rifles, whose units have recently been affiliated with the different groups of Goorkha regiments of the Indian Army, have had, as will be seen in these pages, a career of not far short of a century, full of arduous undertakings and borderland service connected with their duties as Wardens of our long N.-E. Marches of India. They have taken their share in the heat and burden and stress of every expedition officially recognised as such or otherwise, labours which formerly have too frequently passed unnoticed, and in spite of the recent depletion of their ranks, due to temporary economic reasons, it is pleasant to read the remarks of the Governor of Assam in the last Police Review for 1925. These run: "Notwithstanding the reduction in the complement of British officers and men and the undue strains consequently placed on the remainder of the battalions, the Force surpasses its former high standard of efficiency. Generally the last year's record (1924) has been one with which officers and men have every reason to be satisfied, and the Governor-in-Council congratulates the several Commandants who have succeeded in spite of difficulties in maintaining the high traditions of the Assam Rifles."

Floreant custodes terminorum Imperii nostri.

BIBLIOGRAPHY

Mackenzie's "North-eastern Frontier of Bengal."

Assam Gazetteers.

Grange's "Expedition into the Naga Territory of Assam."

Eastern Bengal Gazetteer (Chittagong Hill Tracts).

"History of the Sylhet Light Infantry" (now the 8th Goorkha Rifles).

Butler's "Sketches in Assam, 1855."

Butler's "Life and Adventures in Assam, 1857."

Colonel Lewin's "A Fly on the Wheel."

Dr. Brown's "Manipur, 1870."

Lectures on Assam at the Society of Arts by Sir Charles Lyall, 1903.

Lectures on Assam at the Society of Arts by Sir Henry Cotton, 1900.

General Sir James Johnstone's "My Experiences in Manipur and the Naga Hills, 1886."

Moore's "Twenty Years in Assam."

Gait's "History of Assam."

Rev. Endles' "History of the Cacharis."

Indian Army Transport on the N.-E. and E. Borders by Major G. H. C. Livesay.

Lord Roberts' "Forty-one Years in India."

"The Lushai Expedition, 1871–72," by Captain Woodthorpe.

Report on the Mishmi Expedition 1899–1900, by Captain G. Ward.

J. H. Hutton's "Angami Nagas."

Old Indian Office Records.

"The Chin Lushai Expedition 1889–90," by Col. A. S. Reid, I.M.S.

Col. J. Shakespear's Diaries in the Lushai Hills, 1888–96.

Papers sent by the Inspector-General of Police, Assam.

Information *re* Aijal and the N. Lushai Hills supplied by Col. Loch.

Frontier and Overseas Expeditions.

Diaries of the Superintendent South Lushai Hills, 1890–97.

Cardew's "Services of the Bengal Army."

Dr. McCosh's "Account of the extreme N.-E. and E. Frontiers of India, 1840."

"History of Indian Railways" (Assam section).

"History of the Indian Navy."

"History of Bengal."

Information collected and sent me by the different Assam Rifles Commandants.

Gazette of India, July, 1890.

Letters of the Political Officer, North Lushai Hills.

Surridge's "Romantic India."

R. G. Woodthorpe's "Survey Operations in the Naga Hills, 1877."

R. G. Woodthorpe's "Lushai Expedition, 1871–72."

CONTENTS

	PAGE
FOREWORDS	v
PREFACE	xi
BIBLIOGRAPHY	xv
CONTENTS	xvii
LIST OF ILLUSTRATIONS	xxi

CHAPTER I

General information from 1824 to 1839—The province of Assam in early days—Its progress—Protection—Early frontier line—Armed civil police—Raising of the old Cachar Levy and the Jorhat Militia—Their duties, posts, etc. on the Nowgong border—Sylhet and Cachar—Khasia and Jaintia Hills—Description of frontier posts—Mr. Grange, first Commandant of the Cachar Levy—Naga and other tribes 1

CHAPTER II

General, 1839 to 1850—Grange's first expedition—His visit to Samaguting and Dimapur—Grange's second expedition, 1840—Seriously attacked near Togwema—Lieut. Bigge opens market at Samaguting, 1842—Nagas raid Hosang Hajoo post—Retaliation—Major John Butler—North Cachar Hills rebellion, 1841 to 1844—Asaloo—The Lushai border—Blackwood's first expedition, 1844—Lister's expeditions, 1847 and 1849—Samaguting post established, 1848—The Levy's uniform—Communications — Bogchand at Samaguting — Captain Vincent's expedition, 1849 to 1850—He and Major Foquett attack Khonoma—Fight at Kekrima—Passive policy and Nowgong frontier drawn back—Cachar Levy split into two portions—The Garo Hills 16

CHAPTER III

PAGE

General, 1825 to 1864—Tribes and expeditions on borders north of the Brahmaputra river—The Bhutan war—The Akas—The Daphlas—The Abors and Sadiya—Lowther's and Hannay's expeditions, 1858 and 1859—The Mishmis—Eden's exploit, 1855—Hkamtis and Singphos—Neufville's and Charlton's expeditions—Nagas of the Sibsagor hinterland . . . 33

CHAPTER IV

General, 1860 to 1870—Synteng rebellion, 1862—Shillong—Frontier Police recruiting Depot at Sylhet—Forward policy once more—Gregory at Samaguting—Captain Butler—Change in Nowgong F.P. uniform—Sanction for post at Wokha refused but established 1875—Settlement of Manipur boundaries—Survey work—Butler killed at Pangti—Proposed and sanctioned reorganisation of F.P. units—Matter delayed by Naga rising 1879/80—Military Police Battalions come into being 1882/83—Changes in uniform—First commandants 49

CHAPTER V (1st Assam Rifles)

1863 to 1869. The Surma Valley Frontier Police raised, 1863—General Nuthall's expedition into Lushai Hills, 1868—The Chittagong border and armed Civil Police—Exploration of the Koladyne river, 1848—The Mutiny, 1857—Proposed road connecting with Burma—Early expeditions in the Chittagong Hill Tracts—Lewin and the Arrakan Police on the Koladyne river, 1865—Chittagong Frontier Police organised, 1866—Its frontier posts 58

CHAPTER VI

1869 to 1872. Surma Valley F.P. and Chittagong F.P., *continued*—The expeditions of 1871 and 1872—Chittagong frontier advanced to Demagiri—New arrangement of border posts—Old firearms of Lushais and Naga tribes—Primitive methods of making gunpowder—Difficulty of the country—Rebellion in North Cachar Hills district, 1882 67

CHAPTER VII

1872 to 1890. Surma Valley and Chittagong F.P., *continued*. Survey work on the Chittagong border—Lieut. Stewart's

PAGE

massacre, 1888—General Tregear's expedition—Lung Leh post established—Subadar Major Jitman Gurung—General Tregear's second expedition, 1889/90—Col. Skinner's column—Flying Column to Haka 82

CHAPTER VIII

1890 to 1924. Surma Valley M.P. and South Lushai Hills M.P., *continued*—North Lushai Hills rising, 1890—Its suppression—South Lushai Hills formed into a district, 1891—Composition of Chittagong M.P.—Troubles in the southern hills—Fort Tregear burnt down—Aijal under Col. Loch—Missionary enterprise 95

CHAPTER IX (2nd Assam Rifles)

1859 to 1910. The Lakhimpur F.P., 1864—Lakhimpur Military Police Battalion—Sadiya—Holcombe's disaster, 1875—Aka expedition, 1883—Lushai expedition, 1891—Abor expedition, 1894—Railway surveys and escorts—Mishmi expedition, 1899—New posts—Strikes 111

CHAPTER X

1910 to 1924. The Lakhimpur M.P., *continued*—Abor expedition, 1911/12—Lohit Valley road work and Mishmi survey escorts, 1912 and 1913—Minor expeditions into the Abor and Mishmi Hills, 1914—The Great War and the Kuki rebellion—Riots in Behar—Daphla expedition, 1918—New lines completed at Sadiya, 1919—Elapoin punitive tour, 1920—Sedition and strikes, 1920 to 1922—Rampa State rebellion, 1924 . . . 125

CHAPTER XI (3rd Assam Rifles)

1862 to 1881. The Naga Hills Frontier Police—Change in uniform—Survey work—Fight at Wokha, 1874—Butler killed, 1875—Wokha post established—New roads—Mozema expedition, 1877—Kohima sanctioned as headquarter station—Naga rising, 1879—Siege of Kohima and assault of Khonoma 141

CHAPTER XII

1881 to 1889. The Naga Hills M.P., *continued*—Reorganisation—Change of uniform—Pipers and band—Rifle range—Escorts to tours—Political control areas—Trans-Dikkoo expedition, 1887—Mongsemdi massacre and expedition, 1888/89—Ao Naga country taken over 158

CHAPTER XIII

PAGE

1889 to 1892. The Naga Hills M.P., *continued*—Ao Naga country taken over—New roads—Battalions strength increased—Somra tour, 1890—Manipur rebellions, 1891 170

CHAPTER XIV

1894 to 1924. The Naga Hills M.P., *continued*—Abor expedition, 1894—Patkoi railway survey, 1896—Band replaces pipes—Trouble on the A and B Railway construction, 1898—Trans-Dikkoo tour and Yachumi affair, 1900—Camp of exercise, 1901—Murder of Sergt. Tolley—New class composition—Duty in aid of Civil power, 1907—Makware expedition, 1911—Tour in Taniok area, 1911—Abor expedition, 1911—Mishmi and Lohit Valley escorts, 1911/12 and 1912/13—Chinlong expedition, 1912—Aka expedition, 1913—The Great War—The Kuki rebellion, 1917/19—Aid to civil power, 1920/22—Rampa State Column, 1924 182

CHAPTER XV

1913 to 1924. Further increases to the Assam Military Police—Raising of two new battalions, the Darrang Battalion (4th A.R.) and the 5th A.R., in 1913 and 1920, respectively 201

CHAPTER XVI

The Kuki and the South Chin Hills rebellions, 1917 to 1919 . . 209

CHAPTER XVII

The Kuki and South Chin Hills rebellions, *continued* 224

CHAPTER XVIII

General items of information—Interior economy of the Force, pay, rationing, recruiting, signalling, etc.—The province of Eastern Bengal and Assam—Increase in strength—The Great War—The strikes and riots from 1920 to 1922—Expedition to the Rampa State (Madras)—Conclusion 239

CHAPTER XIX

Points of local interest connected with the areas of certain A.R. battalions 256

APPENDICES 274

INDEX 295

LIST OF ILLUSTRATIONS

FACING PAGE

HEAD-QUARTER COMPANIES NAGA HILLS MILITARY POLICE BATTALION ON PARADE, 1897 . . *Frontispiece*

OLD-TIME REST-HOUSE ON THE BRAHMAPUTRA RIVER, 1894 4

TYPES OF DEFENSIVE POSTS ON THE ASSAM BORDERS:

THE OLD MASONRY BLOCK HOUSE AT DIKRANG, NEAR SADIYA 13

STOCKADED POST AT MONGSEMDI—NAGA HILLS . 13

A FRONTIER POLICE CONSTABLE (GOORKHA) 1877 . . 23

TYPES OF TRIBESMEN ON THE ASSAM BORDERS:

ABORS 43

KUKIS 43

A MISHMI WARRIOR 46

TWO VIEWS OF SHILLONG 49

THE COUNTRY ABOUT CHERRAPOONJI 50

ANGAMI NAGA 54

TRANS-DIKKOO NAGAS 54

A VIEW IN THE LUSHAI HILLS (CHAMPHAI VALLEY) SHOWING HILL SIDES DENUDED OF FOREST FOR "JHOOMING" PURPOSES 70

GROUP OF LUSHAIS 73

RANGAMATTI IN 1888 76

COUNTRY BOATS ON THE KORNAPHULI RIVER USED FOR THE EXPEDITION, 1889–90 76

MAJOR T. LEWIN'S MEMORIAL AT DEMAGIRI . . . 79

CORNER IN THE FOREST NEAR DEMAGIRI—LUSHAI HILLS . 79

FACING PAGE

BAMBOO HUTS BUILT AT DEMAGIRI BY THE FRONTIER POLICE 87

FRONTIER POLICE LEAVING LUNG LEH STOCKADE FOR A TOUR, CARRYING THEIR OWN KITS, 1889 . . 88

OLD STOCKADE AT LUNG LEH, 1890 88

RAFTS ON THE KLONG RIVER BEING LOADED FOR THE NORTHERN COLUMN 94

PASSING BOATS BY HAND THROUGH THE BURKUL RAPIDS, KORNAPHULI RIVER 94

FORT TREGEAR ON THE LUNG LEH—HAKA ROAD . . 99

A CHIEF OF THE SOUTHERN LUSHAI HILLS (MĀMTE) . . 102

ONE OF COLONEL LOCH'S REST HOUSES (NEIDAWN) IN THE NORTHERN LUSHAI HILLS 106

TUIPANG STOCKADE AND DETACHMENT (1ST A.R.) . . 107

LUNG LEH RIDGE FROM THE CIVIL OFFICER'S HOUSE . 109

CIVIL OFFICER'S HOUSE AT LUNG LEH 109

THE 1ST A.R. QUARTER GUARD AT AIJAL 110

THE PARADE GROUND AT AIJAL, DUG OUT BY MAJOR LOCH AND HIS MEN 110

THE STOCKADE AND PICQUET POST AT GELEKI . . 114

GROUP OF LAKHIMPUR FRONTIER POLICE, 1887 . . 114

AN ABOR CANE BRIDGE 122

CONVOY CROSSING A STREAM 128

THE STOCKADED POST AT MISHING—ABOR HILLS . . 128

THE LOHIT RIVER AT TAMEI GHAT 134

DETACHMENT 2ND A.R. AT YAMBUNG POST—ABOR HILLS . 134

SACRED POOL OF BRAHMA KHUND ON THE LOHIT RIVER . 136

SOME TYPES OF TRIBAL WEAPONS (IN COLOUR) . . 142

KHONOMA VILLAGE, LOOKING NORTH 147

ENTRANCE TO HENEMA POST—EARTHWORK . . . 147

VIEW IN THE BARAIL RANGE ABOVE KHONOMA . . 155

THE ZULHEIN VALLEY NEAR PAPLONGMAI . . . 155

TERRACED CULTIVATION IN THE ANGAMI COUNTRY . . 156

AN AO NAGA WOMAN 161

AO NAGA HOUSES 162

FACING PAGE

THE GREAT MORANG OR GUARD HOUSE AT MASUNGJAMI . 162
HEADMEN OF MASUNGJAMI 167
VIEW IN A SEMA NAGA VILLAGE 167
THE FIRST HOUSE IN THE JUNGLE WHERE THE IMPORTANT JUNCTION OF LUMDING NOW STANDS, 1898 . . 184
VIEW OF MOKOKCHANG IN THE AO NAGA HILLS . . 190
KONYAK (TANTOK) NAGAS FROM ACROSS THE DIKKU RIVER 193
KOHIMA PARADE GROUND 199
CAPT. W. B. SHAKESPEAR, CAPT. ABIGAIL (ARM IN A SLING), SUBADAR-MAJOR JAMALUDDIN AND INDIAN OFFICERS, 3RD ASSAM RIFLES, 1921. 199
GROUP OF INDIAN OFFICERS 4TH ASSAM RIFLES, 1922 . 204
THE TAMENGLAO STOCKADED POST, MANIPUR HILLS . 204
A DAPHLA WARRIOR 208
STOCKADED POST ON THE DAPHLA BORDER (5TH ASSAM RIFLES) 208
A CANE BRIDGE IN THE KUKI HILLS 211
PRESENT DAY RESIDENCY AT IMPHAL, MANIPUR . . 211
COOTE'S AND HIBBERT'S COLUMNS AT IMPHAL, READY TO MOVE OUT 216
ATTACK AND BURNING OF LONGYIN VILLAGE . . . 217
COOTE AND HIGGINS INSIDE THE MOMBI STOCKADE . 217
COOTE'S COLUMN HALTED AT THE TUYANG RIVER . . 224
THE D.I.G.'S OF BURMA AND ASSAM WITH COLUMN COMMANDERS AT TAMMOO, MARCH 1918 . . . 224
GATEWAY OF HEAVY SWINGING TIMBERS AT THE KAMJONG STOCKADE 226
CAPTURE OF A KUKI BREASTWORK IN THE CHASSADH HILLS 226
CAPTAINS PARRY AND BLACK BUILDING THE STOCKADE AT POSHING IN THE CHASSADH HILLS 234
TANKHUL NAGAS 234
TANKHUL WAR DRUM 234
CAPTAIN MONTIFIORE'S COLUMN CROSSING THE UPPER BOINU RIVER IN THE SOUTHERN CHIN HILLS . . . 236
THE FIRST BATCH OF KUKI REBELS TAKEN IN ACTION IN THE JAMPI AREA 236

FACING PAGE

RUINED MONOLITHS AT DIMAPUR AS FIRST SEEN . . 257

THE SAME AS RESTORED TO ORIGINAL POSITIONS AND REPAIRED IN LORD CURZON'S TIME, 1902 . . . 257

RUINED GATEWAY IN THE ANCIENT CACHARI FORT AT DIMAPUR 258

ONE OF THE LARGE EXCAVATED TANKS AT DIMAPUR, IN THE NAMBHOR FOREST 258

THE "STONEHENGE" AT TOGWEMA 261

HUGE MONOLITH AT MARAM 261

THE SERPENT PILLAR AT SADIYA 267

ANCIENT HINDOO TEMPLES AT SIBSAGOR . . . 268

RUINS OF THE PALACE OF EARLY AHOM KINGS, AT GARHGAON, NEAR SIBSAGOR 268

STONE STATUES DUG UP AT MAIBONG, IN THE NORTH CACHAR HILLS 269

HUGE BOULDER AT MAIBONG, THE UPPER PART OF WHICH IS CARVED INTO A TEMPLE 269

INSCRIBED STONES DUG UP AT MAIBONG . . . 271

STATUE DUG UP AT MAIBONG 271

SKETCH MAPS

I. THE PROVINCE OF ASSAM . . *At end of Volume*

II. *THE LUSHAI HILLS . . . . . " "

III. *THE SADIYA AND LAKHIMPUR AREA . " "

IV. *THE NAGA HILLS DISTRICT . . " "

V KHONOMA AND ITS DEFENCES, 1879 . " "

VI AREA OF THE KUKI OPERATIONS . . " "

* Showing movements of principal expeditionary columns.

HISTORY OF THE ASSAM RIFLES

CHAPTER I

General information from 1824 to 1839—The province of Assam in early days—Its progress—Protection—Early frontier line—Armed civil police—Raising of the old Cachar Levy and the Jorhat Militia—Their duties, posts, etc. on the Nowgong border—Sylhet and Cachar—Khasia and Jaintia Hills—Description of frontier posts—Mr. Grange, first Commandant of the Cachar Levy—Naga and other tribes.

THE object of this book being to trace from its starting point the history of the force formerly known as the old Military Police of Assam, but now as the Assam Rifles of five Battalions, and to record its services in border defence among strange wild tribes, it will be necessary to describe briefly Assam as it was when it came under British rule a century ago and its development as seen in the present day. Thus the various vicissitudes of the force under the gradually improved conditions in this far-off corner of India may be the better understood.

Assam, known to many only by reason of its flourishing tea gardens and by a certain prominence acquired by it when Lord Curzon's famous "Partition" took place, uniting the district of Eastern Bengal with Assam, and which in 1911 was reversed by Royal Command, has had a long history of its own since ancient times. The Koch and Cachari races warred with each other incessantly until the arrival of the Ahoms about 1220—Shan peoples of the great Tai race from Burma, who gradually conquered the country and governed it with more or less severity for nearly 700 years, until it eventually came under British rule on the conclusion of the first war with Burma in 1824–25.

B

The province, which at first after this war comprised only the country lying between Sylhet on the south, Golaghat and Tezpur on the north-east, and Cooch Behar and Bengal on the west, has been enlarged from time to time until at the present day it extends from the Arrakan border in the south to the furthest confines of the Sadiya district towards South-west China in the north, and from the eastern border of the Manipur State to the eastern boundary of Bengal, or a length of nearly 600 miles by 340 in breadth. It is traversed by two important river systems —the Brahmaputra flowing through Upper and Lower Assam and the Surma through Cachar and Sylhet (Sketch Map 1), the neighbourhood of each giving the only flat country, for the rest is covered with magnificent forest-clad mountain ranges. These are the Himalayas on the Brahmaputra north bank, the Naga, Patkoi, and Manipur hills to the east, the Khasi, Jaintia and Garo hills in the centre, while to the south are the Lushai hills. All these mountain regions are inhabited by wild tribes differing in every conceivable way from those of India proper. A former Chief Commissioner records that it is "a most interesting locality, because there is hardly any part of India where there is a greater mixture or gradation of races than is found in it." The depredations and raids of these wild folk have necessitated at varying intervals their particular tribal areas being taken over by the British, to ensure peace and prosperity as civilisation extended up both river systems. Until 1885 Assam was the eastern frontier province of the Indian Empire when the annexation of Upper Burma advanced this border still further eastward, and it is still such so far as the valley of the Brahmaputra is concerned for some 400 miles of its course. Up to 1874 Assam was incorporated in the province of Bengal, was administered by an Agent to the Governor-General in India, and ruled from Calcutta; in that year it was made a separate province under a Chief Commissioner. Having a much heavier rainfall than India, it is a green land with, except in a few stretches in both great valleys, dense vegetation and forests with magnificent scenery.

In the later years of the Ahom rulers, whose power was deteriorating, the country became filled with the turbulent ruffianism of the great bazaars in Bengal, with disbanded soldiery and fighting fanatics, who pillaged villages and laid waste the fields, reducing the country to ruin. British intervention in 1792, when Captain Welsh's expedition (details of which can be read in the "History of Assam and Upper Burma") to queil the state of civil war and anarchy produced no good effect, was followed by incursions of Burmese forces which only increased the distressful condition of affairs. The latter remained more or less as conquerors till 1824. In that year, as a natural consequence of the declaration of war with Burma, British forces assembled at Goalpara the frontier station of Bengal in this direction since 1765 when that area together with that of Dacca was taken from the Mahommedans. Assam and the Surma valleys were entered, and after a year of fighting the Burmese were expelled and the country was taken over by us, though the district of Cachar did not come directly under our administration till 1830. From being a land devastated from end to end, it now gradually improved. The tea industry, started by Mr. Bruce in the first tea garden at the mouth of the Kundil River near Sadiya about 1832, spread over Assam, to be taken up later in Cachar, where the first garden was laid out in 1855, until both valleys became covered with flourishing tea concerns. Coal and oil were discovered, the forests were found to be a source of valuable timber produce, and with improved communications Assam gradually became a very different country from what it was in 1826.

For very many years the only means of entering and travelling about the province was by large country boats up the two great rivers, by smaller ones and "dug-outs" in the lesser streams, and by the roughest of roads, bridle-paths or tracks in the interior. Major J. Butler (in civil employ) mentions in 1844 that the river journey from Gauhati to Sadiya by country boat (the only means of progression) occupied him a tedious six weeks, while that from Goalundo, the nearest river point to Calcutta, took three months, and often longer. Few houses, either private ones or Rest-houses, had doors and windows, being mostly miserable shanties; in fact, most of the houses occupied by Europeans in Assam in early years were but "wattle and daub" structures with thatched roofs, devoid of any comfort. One reads that many officials when on tour used to carry with them window frames complete, to fix in the rest-houses where they put up. Gauhati and Goalpara were the only places with a few masonry houses where any attempt had been made to ameliorate the conditions of life for the higher officials. The rise of the tea trade brought steamers on to the two main rivers in 1850, while railway enterprise did not start till 1883, and then to connect Dibrugarh and the river with the coal-fields of Margherita and Ledo. This was followed by the Assam and Bengal Railway, some 600 miles in length, to connect the port of Chittagong with Dibrugarh, the first survey in connection with this undertaking taking place in 1893. Construction was begun about 1897, and the whole line, with an extension to Gauhati from Lumding, was open by 1901. About 1910 the Eastern Bengal Railway extended its line from Santahar to Amingaon on the Brahmaputra, nearly opposite Gauhati, and the principal stations of the province were brought into direct and easy touch with the outer world.

In the early days of our rule in this province the Honourable East India Company, being averse to increasing its obligations by taking over more of the country than was actually needed, instructed Mr. David Scott, the first Agent to the Governor-General in India, to hand over the portion of Upper Assam from Golaghat to Dibrugarh (or Muttuk, as it was then called) to Purunder Sing, the last of Ahom royalties, who was to rule in the position of a protected prince, guaranteed against invasion, and was

Old-time Rest-house on the Brahmaputra River, 1894.

[From a sketch by L. W. S.

given uncontrolled civil power. The tract of country, however, east of Purunder Sing's domain, of which Sadiya and Rangarora were the most important places, was retained by the British and held by the Assam Light Infantry to prevent possible incursions by Burmese or Chinese.

Thus the earliest eastern frontier of the newly-acquired country with which we shall be first concerned ran from Nowgong to Silchar, or, to be more correct, as shown in an old map of 1828, it followed the line of the Dunsiri river through the Nambhor forest *via* Borpathar, Mohun Dijoa, Mahur, Semkhor, Lankye, in the north Cachar hills, to the Jatinga valley, down which it ran, skirting the plains as far as Jirighat on the Barak river (Sketch Map 4). From this point the boundary turned south-west, running along the foot of the Lushai and Tippera hills. Beyond this border the country was unknown; the earliest visits into it for very short distances were in 1839 and 1840, save for Captains Jenkins and Pemberton, who sixteen years previously had visited the Manipur State. These two officers entered the hills from the Silchar side and left the State with a large escort of Manipuri troops for the Assam valley *via* Paplongmai and the Naga hills, having to fight most of the way, the records state, eventually reaching the plains at Nagura near Golaghat. It was not till 1844 that the first effort was made to enter the Lushai hills.

From the end of the first Burmese war the country had for many years a large number of troops maintaining order, these being stationed at Goalpara, Bijni, Gauhati, Golaghat, Nowgong, Tezpur, Jorhat, Sibsagor, Lakhimpur, and Sadiya in the Assam valley, and at Sylhet, Cherrapoonji, Jaintiapur and Silchar in the Surma valley, in both cases with a large number of detached posts. The police force (belonging to Bengal) was divided into the armed Civil Police for protection of jails, treasuries, and for guards and escorts, and into the ordinary Civil Police for criminal administrative purposes. This state of affairs, subject to small and gradual reduction of troops, at first by moving those nearest to Bengal, continued till 1838, when the Hkamti–Singpho rising during the following year, in which Colonel White and most of the Sadiya garrison lost their lives, together with Purunder Sing's mismanagement, constrained Government to take over the whole of Upper Assam from the Dunsiri river to Sadiya. In 1840 the station of Dibrugarh was decided on as the headquarters of the administration of this part of the province, and work on it was commenced, while Gauhati remained until the late 'sixties as the headquarters of the Agent to the Governor-General.

Excessive annual expenses in keeping a large force of troops in Assam, when the country had settled down and only depredations of wild hill tribes remained to be guarded against, caused Government to review the situation from the defensive aspect and to reduce the military force, which about 1840 was brought down to four regiments, *viz.* the 1st Assam Light Infantry at Gauhati, the 2nd Assam Light Infantry at Sadiya, the Sylhet Light Infantry in Sylhet, and a Bengal Infantry Battalion at Silchar. As throughout practically all border troubles and expeditions our Frontier Police will be found working in close touch with the first three regiments, it may not be out of place to mention their origin and the dates when they came into existence.

The two battalions of the Assam Light Infantry started life as follows: The older one was raised in 1817 as the "Cuttack Legion" at Chaubiaganj for the protection of the Cuttack district to the south of Calcutta, and in 1823 it was moved to Rungpur in Eastern Bengal, where it was renamed the "Rungpur (Local) Light Infantry." Four years later, after service in Assam, it became known as the "1st Assam Light Infantry" and with its headquarters at Gauhati remained in the province as such till 1864, when its title was changed to that of the "42nd Bengal Infantry (Goorkhas)" and in 1903 to that of the 6th Goorka Rifles, as at present. The younger battalion, raised at Gauhati in 1835 for service in the province and later moved to Sadiya, was known as the "Assam Seebundy Corps (Irregulars)" and was stationed in the Sadiya district, where eight years later its title was changed to that of the "2nd Assam Light Infantry" on being brought on to the strength of the Bengal Army. In 1864 it became known as the "43rd Bengal Infantry (Assam)," and after two other slight changes received its present title of the 2/8th Goorkha Rifles. The Sylhet Local Battalion was raised in 1824 in Sylhet for the protection of that portion of Assam when the first Burmese war broke out, in 1864 its name was changed to that of the "44th Sylhet Light Infantry" on being incorporated into the Bengal Army, in 1901 this Regiment became known as the "44th Goorkha Rifles," and in 1907 this was changed again to the 1/8th Goorkha Rifles, which it has since retained. All these regiments served entirely in Assam and Burma until 1899, taking part in every border expedition, after which year they were sent to serve in other parts of India, the 43rd Goorkha Rifles being the first to be moved to garrison Chitral.

The early uniforms of all these regiments appear to have been red, later changed to green, with accoutrements of black leather; for many years they were recruited locally or from Bengal, until, about 1870, they began to enlist Nepalese in increasing numbers, and in 1885 each unit was given two 6-pounder mountain guns, which in 1903 were handed over to the Military Police battalions.

From 1830 the armed Civil Police had been gradually increased in numbers, and now, with the reduction of the troops in the province, the first idea of a "Levy" or Militia body was put forward, to be a separate force under the Civil Government and apart from the armed police branch. This proposed "Levy" was to be placed on a better footing than the ordinary police, would perform military duties, and would replace the troops in certain parts of the border. As it was to be officered by Civil Police officials it was realised that its drill, training and discipline would perforce be of an elementary nature, but it was expected this might suffice. It was to be a cheap semi-military body, clothed like the Civil Police and armed with the old Brown Bess, but it was badly paid, though slightly better than was the case with the ordinary police. The men were to carry out arduous duties, often involving fighting and danger in what were then most unhealthy jungle localities, and they were drawn from the armed Bengal Civil Police, at first comprising all classes, chiefly from Bengal.

The first unit of this new organisation was definitely raised by Mr. Grange, in civil charge of the Nowgong district, during 1835, and was named the "Cachar Levy," with a strength of 750 of all ranks, *viz.* inspectors, head constables and constables, as they were called until 1883, in virtue of their being a purely civil force. Three years later a similar body, but of lesser strength, the "Jorhat Militia," was raised at Jorhat for the protection of the Sibsagor border and recruited mostly from Shans settled in that area. This unit in old books is alluded to as the "Shan" and sometimes as the "Police" Militia, and after a few years became amalgamated with the "Cachar Levy." The duties of this force were to guard the then eastern frontier of Assam from the Brahmaputra river to Cachar, supported at each end of this line of some 250 miles by strong detachments of troops at Nowgong and Silchar (Sketch Map 4).

Along this stretch, which ran for scores of miles through the great Nambhor forest near the foot of the Naga hills and through the north Cachar hills to the plain of the Surma valley east of Silchar, the Cachar Levy held posts (stockades or block-houses) at Borpathar, Dimapur, Mohun Dijoa, 30 miles south-west of Dimapur, Mahurmukh, Maibong, Hosang Hajoo, Guilon, Gumaigajoo, Hangrung, Baladhan and Jirighat, at the south-east end of the north Cachar hills. At Asaloo (16 miles east of Hafiong) a small administrative station was established about 1845, together with the Levy's strongest detachment. All were in the heart of dense forests and amongst hills, paths between each being cut and kept clear for constant patrolling. Most of these places have disappeared entirely from maps, and the most important ones were those at Dimapur, Mahurmukh, Maibong and Asaloo, these being on routes most used by the Nagas when leaving their hills to trade or raid below, more often than not the latter being their object (Sketch Map 4).

This Cachar Levy thus formed the earliest embodied unit of what eventually developed into the fine force of the five Assam Rifle battalions of the present day. Other portions of the north and north-eastern borders were for many years more guarded by troops and the armed Civil Police of Bengal, with a small body of Hkamtis in the Sadiya area for duty between the Lohit river and the Patkoi range, across which runs one of the routes into Upper Burma. These latter, however, did not last long, and were disbanded as being unreliable. For many years after the Burmese war this tract towards the Patkoi range was a troublesome one, both the Hkamtis and the Singphos, who in some cases received support from Burma, having to be subdued after much fighting between 1826 and 1843. This period was marked by expeditions, at first under Captain Neufville and later under Captain Charlton with the Assam Light Infantry and detachments of other troops. These officers established military posts at Bisa, Koogoo, Ningroo and Nungrang on the western slopes of the Patkoi, which were held till 1850 and then given up (Sketch Map 3). It was at Sadiya in 1839 that the principal Hkamti rising took place with extreme suddenness, when a large body of these warriors surprised the garrison and little station, cutting up Colonel White and 80 odd men and rushing the stockade, which was only retaken after a stiff hand-to-hand fight. It is believed the present earthwork fort, which originally had timber palisading along the top of the parapet, is the same one which witnessed the tragedy, though Major Butler, writing in 1844, mentions Colonel White as having been buried at Saikwa, on the opposite bank of the Lohit river. As this part of the country did not concern the Cachar Levy, it is at present unnecessary to go into further details of military action here.

With regard to the districts of Cachar and Sylhet, forming what is known as the Surma valley, the latter, which lies at the foot of the Khasi and Jaintia hills, had been taken over by the British at the same time as Dacca and Rungpur, *viz.* in 1765, but, owing to turbulent Mahommedan inhabitants and utter lack of communications, had been much neglected and really was but little known till 1824. The few English officials who were there in early days seem to have busied themselves, one reads, in amassing fortunes from the valuable limestone quarries lying along the outer spurs of the Khasi hills, their superintendents and quarrymen frequently, by injudicious conduct, irritating the hill people, thus causing an unsettled state which often ended in retaliation and murder.

The Cachar district, which for some years prior to the first Burmese war had been more or less under the influence of the neighbouring State of Manipur, was visited for the first time in 1763 by Mr. Verelst, the Chief of Chittagong (as the high Government official was styled in those days), who marched a body of troops through Sylhet and Cachar to assist Manipur against Burmese aggression. He did not, however, enter the hills beyond the Barak river owing to great transport difficulties and much sickness in his force. Cachar was brought under British political control in 1826 after considerable opposition by a Burmese force of 8000, which had come through Manipur and had advanced to the vicinity of the Khasi hills. This force was engaged by General Shuldham's troops near the present site of Badarpur Junction, severe fighting surging round the old fort, the remains of which are to be seen just above the railway bridge on the left bank of the Barak river. Driven back, the Burmese made a last stand on the Tilain Tilas, a ridge of low hills between Salchapra and Silchar, where they were finally defeated and pursued into the Manipur hills to a point a little beyond Aqui, a few miles north of Nungba on the present Silchar-Imphal road (Sketch Map 2). In 1830 Cachar was taken over definitely as an administered district, its first superintendent being Captain Stewart, who held the position at Silchar for many years, and maintained order with the aid of the Sylhet Light Infantry and a Manipuri Levy raised amongst the large numbers of those people who for years had settled in this part of the country. Two years later this Levy was made over to the Manipur State, being replaced in Cachar by an increase to the armed Civil Police. The North Cachar Hills district was, until about 1864, administered from Nowgong, after which it was made over to Cachar.

During the period 1826 to 1833 the unsettled state of the Khasi and Jaintia hills was a source of much trouble. The people (Syntengs) inhabiting this area have characteristics different from any of the other tribes met with in this part of India in that, though like the Shans, Singphos, Hkamtis and others of Indo-Chinese origin whose early home in ancient times, according to Sir Charles Lyall, K.C.I.E., a former Chief Commissioner of the province, lay probably in North-west China, the Syntengs' language, habits and matrimonial customs are those of the Mong Kmer peoples of the Cambodian side. They appear to be an isolated remnant of the earliest wave of Indo-Chinese migration westwards, with no relatives now left within the province, their nearest kindred being the Palaungs and Wās in Upper Burma. But they belong to the same racial group, which, much more advanced in civilisation, is represented to-day by the Talaings of Pegu and Tenasserim and the Cambodians, all living hundreds of miles eastwards of the Khasi hills.

Mr. David Scott, who in the early part of the war had been the first European to cross the Khasi hills with an escort of troops and armed Civil Police from Sylhet to Gauhati, strongly urged a road being opened through them to connect the Surma with the Assam valley. This was sanctioned and begun in the winter of 1827 from Cherrapoonji *via* Nunklow, 20 miles west of Shillong. By 1829 it was finished and was known as "Brigg's Trace," though so rarely used that by the time Shillong came into being it had practically been abandoned. At Nunklow in 1829 the Khasias rose, attacked Lieuts. Bedingfield and Burlton, killing both, together with most of their men guarding the road-working parties. A punitive expedition entered the hills, consisting of the Sylhet Light Infantry, 23rd Bengal Infantry, and a strong detachment of armed Civil Police, all under command of Captain Lister, with whom were Lieuts. Townshend, Vetch and Brodie, who were actively employed till 1833, when these hill tracts were subdued. During this period Cherrapoonji in the Khasi hills came into existence as a combined civil and military station from which to control the people and administer the region. Armed Civil Police posts were also placed at points further into the hills. From these brief accounts it will be seen that the armed Civil Police, forerunners of the Assam Rifles, took their share in almost all military activity connected with the settlement of the new British acquisitions.

Returning to the Cachar Levy, or Police Militia as it is referred to in some old books, we find very few records of its earliest years of existence along the eastern frontier line; and what there are show that life for them must often have been solitary and monotonous, cut off as the men were from the amenities of civilisation and settled life by long distances and difficult country. Their occupation lay in constant patrolling towards posts on their right or left in parties of ten or four, according to the strength of the posts, in keeping these in a complete state of repair and defence, in escorting ration or treasure parties, in sending assistance to neighbouring posts or warding off attacks on their own post, or in acting on instructions by which a raiding party might be headed off or rounded up. Numbers of small skirmishes occurred which were never

THE OLD MASONRY BLOCK-HOUSE AT DIKRANG, NEAR SADIYA.

[From a sketch by L. W. S.

STOCKADED POST AT MONGSEMDI IN THE NAGA HILLS.

Types of defensive posts on the N.E. Frontier.

heard of outside the Police, or were unrecorded as being all in the day's work, and very likely gallant services went by unnoticed and unrewarded. Life at these frontier posts was but rarely enlivened by visits from the one European officer in command, such probably occurring but once in the year, if then; for the reason that he could not get more often over his long extent of borderland with all his district work to do as well, and it also was not often that a junior official could be spared to go on tour for so long.

Frontier posts in those days were usually earthworks with a ditch outside and a loopholed palisading along the top of the parapet—examples of these are still to be seen in the old post to the north of the ferry at Jirighat and in one close to Charduar near Baliapara in Tezpur district; or they were plain timber stockades with a deep fringe of abattis work running round the outside, to prevent an enemy getting close to the timber wall, or again, where nearer to civilisation and material was available, the posts were masonry block-houses, of which the present Rest-house at Borpathar, near Golaghat, and the old post at Dikrang, near Sadiya, are extant examples.

With 1838–39 the eastern frontier entered on more interesting and stirring times for the Cachar Levy under command of Mr. Grange, who has been called the "Father of the Frontier Police." This officer was also the principal civil official at Nowgong, a place on the Kullung river, some seventy miles from the border of those days, which six years earlier had replaced the first administrative station at Raha, near the present-day railway station of Chaparmukh (Sketch Map 4). Burma was again causing anxiety, giving expectation of a fresh war, and Captain Gordon, then Political Agent in the State of Manipur, reported the intention of its Raja to bring the Naga hills permanently under his rule, action by no means approved of by Government. These, together with constant tribal raids and depredations across our border, constrained greater notice being taken of the Naga tribes, with a view to bringing them under British influence and their chiefs to friendly terms.

A few words may here be said relative to these tribes and their origin, hitherto scarcely known to us. The Naga and Kuki tribes, with which latter the Lushais are included, with whom our dealings and troubles along the eastern and southern border lands are concerned, belong—again to quote Sir Charles Lyall—to the Thibeto-Burman racial division who inhabit all the hills not occupied by the Khasias. The aborigines of Assam would appear to have been largely of Dravidian stock, but in the main this country, according to certain authorities, was peopled from North-west China, Mongolian tribes, swarms of whom in far-off times found their way into Assam, Bengal, and up the Tsan Po river, while others moved southwards down the Chindwyn, Irrawadi, and Salween valleys, peopling Burma, Siam, etc. Pressure from those behind caused the earlier swarms to turn aside from the large valleys and to enter the hill areas. Scientific analysis of the speech of these tribes (with the exception of the Khasias), which classes the various tribal languages as Thibeto–Bodo, together with in most cases their Mongoloid appearance, vouches, it is said, for this statement as to their original homeland.

Another school of thought gives them a southern origin, classing them as akin to the great family of the Borneo Dyaks and Malay peoples, who in the dim past probably trekked northwards until stopped either by the wall of the eastern Himalayas or by the southward migration of other races. Their views for this are based on head-hunting propensities which the Dyaks have, on similarity in village arrangements and styles of building, on certain slight affinity in language, and in the love of the tribes for marine ornaments, shells, etc. Mr. J. P. Mills, for many years a civil officer in the Naga hills, and an authority on tribal matters, states that the huge war drums made from hollowed-out tree trunks and used by many hill tribes show unmistakable signs of having been developed from old-time canoes. He also says that many words used by these people would be easily understood by the Maoris of New Zealand. These points, it is thought, give evidence of an ancient home near the sea, whereas they are now far inland-dwelling communities. As if bearing out this theory in our own times, we find the Kukis still continually pressing northwards, while in Upper Burma the great Kachin (Singpho) tribe were still moving southwards, threatening to oust the Shans, until the British annexation in 1885–86 put a stop to such a possibility. Many of these tribes, the Angamis and the Semas of the higher ranges in particular, are very fine specimens of humanity—handsome, athletic, and accustomed for long generations to dominate their surroundings.

The Manipuris or Meitheis, who also will concern this history later on, belong to the same Thibeto-Burman group. According to Colonel McCulloch, who was Political Agent in Manipur for many years up to 1867, the Meitheis were the strongest of several clans inhabiting the Manipur valley, who eventually obtained the mastery and gave their name to all the other clans; but their origin is somewhat obscure. Captain Pemberton, one of the earliest visitors to and writers on this region, believes they hailed from China and came south. The race of Meitheis has been continuously fed by intermarriage with and additions from various hill peoples surrounding the valley, and from paganism and serpent worship, etc., the entire Meithei tribe became converted to Hindooism about 1750. Since then they have become most bigoted in that religion.

CHAPTER II

General, 1839 to 1850—Grange's first expedition—His visit to Samaguting and Dimapur—Grange's second expedition, 1840—Seriously attacked near Togwema—Lieut. Bigge opens market at Samaguting, 1842—Nagas raid Hosang Hajoo post—Retaliation—Major John Butler—North Cachar Hills rebellion, 1841 to 1844—Asaloo—The Lushai border—Blackwood's first expedition, 1844—Lister's expeditions, 1847 and 1849—Samaguting post established, 1848—The Levy's uniform—Communications—Bogchand at Samaguting—Captain Vincent's expedition, 1849 to 1850—He and Major Foquett attack Khonoma—Fight at Kekrima—Passive policy and Nowgong frontier drawn back—Cachar Levy split into two portions—The Garo Hills.

REVERTING to the tribes as found in those early days, the strongest and most turbulent of the Angami Naga villages were those of Mozema, Khonoma, Jotsoma, Kohima, and Kekrima, all of which at that time were well defended and contained each from 700 to 800 houses, though these numbers have declined somewhat since. The nearest to our border and most influential ones were Khonoma and Mozema, 25 miles into the hills, while Kekrima lay a full 30 miles further east. It was the two first-named villages which for long were the principal offenders in breaking the peace of the border lands by raiding into the districts of Nowgong and Cachar, often to obtain slaves through the agency of Bengali traders, a class who, it was found, carried on a regular slave trade. The time had now come to stop this, to show ourselves among the tribes, and to punish offending villages.

To this end, then, Mr. Grange was directed to conduct the first expedition into the Naga hills, and in January 1839 he set out with 50 men of the Cachar Levy and a small detachment of the 1st Assam Light Infantry. He marched *via* Doboka to Mohun Dijoa, thence along the border southwards to Gumaigajoo in the north Cachar hills visiting his various posts, and then, entering the southern Naga country, reached Berema *via* Semkhor and Henema. The route lay along rough tracks entailing much climbing through forest-clad ranges over 5000 feet in altitude, with no actual fighting, though hostility showed itself on the way. On one or two occasions there was a little firing, and a few men were speared and killed by hidden Nagas while going singly for water, two sentries being also cut down at night. This, together with sickness from the cold in the higher ranges, weakened the small force by the time Berema was reached, where, feeling himself not strong enough to move against Mozema to punish that clan, Grange halted and summoned the two headmen to come to him (Sketch Map 4). These duly appeared and took an oath, not kept for long, not to molest British villages again, the oath being made by both headmen and Grange holding the opposite ends of a spear while it was cut in half. Having no support near and not being strong enough to enforce the restoration of the slaves alluded to, Grange left the hills *via* Jalookama, Samaguting, and Dimapur, which last-named place was visited for the first time and of which nothing had been known before. Here he was shown the remains of the old Cachari fort containing many huge and elaborately carved monoliths, the object of which has never really been discovered, also several large excavated tanks and other signs attesting the presence long ago of a large city on the banks of the Dunsiri river now buried in almost primeval forest. All gave evidence that the city must have been the chief seat of a people far in advance, both in power and civilisation, of the simple tribesmen of the present day. Later historical research showed Dimapur to have been the capital of the old Cachari kings, and destroyed by the Ahoms about 1570. A fuller description of these remarkable remains is given in Chapter XIX. He also records

C

having found gold washing being carried out in the Dunsiri river.

Struck by what he considered the advantageous position of Samaguting at 2000 feet on the outer range overlooking the Nambhor forest from which to control the tribes, and of Dimapur as another post in support, he advocated taking action in both cases; neither recommendation was, however, accepted.

A year later Grange was again deputed to enter the hills to meet leading Naga headmen, annual visits with escorts being the line taken by Government as a means of acquiring influence and power over the clans, and thus frustrating Manipuri interference. He was also to meet a deputation from Imphal, the capital of the native State of Manipur, at or near Paplongmai the chief village of the Mezama or Kaccha Naga clan, with whom the question of boundaries was to be discussed, and who were to co-operate with him if the people gave trouble. With a stronger force this time, formed of detachments of the Cachar Levy, the Jorhat Militia, and 50 men of the 1st A.L.I., while some of the Jorhat Militia were left in support at Samaguting, which was none too friendly disposed now, the force marched *via* Raziphima up the Chatthe valley, climbed the western slopes of the great Barail range through Lemhama and Chama, over the Paona ridge at 8000 feet, and crossing the Zulhein valley reached Paplongmai, well situated at a height of about 6000 feet. Grange was now in the heart of the Barail mountains with the towering peaks of "Japvo," 9900 feet, and "Kahoo," 8700 feet, forested to their summits, overlooking the village and the deep valley of the Typhini (Zupvoo) river stretching away to the south, its waters joining the Barak river in the far distance.

Here he waited a few days, and as no Manipuris arrived he marched on down this valley for two days to a point near Togwema (Uilong), expecting to meet them. But here he learnt the deputation had merely come as far as this point, and not finding Grange, had turned back. It was also found the Angamis evinced great hostility towards Manipur, whereas it had been thought they were on tributary and fairly friendly terms—a hostility Grange was soon to discover for himself, the tribesmen imagining him to be an ally of Manipur, and one whose methods of oppression were probably the same.

As it was useless to remain at Togwema the force turned back, intending to make for Khonoma, but the moment Grange started up the Typhini valley he was attacked, a series of fights ensued, and the march was much harassed and interrupted by the enemy, who set fire to the long grass and rolled rocks down the hillside on to his men. Chekwema (Ỳang) village was attacked by the force and burnt, three other villages suffering the same punishment, but in the narrow defile which closes the valley and out of which the ascent led to Paplongmai, the people of that and other villages ambushed the force. A fierce fight took place, continuing up to the village, which was then destroyed with all grain and property that could be found. Both sides suffered considerable casualties, and 11 Nagas prominent in the attacks were captured. Grange's force reached the plains in mid March 1841, having learnt that the Angamis, although armed only with spears, daos, and a very few old muskets, were a foe by no means to be despised.

Having left his wounded at Dimapur, he re-entered the hills to punish the nearer villages of Piphima and Sephema for having joined in the recent attacks on him, and after two short skirmishes destroyed both places. Dimapur was now allowed to be included among the frontier posts, and a stockade was built at the Dunsiri river crossing just below the present bridge, for a detachment of the Levy.

Between 1841 and 1845 two visits into the hills were made by Lieut. Bigge and Captain Eld, who respectively followed Mr. Grange (promoted elsewhere) as civil officers in the Nowgong district and in command of the

Cachar Levy; visits at which agreements were made by various Naga notables with Government, but which were never kept for long. The former officer established a salt depot and market at Dimapur and cut a bridle-path towards Samaguting. Neither, however, penetrated far into the hills, and Eld had to carry out one small punitive outing. During 1844 an attack on the Hosang Hajoo post in the north Cachar hills and the loss of several of the Levy, being traced to the village of Asaloo assisted to a certain extent by Mozema men, Mr. Woods, Sub-Assistant at Nowgong, was sent over the border with 50 men of the 1st A.L.I. and 70 of the Cachar Levy, when he burnt both villages with but slight opposition.

In 1845 Captain Eld was succeeded by Captain J. Butler as Principal Assistant at Nowgong and in charge of the Levy, who remained in the billet some years. He is the first to have left good accounts of this part of the border lands, its tribes, expeditions, etc., and his name, together with that of his son, who followed later in the same billet, is still remembered there. His books, " Travels and Adventures in Assam " and " Sketches in Assam," are interesting as showing the difficulties and discomforts of life in those early days on the frontier.

Not only were things livening up at the Nowgong end of the border, but the southern end from 1841 to 1844 was in a disturbed condition, for in this area, *viz.* the north Cachar hills, the Levy's detachments were kept busy. This was due to one Tularam Senapatti, the principal chief of that region, who had had certain lands assigned him by Mr. David Scott when the district was taken over by Government, and who now caused a revolt in the hope of gaining the whole area for himself. Detachments of the Cachar Levy were employed for one and a half years in rounding up or dispersing Tularam's gangs, which involved some desultory fighting, until that worthy gave in and retired from the scene. In consequence of this disturbance Asaloo, 15 miles east of Haflong, was decided on as a pl[illegible] from which these hills, so remote from Nowgong, could be administered; and a small civil staff was located there together with a strong detachment of the Levy.

Prior to this the Kuki and Lushai tribes beyond our extreme southern frontier line in the Cachar district were hardly known, though long before this people within our borders had suffered from tribal raiders. These raids becoming of frequent occurrence necessitated the Sylhet Light Infantry being called on to place detachments at two points in the Hailakandi area for protective purposes. The first expedition across this border on a small scale was made by Captain Blackwood, with parties of the Sylhet Light Infantry and the armed Civil Police at the end of 1844.

He did not get far, but going *via* Koilashur on the north-east border of the Tippera State (now called by its old time name, "Tripura") he managed to surround one of the offending villages, capturing its Chief, Lalchokla. During 1845 and 1847 the Lushais (or Kukis, as the old records call them) carried out several serious raids both in the Manipur State and in Sylhet, in the latter case obliging the move of the Sylhet L.I. up to that part of the border, and there, after a conflict with a large body of tribesmen in which Captain Lister was wounded, they were driven back into their hills. In 1849 a village within 10 miles of Silchar was raided with great boldness, many persons being killed and 42 were carried off captive. This called for serious notice and action, and Major Lister, as he now was, conducted an expedition to punish certain villages three days' march along the Chattachoora range. The force consisted of 100 of the S.L.I. and 150 armed Civil Police, and by the 4th January, 1850, he had surprised and destroyed the large and troublesome village of Mora (Gnura) with its 800 houses and granaries, later rebuilt and known as Shenklang, a little north of Neiboi. This success also released a number of British subjects in captivity. Although the force had only a few casualties Major

Lister was again somewhat badly wounded (Sketch Map 2). On returning out of the hills his march was considerably harassed by the Lushais, obliging Lister at one point to destroy a quantity of stores which could not be got away.

A small body of local Kukis 200 strong and later increased was this year (1850) formed into a Kuki Levy at the suggestion of Major Lister, to assist the armed Civil Police in controlling and protecting the borders and also to give employment to those Kukis living in our area, and during this year Sookpilal, a prominent Lushai chief living much further into the hills, sent an embassy of four notables to visit and establish friendly relations with the British officials at Silchar. This produced peaceful conditions for a few years.

Turning back to the Nowgong frontier, Captain Butler in 1848 had again visited the Naga hills and reached Khonoma, where tribute was received in the form of ivory, clothes, etc. Oaths were again made, though they were never kept, for the Angamis continued their depredations at intervals. As a result of this visit Butler, having urged the establishment of a permanent post in the hills as the only means of maintaining peace, was allowed to arrange for a small Levy post and a market to be opened at Samaguting. He also in this year (1848) opened up rough cart roads from Borpathar and Mohun Dijoa to Dimapur and cut a bridle-path up to Samaguting, which was taken up the spur on which the Nichuguard Thana now stands. It was hoped by this means to stimulate trade, and with trade, peace. Though it certainly did tend to increase the former it did not establish the latter, for the stronger Naga clans still continued to harry our side of the border.

With a view to opening up this line of frontier and to link up the Surma valley with that of Upper Assam, it was proposed in 1849 to make a cart road from the highest navigable point on the Jatinga river where it emerges into the plains below Damcherra, through the

A Frontier Police Constable, 1877 (Goorkha).

Nambhor forest to a navigable point on the Dunsiri river, which would have followed much the same alignment as the Assam Bengal Railway now takes. As a commencement to this project survey work began, and was carried from the Silchar side to a little north of Haflong, but was given up owing mainly to the difficulty presented by impenetrable forests and unhealthy local conditions.

In Butler's early days the Cachar Levy was given a different uniform from that of the armed Civil Police hitherto worn, and we now find them in jacket and trousers of black serge with white metal buttons, weapons and accoutrements of Waterloo days, *viz.* the old muzzle-loading Brown Bess musket with long bayonet, two broad black leather cross-belts supporting the bayonet on one side and a large expense pouch on the other, both kept from swinging loose by a black waist-belt. A short sword attached to the belt was also carried for a good many years, which must have impeded a man's progress through jungle, until about 1865 the more useful "kookerie" was substituted in its place. For head-dress the black Kilmarnock (or pork pie) cap was worn, also native shoes, while for many years, as no knapsack was given to the men when on line of march in which to carry spare kit, food, etc., these had to be arranged for in a "chudder" (sheet), the ends of which were tied either across the chest, or the weight on the back was supported from the forehead. A change in recruitment was also made by Butler, who from this time on enlisted Nepalese, Cacharis, and Shans, as being better men for hill and jungle work; but they were still known by their civil titles in the different grades.

When the new market and post were completed, a capable Police officer, one Bogchand Daroga, was placed in charge of Samaguting. This officer had been at Dimapur some time and knew something of the tribes, having been in more than one "rough and tumble" with them. On one occasion in 1847, when sent with

40 constables of the Levy to Lakema and Mozema to inquire into certain aggressions by men of those villages, while returning from the latter place his party was ambushed by a large mob of Angamis, who caused several casualties with their spears. Bogchand and a head constable, Ahena Cachari by name, led a charge after two or three volleys, and with difficulty succeeded in cutting their way out and gaining Merema, a friendly village, whence they were able to reach the plains.

For a time all went well with the new post, and the tribesmen freely came down to trade. Being an ambitious man and intent on pushing further into the hills, Bogchand's continued representations as to the desirability of locating a post at Mozema to control those turbulent clans met with approval at last. In April 1849 he set out with a small Levy escort and a party of friendly Nagas, with intent to arrest certain men prominent in raiding and to establish the sanctioned post. A rapid march brought him to Mozema, a large village situated at well over 5000 feet, overlooking a deep valley with the still larger village of Khonoma on the opposite side, and where his visit was unexpected. The two headmen met him, agreed to the location of the post and told their people to commence building the stockade for it. Bogchand then inquired after the men concerned in recent troubles, and on these being pointed out he immediately arrested them—an unwise act at the time, considering the smallness of his party. This started a ferment, and thinking it wiser to leave the matter of the post to another time, he retired with his prisoners towards Samaguting. Halting for the night at Piphima (Sketch Map 4) he was attacked by a large body of Angamis, his friendly Nagas deserted, ammunition ran out, and before morning he and most of his men, fighting desperately, were overwhelmed and killed, few escaping. In all 22 were killed at Piphima and several wounded who got away were cut up in the pursuit. News of this disaster reached Butler who withdrew the post, owing to threatened attack, from Samaguting to Dimapur. This outrage could not go unpunished, and Government sanctioned a military expedition under Captain Vincent with 150 men of the 2nd Assam Light Infantry and a detachment of the Levy, which entered the hills in the early part of the winter 1849–50. Captain Vincent, the only British officer with the force, however, fell ill and it had to return, having accomplished nothing and having lost a large amount of stores at one camp, which the Nagas managed to set fire to. In March 1850 Vincent and Butler with Lieut. Campbell and a stronger mixed force from the A.L.I., Cachar Levy, and Jorhat Militia, with a supporting body stockaded at Samaguting, re-entered the hills and successfully attacked both Mozema and Khonoma, burning the two most troublesome "Khels" in each, without very much fighting.

It had by now been found out by Butler that Naga villages were not formed of one entire community working harmoniously together, but were divided into exogamous sub-divisions called "Khels," of which there were often three to five in a village. It had also been learnt that in one village, for example, one or two "Khels" would be averse to fighting the British and would indeed sometimes even help them, while the other "Khels" fought. These sub-divisions frequently fought each other in the same village, producing a chaotic state of turmoil which the headmen were unable to contend with, but occasions did arise when all would combine against a common foe, for they are greatly attached to their sites and well-defended villages, the houses of which are substantially built of heavy timbers, unlike the lighter buildings of several other tribes with nomadic tendencies, such as the Kukis and Lushais.

After this success Vincent and Campbell established themselves in a strong stockade on the Bassoma spur overlooking the valley, where they not only maintained themselves for several months with the aid of Mozema, which submitted entirely and provided them with rough supplies, but they also managed by a series of rapid moves to punish more distant villages which were connected with raids. The writer was informed in 1897 by old men of Khonoma that this spur, where Vincent's stockade stood, is the one overlooking Khonoma from the east in the great loop made by the present road from Jotsoma to Khonoma.

What with casualties and sickness and the steadily growing hostility of all the more important Angami villages, Vincent, feeling himself in a position not easy to get out of or to do much more in and with Khonoma defiant and being rebuilt and fortified, felt obliged by November 1850 to call for assistance from Nowgong. This was sent up in a strong reinforcement of 500 sepoys of both the 1st and 2nd A.L.I. and 200 men from the Cachar Levy and Jorhat Militia, all under command of Major Foquett, with Lieuts. Reid and Bivar. Two mountain guns and two mortars under Captain Blake also accompanied the force. These entered the hills in December, dropping posts to keep open the line of communications and to guard and escort prisoners, etc.

Having made their stockaded base at Mozema, now submissive and friendly, and being joined by Captain Butler with more of his men, the force moved across the valley to attack Khonoma, defiant still, and whose men managed to harry the L. of C. posts considerably at first.

This village, which had been rebuilt and crowns the top of the northern spur of a steep hill jutting out into the valley lying between it and Mozema, was now well defended by rough loopholed stone walls running round the upper portion, which was strongly fortified and barricaded; there were also many "sangars" and barricades at intervals up the spur, the whole making a strong position of 700 yards in depth to be taken, which was held, it was computed, by over 5000 Angamis. At 2 p.m. on the 10th December the guns opened to cover the advance, but the distance being too great to be effective, they were pushed up to within 150 yards of the lower defences. After these had been well battered the force was able to push its way up the spur, overcoming sturdy opposition at different defended points, till the main fort and heavy timber barricades near the top were approached late in the day. The Nagas disputed the advance with showers of spears and rocks, causing 36 casualties among the A.L.I. and the Levy, retiring eventually into the upper fortified position, which the guns failing to breach, escalade by the leading troops was ordered. At this point the troops were confronted by a deep ditch studded with bamboo stakes, beyond which was a thick wall crowded with the enemy, whose showers of spears caused Major Foquett's men more casualties, so as night was coming on he decided to withdraw, bivouac on the ground so far won, and assault again at dawn. Before that hour scouts from the Levy and some friendly Nagas crept up to the position and reported it to be deserted, the enemy having retreated with their wounded into the higher ranges during the night. There were evidences of heavy casualties among the Khonoma men, one record placing their dead at 200. This village, reputed to be the strongest amongst the Angami clans, was then burnt and all defences were destroyed (Sketch Map 5).

The bulk of Major Foquett's force was now sent back to the plains, leaving Captains Vincent and Blake and Lieut. Reid with the two guns and 250 men of the 2nd A.L.I. and Cachar Levy to make a tour further into the country, as it was desirable to punish certain other villages which had sent men to assist Khonoma against us, and which had also been guilty of raiding. Owing to distances such villages had not yet been reached. Jotsoma, Kohima, Kigwema, and Kezuma were visited and only slight opposition was experienced when two "Khels" in Kigwema and one in Kohima were burnt. On arriving in the area of the Sopvoma group of villages (Mao Thana) two of them came in, submitted, and paid tribute, but the people of the others refusing supplies or assistance and offering opposition, a village was destroyed, which brought them all to heel. The force then moved down the ridge dividing the Sijoo from the Zulloo rivers, having a skirmish near Kezuma village, and here on the 8th February, 1851, two notables from the large village of Kekrima across the Zulloo river (Sketch Map 4) appeared in Vincent's camp. They brought a challenge from their clan to come and prove who had the greater power in the hills—they or the British? The men were well received by the British officers, who showed them muskets and guns. Apparently these did not impress the warlike savages, who scornfully remarked: "Your men are flesh and blood like ours—come and fight man to man—here is a specimen of our weapons," and handing over a handsome spear and dao to Vincent, they withdrew. As Kekrima was believed to be an offending village and lay not far off the route of the tour, it would have had a most injurious effect on other clans if he had returned to Mozema without meeting the challenge, so Vincent marched across the Zulloo valley. On nearing the top of the steep ascent on the far side his rear guard was attacked, and on reaching the top the advance guard found itself on a fairly broad, level, and open ridge which sloped gently up to Kekrima village a mile off. Across this ridge, barring the way further, was a dense mass of armed Nagas who spun their spears as they shouted their challenge and abuse. The main body and guns rapidly followed, getting into the best position possible, just as the enemy began their attack by a charge *en masse* in front, while parties assailed the flanks, where a few sepoys were speared. Suffering heavy losses from volleys and Blake's mountain guns, which the Nagas once nearly reached, the enemy retreated to the village, from which a few shells dislodged them, and the place was then destroyed. The enemy lost on the field nearly 250 men, while another account puts the number at over 300 during the day. The troops bivouacked near the spot for the night, disturbed by Nagas creeping up, who managed to inflict a few casualties among the sepoys, one of whom was killed by a spear while sitting close to a mortar which was being fired at the time. Vincent's casualties were small, only 3 killed and 20 wounded.

The force now began its return march, experiencing no further opposition, and after a few days' halt at Kohima reached the plains in late March 1851. Captain Vincent wrote an excellent account of his doings and of the tribes and country, which, it is said, was ably illustrated with sketches by his wife, who joined him towards the close of the expedition and was the first Englishwoman to cross the border into the hills. Unfortunately, this account, which was in manuscript, was destroyed with all other records in the siege of Kohima, 1879. Captain Williamson, I.G. Police, 1879, recorded that he had seen this manuscript of Vincent's.

For a time this visitation produced a salutary effect on the tribes, but in a year or two raiding commenced again; and Government, unwilling to incur the great expenses of military expeditions, agreed with Major Butler's new views in regard to leaving the tribes entirely alone, directing him to withdraw the post which had been placed in Mozema, and generally to draw back the frontier line to its original position. Samaguting and Dimapur were therefore abandoned, Borpathar and Mohun Dijoa becoming once more the advanced posts at this end of the eastern border. This policy, which at one time inclined towards a complete withdrawal from the north Cachar hills as well but which was not carried out, continued for twelve years, and the tribes, naturally emboldened by our passive attitude, raided at will, nothing being done to check them.

About 1852, it being found difficult to control adequately from Nowgong the long line of border posts stretching from Borpathar to Jirighat in Cachar, the old Cachar Levy was split in two; the portion in the north Cachar hills was increased in strength and placed under the command of the civil officer at Asaloo.

The Jorhat Militia ceased to exist as such and was amalgamated with the Nowgong portion of the old Levy. With this change the old titles were given up, and the forces on this frontier became known as the "Frontier Police of Nowgong" and of the "North Cachar Hills," which two bodies subsequently, and after other changes, became the 3rd and the 1st Battalions Assam Rifles respectively.

The north Cachar hills were largely peopled by clans of Kukis, a self-reliant, sturdy folk, who originally dwelt in the hill country south of Cachar, but who had moved and were still moving north under pressure of the Lushai tribes behind them. They live under the autocratic rule of their own Rajas and therefore invariably combined together for any purpose, defensive or offensive. For this reason, together with their fighting capacity and weapons (chiefly bows and arrows, with which they are experts), they were somewhat feared by the Nagas, who, being essentially democratic and obeying no particular chief except when it pleases them to do so, can but rarely combine effectively.

So far the Garo tribe and their country lying west of the Khasia hills and between them and the Mymensing district of Bengal (Sketch Map 1) have not been mentioned, but may here be touched upon as showing some of the activities of the early armed Civil Police. The Garos are a wild people, having little to do with either the Khasias or the plainsmen; they belong to the Thibeto-Burman ethnological group, with a language classed as among those of the Bodo linguistic divisions, and were probably driven into these regions either by early invaders from India or by the pressure of other migrating tribes.

Their country, entirely mountainous with ranges running up to 5000 feet trending down gradually to the plains of Mymensing and about Goalpara, is densely wooded, and the Garos were the first of these wild tribes the British came into contact with, when in 1765 the districts of Dacca, Mymensing, and Rungpur were taken over from the Mahommedan Diwani of Bengal. Troops were then located in Goalpara on the Brahmaputra river and in the old fort at Jogighopa on the opposite bank, which until the first Burmese war constituted our extreme eastern frontier stations. The Garos, not being a very warlike race, have only caused a few small expeditions in the past, with but little fighting, and need only be briefly mentioned here.

In 1837, unrest starting amongst certain tribal sections of the Garos, a first visit to their country was made by Mr. Strong the Deputy-Commissioner at Goalpara, with a Police escort, and from then till 1861 only three small raids had to be punished with, in one case, the burning of a village, but there was no active opposition. This tract then became a separate district under a British officer who in 1866 was located at Tura, but its general administration was still dealt with from Goalpara. In 1871 Major Godwin Austen and Captain Williamson with an armed Civil Police escort were the first to traverse the Garo hills for survey purposes, and were unmolested. Two years later the Garos of Pharangiri broke out and attacked the Police post there, causing some casualties, and their village was destroyed by Captain La Touche with 40 armed constables.

In 1874 the tribe was completely subjugated by a force of 200 sepoys and 500 armed Civil Police divided into three columns under Captains Williamson and Davis and Mr. Daly (Police). With them went Lieut. Woodthorpe (later Surveyor-General in India), who completed the mapping of the region, through which roads and paths were opened. In 1879 the headquarters of civil administration were moved from Goalpara to Dhubri, the Garo hills thereafter being controlled entirely from the little station of Tura (1800 feet), where also a force of Frontier Police of 300 men was located with three posts further into the hills. This body was raised chiefly from Nepalese and Cacharis among the armed Civil

Police, and on the reorganisation of the whole of the Frontier Police into Military Police Battalions it became the Garo Hills M.P. Battalion, doing duty there for some twenty years. In 1908 its strength was reduced, 200 men being sent to make up the complement of the Dacca M.P. Battalion, as the Assam Province now included Eastern Bengal, and the Tura post remained at that strength (100) till 1913, when the detachment became part of the newly-raised Darrang M.P. Battalion, now the 4th Assam Rifles. Here we can leave this somewhat uninteresting locality.

CHAPTER III

General, 1825 to 1864—Tribes and expeditions on borders north of the Brahmaputra river—The Bhutan war—The Akas—The Daphlas—The Abors and Sadiya—Lowther's and Hannay's expeditions, 1858 and 1859—The Mishmis—Eden's exploit, 1855—Hkamtis and Singphos—Neufville's and Charlton's expeditions—Nagas of the Sibsagor hinterland.

We now may look round the other parts of the Assam frontier, *viz.* the northern from Bhutan to Sadiya, and the north-eastern portion where the Patkoi range and other hill tracts border the Sibsagor and Jorhat districts (Sketch Maps 1 and 3), and note how they progressed. Here, as for many years there was no special body of Police formed for duty, protection from tribal aggression was maintained mostly by the military, assisted to a certain extent by the armed Civil Police of Bengal, who held a few of the less important posts on the border, and bore some small share in various expeditions.

Taking the northern border lands first, the British, after the annexation of Assam, 1825–26, found themselves in contact with a variety of hill tribes occupying contiguous areas along its whole length, with different languages, dress, and habits. Some of these had taken advantage of the confusion reigning in the country prior to and during the war, and had occupied territory in the plains to which they had no rights. The gradual ejection of these people from such areas as they had spread into gave the British officials their first acquaintance with many tribes, none too easy to keep in subjection, though not so persistently hostile as the Angamis, the Abors or the Lushais. In spite of these being of a less warlike type, the history of this part of the frontier is chequered during the succeeding decades until 1920, with troubles of varying degrees of intensity.

As only the armed Civil Police for many years are connected, and but slightly, with this stretch of frontier, the general control of which lay as stated with the military, events here need only be briefly recorded now. These Police, forbears of the Lakhimpur Frontier Police, were chiefly employed in holding a few border posts, and in guard and escort duties, taking only a small share in expeditionary work up to 1862–64, when the first body of Frontier Police was definitely formed for border defence along this line, and whose history from that year forms the subject of a separate chapter.

Commencing, then, with Bhutan at the north-west end of the border where Assam touches Bengal and working eastwards, we find after the ejection of the Bhutanese from the plains a series of minor annoyances arose, which led in 1837 to the first mission of Captain Pemberton to the Bhutan capital Ponaka, from which no effectual or permanent result accrued. A large market and fair were started at Udalguri by Captain Rutherford, civil officer of the Darrang district, with a view to increasing trade and promoting friendly intercourse with the Bhutanese, and these, being a success, have continued to be held to the present time. Here at the time of the fair gather traders not only from Bhutan but also from Thibet and places beyond Lhassa, people clad in Chinese dresses and looking to all intents like those of the Celestial Land. In 1852, a Thibetan invasion of Bhutan threatening the peace of the border as Lhassa troops were approaching it, a detachment of 400 Native Infantry with 2 light guns, under command of Lieuts. Reid and Campbell, moved up to the frontier, which checked possible trouble, and an agreement of a friendly nature was made by these officers with one of the Bhutan Rajas. A few years later various aggressions led to another mission under the Honourable A. Eden being sent to Ponaka in 1863. This mission was subjected to great annoyance and insult, and was detained until the leader signed, under protest, a preposterous treaty as the only means of ensuring the safe return of himself and his escort of 100 sepoys. This treaty was at once disavowed by the British Government and led to war with Bhutan in 1864, which, although not uniformly successful throughout, compelled the Court at Ponaka to make submission.

This war, now forgotten, was begun by Brigadier-General Mulcaster and completed by General Tombs, and occupied a large force, consisting of the 55th and 80th Foot, the 43rd A.L.I., the 44th S.L.I., 11th B.I., 18th, 19th, and 31st P.I., 4 companies Sappers and Miners, 6 squadrons of Cavalry from the 5th and the 14th B.C., and 7 mountain guns, our friends of the armed Civil Police assisting by holding some of the posts behind the troops. These troops advanced into the hills in early December 1864 in four columns from Gauhati, Sidli, Cooch Behar, and Jalpaiguri, which places formed the bases for operations. Severe fighting occurred at Daling, east of Darjiling, where the fort of Dalingkot was only taken after considerable loss, and at Dewangiri, which was taken by Captain Macdonald with a small force of the 43rd A.L.I. and some of the armed Civil Police, who reached the place by another route before the arrival of Brigadier-General Mulcaster's main column. The regrettable affair at Dewangiri, where some of the Police formed part of the garrison, occurred when the bulk of the troops had withdrawn to the plains and orders had just been issued for the Field Force to break up. Here, as well as at other posts left temporarily in the hills, the Bhutanese suddenly attacked in strength.

Dewangiri was surrounded and water cut off. Serious attacks (for the enemy were no mean fighters) cost the little garrison 1 British officer and 5 men killed and 32 wounded. The position being untenable, Lieut.-Col. Campbell began a retreat, but the column lost its way in the forests and panic set in under the ceaseless attacks of the enemy, the two guns and some wounded being abandoned as well as all baggage in the rout. Later the disaster was retrieved by fresh troops, who recaptured Dewangiri with a casualty list of 7 killed and 99 wounded, amongst the latter being 4 British officers, the enemy leaving nearly 400 dead behind them. At the same time the stockades at Balla were successfully assaulted by the 18th and 29th P.I. after a stiff fight which ended the operations. The Bhutan Court, however, not acceding to our terms or returning the 2 captured guns, another force of 2 British and 6 Native regiments entered the hills again in 1866, when after one action at Salika, 15 miles north of Dewangiri, the Bhutanese finally submitted, complying with all terms, and have given no trouble since.

The next tribe eastward, *viz.* the Akas, first came to notice about 1830 through the depredations of their Tagi Raja, who caused considerable trouble along the border of the Darrang district (Sketch Maps 1 and 3), culminating in a successful attack on the Charduar stockade near Baliapara, where the little garrison of the 1st A.L.I. was cut up. A blockade of this tribe was deemed sufficient punishment and certainly kept them quiet for a number of years, as we hear of no further trouble till 1883, of which an account is given later.

Their neighbours to the eastward, the Daphlas and Miris, beyond the Tezpur and north Lakhimpur borders, are not very dissimilar to the Akas, though their language is different. First acquaintance was made with them after a raid, which was punished by Captain Mathie, in charge of the Tezpur district, with a small force of armed Civil Police after a little desultory skirmishing. No further raiding took place until 1871, when the Daphlas suddenly attacked a village inside our border, carrying off 35 persons and killing others. The reason for this outrage was curious. It appeared a severe epidemic of whooping cough had broken out amongst the plains Daphlas dwelling on and inside our frontier line, and this malady had spread to the hill clans. These latter then demanded compensation from those in the plains and lower hills amongst whom it had started. As this was refused the hill clans came down and raided. A force of 600 of the 1st A.L.I. and a strong detachment of the Nowgong Frontier Police under Major Corry were sent into the Daphla hills, but friction occurring between Corry and the civil officer accompanying the column, nothing was accomplished beyond a futile blockade. This emboldened the tribe, which became more aggressive, and a strong force of 1000 rifles of the 1st and 2nd A.L.I. and Frontier Police detachments from Dibrugarh and Nowgong under Colonel Stafford was sent against the Daphlas. These, not being really a warlike people, made no opposition, returned the captives, and paid the imposed fine, on which the force returned amidst a clamour from Government over money wasted. As this tribe does not concern this history further at present, we can now leave them.

The next tribe to be noticed are the most truculent and troublesome of all dwelling along the border north of the Brahmaputra, *viz.* the Abors, who, with their close neighbours the Miris to the west and Mishmis to the east, inhabit the outer ranges of the eastern Himalayas through which flow the great rivers, the Dihang, Dibong, and Lohit, which, uniting below Sadiya, form the Brahmaputra river (Sketch Map 3). Ethnologists class these tribes as well as those previously mentioned as offshoots of one race—the Thibeto-Burman, but they are now independent of each other and speak different languages. They inclined to the belief that, of the migrations in a far-off past, the Abors are the last arrivals, and as such have retained more of their pristine savagery and hardihood. Their country is densely forest-clad, as may be said of that of all the tribes alluded to in this chapter, owing to a much heavier rainfall in this part of the province. From the Brahmaputra for 20 to 30 miles when the border is reached, the level country is covered with thick jungle everywhere and much intersected by streams, which in the wet season overflow, converting the locality into a vast morass. Near to and beyond the border the forests occur, enormous trees with dense undergrowth flourishing up to 8000 feet, the whole forming a country most difficult to operate in.

Up to about 1840 fairly friendly terms seem to have existed between the Abors and the officials at Sadiya, even to the extent of some sections of the tribe helping us against the Hkamtis and Singphos in the troubles of 1838–39, with whom the Mishmis at that time were in alliance. The first recorded trouble with the Abors arose in 1848, which originated over the gold-washing pursuits of the Miris and certain Cacharis who worked in the rivers flowing out of the hills. The tribe, while on intimate terms with the Miris, had for long asserted their right to a percentage of gold and fish taken from rivers flowing from their hills, and this year disputes with the gold-washers led to a raid across the border in which several Miris and Cacharis were carried off. Captain Vetch with a party of the 2nd A.L.I. from Sadiya, following up the raiders, burnt an offending village, thus starting a long series of retaliatory raids and outrages, which continued at intervals up to 1911. Most of these were either more or less ignored by the authorities, or a blockade of their hills was instituted, so these pages will only deal with the more prominent raids necessitating active punitive measures.

Before relating these, a few remarks on Sadiya and past troubles in this part of the province may not be out of place, as the disturbed state of this part of Assam in the early years following the first Burmese war and before the country settled down, continued for some time.

The Singphos, who are of the same tribe as the Kachins or "Chhingpaw," as they call themselves, of Upper Burma, appear to have been a warlike people of the Patkoi ranges and of those further to the east, for at the opening of the war of 1825 they managed to defeat a

Burmese force, and much encouraged thereby they ravaged the Sadiya and Dibrugarh areas almost to Rangpur, near Sibsagor. As the British forces advanced into Assam Captain Neufville in 1826 was detached with a body of Native Infantry and 2 gunboats of the Indian Marine up the Brahmaputra against the tribe.

Proceeding up the Noa Dihing river he entrenched 25 miles above its junction with the Tengapani, where the gunboats and a detachment were left to protect the river crossing. The next advance brought about actions at Daffa on the 6th June, 1826, and at Bisa, where he defeated a mixed force of Burmese and Singphos, pursuing them over a pass in the Patkoi. Neufville withdrew, leaving posts at Bisa, Koojoodoo, Ningroo, and Nungrang, and for a time there was quiet. From 1835 to 1843 the Singphos caused much trouble, particularly in the former year, when they overwhelmed the post at Bisa, causing much loss of life. They also attacked the other posts, though without success, as these were commanded by British officers. This fighting was the way of the savage to vindicate his right to capture slaves, which custom the British were putting a stop to. Various expeditions during this period were conducted by Captains Neufville and Charlton mostly with troops, but old records show that parties of the armed Civil Police were also employed. It was not till 1850 that a settled condition in this area permitted the withdrawal of these posts (Sketch Map 3).

Sadiya was occupied by the British on conclusion of the first war with Burma and was held by a regiment of Native Infantry, aided by gunboats manned by the Indian Marine, who patrolled the rivers. From old maps the little station seems to have been located on practically the same site as at present, though for a few years it was moved to Saikwa, on the opposite (left bank) of the Lohit river. Dr. McCosh, in his account of the extreme north-eastern frontier in 1835, writes of Sadiya as " situated on the right bank of the Lohit near the mouth of the Kundil river. Trade is rapidly increasing, all the necessaries of life are procurable, and it is a place of rising importance. It is the most advanced post in this direction and is the headquarters of the 2nd A.L.I., of whom 3 companies are in garrison here, the remaining ones holding posts in the neighbourhood. Two gunboats, each mounting a 12-pounder gun and manned by the Royal Naval Brigade commanded by Lieut. Bruce, R.N., patrol the river. It was this officer's brother who started the first tea garden shortly after 1826, assisted by Lieut. Charlton, which was laid out close to the station towards Kundilmukh. Bruce also was the first European to visit Rima from Sadiya in 1828 with a small escort, which he accomplished in 20 days' marching. The barracks and houses for officials at Sadiya are huts of wattle and daub, and in the centre of the place stands the fort, a fair-sized earthwork enclosure with ditch, surmounted by a timber palisade, while inside are masonry buildings for the magazine, treasury, stores, and a barrack for the detachment on duty there." This old fort is still in use and is the one which witnessed the massacre of Colonel White and a large number of his men by the Hkamtis in 1839, and to whose memory a few years later the new church at Dibrugarh was dedicated. An old map of Sadiya in 1828 shows barracks and officers houses much on the same site as at present, even to the racecourse, which apparently was laid out as far back as that year. In those early days after the war the Hkamti tribe, who inhabited the area above the Tengapani river to the foothills of the Himalayas and were under a chief known as the Sadiya Kowa Gohain, furnished a body of Militia, 200 strong, which took part in Captain Neufville's first expeditions against the Singphos of the Patkoi range. Dr. McCosh also states that in his day strong suggestions were made to open a road from the last navigable point on the Noa Dihing river *via* the Hukong valley beyond the Patkoi to the Irrawadi in Burma. The idea being approved, a beginning was made by Lieut. Bennet with an escort of the 2nd A.L.I. but he, while reconnoitring one of the passes of the Patkoi, was attacked by the Singphos and driven back, many of those with him being killed. This led to one of Neufville's expeditions, after which the project of a road through to Burma was given up, not to be revived again for some sixty years and then for railway purposes.

Reverting to the Abors in 1858, a large body of the Minyong clan (the tribe having four large clans—Minyong, Padam, Pangi, and Shimong) attacked and destroyed a village barely 6 miles from Dibrugarh, and great uneasiness was felt lest that station itself should be raided, where a detachment of the Nowgong Frontier Police was now on duty in addition to some Regulars. Troops were at once sent in pursuit of the raiders, but owing to various mischances they failed to enter the hills, and returned with loss of credit to those in command. This only heartened the tribe, and an expedition was decided on consisting of 140 men of the 2nd A.L.I., a detachment of the Frontier Police, and two 12-pounder guns from Sadiya under Captain Lowther, with whom went the Deputy-Commissioner of Lakhimpur. Kebang, the principal village of the Minyong Abors, was unknown, but was believed to be only 4½ days' march beyond the border. On the 19th March, 1858, the little force reached Pasi, where the Dihang river debouches from the hills, and the following day advanced towards Kebang. The first 15 miles were traversed in small boats as far as Pangi, the guns being carried along the bank by elephants, and here they had to be left with the boats, as it was found impossible from the nature of the country to carry them further. On the 22nd March the force, naturally reduced by having to leave behind guards for boats, guns, and ration escorts, continued its advance under considerable difficulties, mainly due to the tribesmen, who attacked two ration escorts, driving them back. Thus the force, meeting with much opposition and receiving no supplies, was ordered to retire, although, unknown to the officers, they had actually reached a point within 2 miles of Kebang village and where one good effort would have achieved the desired end. The retirement was greatly harassed by the Abors and many casualties occurred; and seeing the discomfiture of the troops many other villages also joined in the pursuit. On reaching the boats the force evacuated the hills as quickly as possible without having effected anything. This failure was not only due to bad commissariat arrangements and inadequate escorts to the same, but the fighting strength was too small for its purpose, and the expedition also suffered from the unfortunate state of friction existing between the O.C. troops and the Civil Officer with it, who tied the former's hands—a condition of affairs too frequently occurring in those days and which militated against the success of many border expeditions.

The Abors now left their hills and occupied Pasi, where they built strong stockades and at Rungkang in the same neighbourhood, whence they proceeded to harry villages on the plains, causing an intolerable state of affairs. An expedition in greater strength had therefore to be arranged, consisting of 300 men of the 2nd A.L.I., 150 armed Civil and Frontier Police from Nowgong and Dibrugarh, 62 men of the Naval Brigade, and a native artillery detachment of 56 men with two 12-pounder howitzers and a couple of mortars, the whole under command of Colonel Hannay, 2nd A.L.I., with 5 officers.

This force left Sadiya on the 21st February, 1859, by boats to Pobamukh, whence it marched through swampy lands and forests to within a short distance of Pasi, where the enemy had erected several stockades, as well as others near Rungkang village, which they were said to be holding in strength (Sketch Map 3). Reconnoitring parties sent out at once were able to locate four out of the many stockades, which friendly Abors declared had been built between Pasi and Rungkang. Early on the 27th February Hannay attacked and at once found, as his despatch states :—" A stubborn opposition to our advance, which the enemy's knowledge of the ground, his skill

ABORS.

KUKIS.

with bows and arrows and spears, and his formidable stockades rendered easy. Of these latter several were defended to the last, while in three cases it was necessary to use the howitzers to open a way for the assault. The first series of positions at and above Pasi was taken by detachments of the Naval Brigade (Indian Marine), the A.L.I., and the Police, with the guns under myself and Major Reid; the farther ones and Rungkang village being taken by the Marine detachment and one of the A.L.I. Three of these latter were taken at the point of the bayonet, in which assaults Lieut. Davies and Midshipman Mayo were badly wounded, the former in three places."

Lieut. Lewis, in command of the Marines, in his account of the operations, which is apparently the only one in any detail, writes:—"For about 3 miles from our camp below Pasi we were unmolested, and we then began to experience slight opposition from trees felled across the rough track through the forest and from arrows fired at us from the jungle on either flank. On approaching the first stockade a howitzer was brought up by Major Reid and several rounds of grape shot were fired into it, after which, more troops having come up, the place was assaulted, many dead Abors being found inside. Beyond this ran a small river with a high bank on the far side on which stood another large stockade. Again the howitzers came to the front and battered the defences while the troops crossed and climbing the steep bank carried the position, only to find another one beyond and above us, which greeted the advancing troops with heavy showers of arrows and a few musket shots. Several more casualties occurred here, and under covering fire from a section of the A.L.I. the whole force moved forward and assaulted. It was found the capture of this stockade enfiladed two others further on from which the enemy bolted almost at once. The force was now well into the hills above Pasi, the country was most difficult, being steep and jungle covered, and some distance higher up stood another large and strong stockaded position barring the way to Rungkang village. The spur on which this one was located was almost precipitous and here the Abors made the longest and most determined resistance of all.

"The troops had to climb under prolonged discharges of arrows and rocks rolled down on them, until they reached the bit of level on which the stockade stood. The Naval Brigade men and some of the A.L.I. and the Police, who were first on top, charged and got up to the stockade palisading, through interstices in which the enemy thrust their spears and let fly showers of arrows. Efforts were made to climb over the palisading but failed, many being wounded in the attempt. Owing to the nature of the ground the guns could not be used, and the only way to effect an entrance was by gradually cutting and breaking down a portion of the timber defences. Here Lieut. Davies and Midshipman Mayo were badly wounded, the former in three places, while directing the men. Davies kept going in spite of two wounds, and just as he was hit the third time managed to thrust his revolver between the timbers and shot his assailant dead before he collapsed and was carried to the rear. Many men of all units, including three or four of the Police who were engaged thus, were hit, but at last a way was broken in, when resistance ceased, few remaining to contest the entry of the troops, the rest bolting into the forest leaving numbers of dead and wounded. The last stockade was abandoned without any fight and Rungkang a little way on was in possession of the force by 2 p.m. and was destroyed, after 7 hours of uninterrupted hard fighting and climbing in exceedingly difficult country. The total casualties in the force were 52, and from Abors who now came in and made submission, it was stated the fighting strength of the enemy had been 1400."

Unfortunately no map accompanied Lewis' account, and as Rungkang has long since disappeared it is not easy to make out where the hostile positions were or the actual route taken. After destroying three other villages

Hånnay withdrew his force, enough punishment, it was thought, having been inflicted. The opposition and fighting qualities shown by the Abors in this expedition exceeded any they have since displayed in either the operations of 1894 or 1911, excepting the fight they put up at Dambuk in the first-named year.

A chain of posts to be held by the military along this part of the frontier and their connection by means of a road were now strongly advocated, but as Government would not agree to this owing to financial reasons, the local authorities took protective measures "on their own," and using convict labour carried out the scheme of road communication. All this work, which occupied some considerable time, so impressed the Abors that some of their leading men came to a conference with the Deputy-Commissioner, held at Lallimukh near Kobo, and concluded friendly agreements, which were duly adhered to for a few years. Their raids, however, into the Mishmi hills, where they practically controlled one of the trade routes, together with their tendency to come down across the Dibong river into the plains, obliged the establishment in 1876 of strong military posts at Nizamghat and Bomjur (Sketch Map 3) to keep the Abors in check. The latter was held for many years and given up about 1900, and Nizamghat, for years held by the regiment at Sadiya, was made over to the Lakhimpur Military Police Battalion about 1890, and is still retained as a post.

The Mishmis to the east of the Abors (Sketch Map 3), who had taken no part in the operations just narrated, had been known but slightly from 1830, and six years later Dr. Griffiths paid a short but friendly visit to their country. Then came the Hkamti rising of 1839, in which small parties of the tribe joined, and in 1845 Lieut. Rowlatt, on duty at Sadiya, entered their hills and was well received. They also are divided into four clans—Chulikatta, Bebejiya, Digaru, and Meju—but differ from their neighbours in both language and customs, although, like all these tribes, they originated from the same stock. It was the murder of two French missionaries, MM. Krick and Bourri, in the end of 1854 by Kaisha, a Chulikatta chief, which caused the first punitive entry into the Mishmi hills in retribution for the outrage. Lieut. Eden was deputed to carry this out, and took a carefully selected party of 20 men of the 2nd A.L.I. and 40 Shan volunteers from the armed Civil Police at Dibrugarh, these latter being men most likely to do well in those parts, and with a few porters he left Sadiya in early February 1855. His march and its results have been recorded as "one of, if not the most successful minor expedition of all our punitive outings in Assam," and shows what can be done by a small party of hardy, resolute men, well led. The record goes on to state that "after eight days' forced marching, swinging over dangerous torrents on bridges of single canes, experiencing bitter cold in the higher ranges, and showing wonderful endurance of great hardships inseparable from rapidity of movement, Eden and his men, in the grey dawn of a misty morning, reached and surprised Kaisha's village on the Du river."

A friendly Meju chief, by name Lumling, with some of his own followers, joined Eden in time for the sharp fight which at once ensued, in which Kaisha was captured, his two sons and many of his men were killed, and the village was destroyed. The murder of the missionaries was amply avenged, their Singpho servant was released and the greater part of the stolen property was recovered; while the news of such an exploit spread through the hills and did not fail to astonish and overawe neighbouring tribesmen. Eden brought Kaisha back, who was duly hanged at Dibrugarh, but not before the sturdy ruffian had managed to kill two warders. The outcome of Eden's success where the friendly Meju chief was concerned was regrettable, for Government declined to aid Lumling in the inter-clan fighting which followed. In this the relatives of Kaisha with the bulk of their clansmen completely exterminated Lumli ·. his family, and many

MISHMI WARRIOR.

of his people. Since then the feelings of the Meju Mishmis towards the British have not been of the most cordial. Peaceful relations, however, reigned with this tribe for nearly forty years.

Mention having already been made regarding the Hkamtis and Singphos with Neufville's and Charlton's expeditions towards the Patkoi range, we can follow the border from Sadiya district in a south-westerly direction, when we find various tribes of Nagas dwelling in the mountains south of Sibsagor and Jorhat, or roughly from the Singpho country to the Dikkoo river. In general these people, though of the same ethnological stock as the Angamis, are much less warlike and aggressive, and from early days used to come freely to trade in the plains. The most troublesome among them have been the Jaboka, Banfera, Bor Mutania, and Namsangia sections, with whom a first acquaintance was made in 1840 by Captain Brodie, then Principal Assistant at Sibsagor to the Governor-General's Agent in Assam, and with whom they made agreements not to molest the plains villages or the tea gardens then coming into existence in this part of the province. Two years later he made the first tour through their hills with an escort of the Jorhat Militia (Police) and was well received. For some time the tribes confined their hostility amongst themselves, but in 1844 this border became so disturbed that Brodie had to lead two minor expeditions with his Jorhat Militia into the hills to enforce quietude. In neither do the records show any fighting as having taken place, and for many years it was found that a blockade of their hills was sufficient to bring the different sections to reason when trouble seemed probable.

Two missionaries (Americans) deserve mention here for their remarkably good work in these hills, *viz.* Mr. Bronson, from 1842 to about 1852, and Dr. Clarke, from the early 'sixties till 1898. The latter with his wife, and joined later by a friend, established themselves in the village of Molongting, on the outer range overlooking the present Amguri tea gardens. They soon became a great influence for good amongst the tribes by reason of their extensive and continuous tours, during which they made friends with the Nagas and gave unremitting attention to their sick people. In many cases they were able successfully to use their influence to prevent raiding and trouble. About 1893 Dr. Clarke and his wife, joineed by three other American missionaries, left Molongting and started the little mission station at Impur, 12 miles from Mokokchang in the Ao Naga country, which exists still, but those who followed on in the work on the Clarkes leaving for good, lacking the zeal, energy and personality of those who had departed, cannot be said to have excelled or even approached the example set them.

This brings us back to the Angami Naga, Khasi, and Lushai hills with their various disturbances, which were due, as previously stated, to the passive attitude of the Government after 1851 and Vincent's expedition.

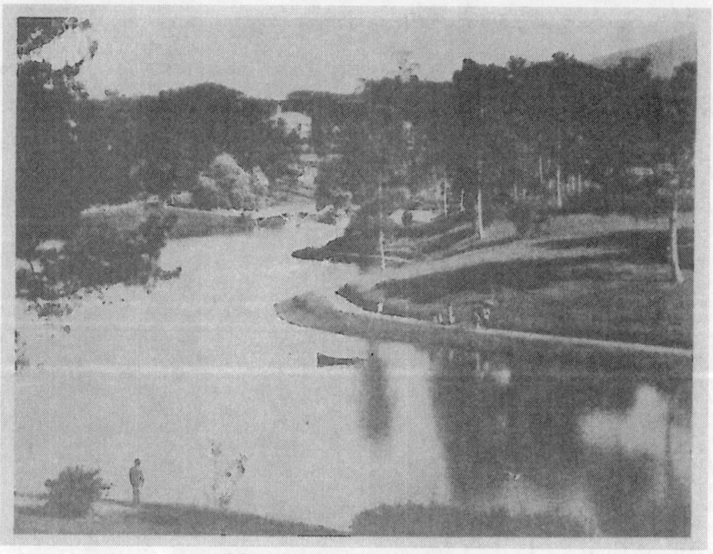

Two Views of Shillong.

CHAPTER IV

General, 1860 to 1870—Synteng rebellion, 1862—Shillong—Frontier Police recruiting Depot at Sylhet—Forward policy once more—Gregory at Samaguting—Captain Butler—Change in Nowgong F.P. uniform—Sanction for post at Wokha refused but established 1875—Settlement of Manipur boundaries—Survey work—Butler killed at Pangti—Proposed and sanctioned reorganisation of F.P. units—Matter delayed by Naga rising 1879/80—Military Police Battalions come into being 1882/83—Changes in uniform—First commandants.

DURING 1860, after many years of quietude in the Khasi and Jaintia hills (Sketch Map 1), these people suddenly became troublesome, eventually breaking out into open rebellion a year later. This was known as the "Synteng Rebellion" and was due to taxation which had been imposed on the inhabitants of these hills, and which was followed by injudicious police restrictions regarding the burning of their dead. The force under Colonel Dunsford employed to suppress this rising comprised the following troops: the 21st and 28th Punjab Infantry, 33rd Native Infantry, 2nd A.L.I., S.L.I., the Kamrup Regiment (later transferred to the Civil and the Frontier Police), Rattray's Sikh Military Police (later 45th Sikhs), 200 Frontier Police from Nowgong and the north Cachar hills, and a battery of Artillery. The principal scenes of action were in the area round Jowai, 32 miles east of Shillong, which was besieged by the rebels for nearly three weeks, and was only relieved with much difficulty, fighting, and a number of casualties. It was not till November 1863, after every glen and jungle had been searched out by the troops and Police (the latter having 3 killed and 19 wounded in the operations) and the last rebel leader had been captured, that the trouble in these hills was stamped out and has not recurred since. Jowai was held by a military detachment until 1885, when it was handed over to Civil Police protection, and thereafter declined in any importance it ever had.

The year after these operations were closed a change in the location of the Civil Administration's headquarters was found desirable.

For some years previously, in spite of its pleasant surroundings, Cherrapoonji had been found far too wet for the health and comfort of the troops and officials stationed there. Standing as it does on the edge of a range 4300 feet above sea level and directly overlooking the plains of Sylhet, it receives the full brunt of the monsoon from the Bay of Bengal, this giving it an annual rainfall averaging up to 450 inches, making it about the wettest place in the world. During 1861 actually over 800 inches were recorded. Therefore during the quieter intervals of the operations just mentioned opportunity was taken to search for a locality better suited climatically to the needs of a large and important station. This was found on an undulating plateau along the northern slope of the Shillong range at an elevation of 4900 feet, overlooked by the "Peak," 1400 feet higher. Here, although only 30 odd miles from Cherrapoonji, the annual rainfall was found to be only about 84 inches, so all circumstances being favourable building was commenced, roads were laid out and communications opened direct with Gauhati. Cherrapoonji was then abandoned and in 1866 the seat of Government was transferred from Gauhati to Shillong, which in course of time developed into what we now see—the best kept and most desirable headquarters station of all the local Governments in India.

The winter 1862–63 saw a change take place in regard to the armed Civil Police and the protection of the southern borders of Cachar and Sylhet. This was the formation of a new body of Frontier Police for Cachar on the lines of the old Cachar Levy, who were to take on in a large measure the watch and ward of the border lands, with headquarters at Silchar. Hitherto these

The Country about Cherrapoonji.

duties had been carried out partly by the Sylhet Light Infantry and partly by the armed Civil Police together with a small Kuki Levy of 200 men raised some ten years before by Majors Lister and Stewart. This Levy and the North Cachar Hills Frontier Police were now amalgamated, added to by recruitment, and the Cachar Frontier Police force (later renamed the Surma Valley F.P.) came into being in late 1863, commanded by a Civil Police officer and dressed, armed and equipped as the other F.P. units were. From this year on the history of this body forms the subject of a separate narrative.

In 1865 a recruiting depot for all the Frontier Police was opened at Sylhet for the enlistment of Nepalese, Cacharis and Jaruas, and at this time also European Police inspectors, some of whom had been in the Army, were attached to all F.P. headquarters to supervise the military training and musketry of the men on lines similar to those in force in Light Infantry regiments. From 1866 onwards selected F.P. men were sent periodically for training to either the Assam or the Sylhet Light Infantry, and were then employed as drill instructors in the force.

At last by 1865 passive resistance and blockading the tribes along the Nowgong and north Cachar hills border having produced only an impossible and chaotic state of affairs, in which nothing was done to check the continuous raiding, Sir Cecil Beadon's strong recommendation of four years earlier for a more vigorous forward policy bore fruit, and strong measures were sanctioned. Major John Butler having retired, Lieut. Gregory, an officer of much tact and energy in charge of the north Cachar hills district, was transferred to Nowgong in his place.

The frontier line was pushed forward once more, Dimapur and Samaguting being reoccupied, and to this latter place Gregory with 150 of the Nowgong F.P. was sent (Sketch Map 4). He was to exert a conciliatory influence over the Angami clans, and if this failed was empowered to undertake punitive measures at once. No sooner had the new arrangements been completed than the village of Raziphima in the Chatthe valley went on the war-path, and raided Sergamcha on the north Cachar border. Directly the news of this reached Samaguting, Gregory with 80 of the F.P. marched for Raziphima and after slight opposition destroyed it and its granaries, and capturing most of the community deported them elsewhere. This salutary lesson, together with the knowledge that a British officer with powers of immediate action was now permanently settled within reach of them, had the effect of stopping raids for some years, thus enabling Gregory to make several tours with F.P. escorts to various Naga villages of importance, whereby our knowledge of the country and its people was increased.

Lieut. Gregory was succeeded in 1868 by Captain Butler (son of Major John Butler), whose first visit with a strong F.P. escort far into the Naga hills took place the following year in connection with the settlement of the boundaries between British and Manipuri spheres of influence. Dr. Brown, then Political Agent in the Manipur State, was met at Mao Thana and boundary matters were arranged without trouble, much as they stand to-day.

About this time it was found desirable to change the headquarters of administration in the north Cachar hills from Asaloo to Gunjong, some 20 miles further west, where a higher and healthier site had been found; the first-named place then dropped to the level of a small F.P. post, and was given up entirely fifteen years later.

The Frontier Police uniform generally appears to have been now (1868) changed for one of dark blue cloth with white piping round cuffs and collar and down the seams of the knickerbockers, some units adopting black putties, others a stiff brown canvas gaiter, but, as seen in the illustration, knickerbockers were often discarded. Buttons were of white metal and a silver bugle badge adorned the Kilmarnock cap or the "pagri," which latter headdress was worn for long by the Cachar F.P. Personal knowledge of this uniform was acquired by the author when, as Commandant of the Naga Hills M.P: 1897–1902, an old native officer of the battalion, Jemadar Belbong Ram, who had enlisted in the 'seventies and had been in the Khonoma operations of 1879–80, brought his old uniform, carefully preserved, to show him. The black leather equipment remained the same, but the sword had given place to the more useful kookerie. Black greatcoats were given the men free in 1879.

We now approach the period which saw the greatest change in the life and conditions of the whole of the Frontier Police Force of Assam, *viz.* its reorganisation into separate Military Police battalions arranged territorially. Up to this time (1875), as has been shown, the Assam borders were protected by four Regular battalions of the Indian Army, aided by the Frontier and the armed Civil Police. The 42nd and the 43rd A.L.I. and the 44th S.L.I. had their headquarters at Gauhati, Shillong and Dibrugarh, with strong detachments at Golaghat, Sibsagor, Tezpur, Jaipur, and Sadiya, while a Bengal regiment was still stationed at Silchar. The frontier posts were 50 in number, of which 36 were held by the F.P. with 734 men, and 14 by the military with 646. After the Lushai expedition of 1871–72, narrated in Chapter VI, and various troubles connected with survey work, it became apparent that the border and internal defence needed revision and rearrangement under a better system, and as the border lands after 1875 generally appeared quieter, the matter came under discussion, which, lasting as usual a considerable time, was brought to a head by events four years later.

That such reorganisation was eminently desirable was shown thus. The frontier posts and defence generally had hitherto been arranged without any definite system, and as military units, Frontier and armed Civil Police were mixed up indiscriminately, administrative unity was impossible as the posts were held by men of different organisations. Hence they ceased to form a connected chain of posts ready to co-operate with each other. The military would not act without instructions from their own commanding officers, although they were under the orders of the civil officer in charge of the district in which they were serving, and this naturally led to delay, to circumlocution of orders, and also in many cases to friction between the civil and the military elements. Regimental C.O.'s greatly disliked seeing their commands split up in posts difficult to reach, which not only caused discipline and training to deteriorate, but led also to great expense in rationing, transport, etc. In those days it was computed a military sepoy cost Government 337 rupees per annum, while 187 rupees represented the yearly cost of a Frontier Police constable.

It seemed the time had undoubtedly come when border posts might well be taken over by the Frontier Police force, as had successfully been done by the Bengal Government in the case of the Chittagong Hill Tracts, and that the military units might be still further reduced.

But to carry out all duties required of them efficiently the F.P. needed both increase in strength and reorganisation; also it was highly desirable that they should be placed under officers of the Regular Army, lent to the Assam Government for a certain period of years for purposes of efficiency in drill, training, discipline, and internal economy. On all these points endless discussions took place between the provincial Government and that of India, and at last it was decided to remove the Bengal Infantry Regiment at Silchar, leaving the three local regiments (42nd and 43rd A.L.I. and 44th S.L.I.), to which were still attached 6 mountain guns under a R.A. officer, and to maintain sufficient transport elephants, mules, and coolies to enable half of each to move out at twenty-four hours' notice. Then followed the reorganisation of the old Frontier Police force which had been in existence as such, in the case of the Nowgong and the North Cachar F.P. since 1835, that of Lakhimpur since 1864, and that of Cachar since 1863.

Up to this time the total strength of the F.P., increased

Angami Naga.

Trans-Dikkoo Nagas.

and reduced from time to time, stood at 2400 of all ranks, and it was proposed to raise this number to 3300. It was also recommended that the force should be arranged in battalions territorially, on a proper military system, to be styled the Assam Military Police Battalions of the Naga hills, Lakhimpur, and the Surma valley (Cachar), each of 750 men, with a small battalion of 330 men for the Garo hills. Later these strengths underwent slight alterations. The Naga hills and the Lakhimpur Battalions were to be each under an officer of the Army, while those of the Surma valley and Garo hills would remain under their Civil Police officers, Messrs. Daly and Fisher, respectively.

It was also recommended as an aid to better recruitment that the titles of all ranks should be assimilated to those of the Army, *viz.* Subadars, Jemadars, Havildars, and Sepoys, with pay at 150/-, 60/-, 16/-, and 8/- a month, respectively.

Posts decided on to be held by each battalion were as follows :—

Naga Hills Battalion (Kohima)	*Lakhimpur Battalion* (Dibrugarh)	*Surma Valley Battalion* (Silchar)
Borpather	Daimara	Adampur
Dimapur	Baliapara	Alinagar
Nichuguard	Lalukdoloni	Langai
Piphima	Bordoloni	Oliviacherra
Wokha	Dijmur	Mainadhar
Vishwema	Dikrang	Jatinga Valley
Henema	Disoi	Gunjong
	Diphoo	Hangrung
	Sonpura	Baladhan
	Sadiya	Aisacherra
	Makum	Jaipur
	Jaipur	Jirighat
	Behubar	
	Geleki	

Detachments were also to be placed at Tezpur and at Sibsagor, furnished from Dibrugarh, and the Garo hills unit with headquarters at Tura was to hold two posts in the interior. The only posts from now on to be still held by the military were to be those of Pobamukh, Sesseri, Bomjur, and Nizamghat in the Sadiya area, and in that of the Surma valley at Jalnacherra, Doarband, and Monierkhal.

When decisions had at last been arrived at, but before any action could be taken to carry them out, serious trouble broke out delaying all reorganisation on the lines advocated and sanctioned, which are narrated in detail in Chapter XI on the Naga Hills M.P. Battalion.

It was therefore not till 1882, when border quietude reigned once more, that the reorganisation of the Assam Frontier Police force could be taken up as sanctioned in 1877–78. By early 1883 we find the new Military Police Battalions, as previously named, had come into being, the Naga Hills M.P. Battalion having been raised by its first Commandant, Captain C. Plowden, 5th B.C., that of Lakhimpur by Captain E. Molesworth, 44th S.L.I., the Surma Valley and Garo Hills M.P. being commanded by Civil Police officers, as mentioned a little earlier. The three full-strength battalions were also given the services of a sergeant from a British regiment to assist Commandants with recruits and internal economy. Battalions at first wore their old uniforms until khaki was introduced in 1885, when each unit adopted its own distinctive silver buttons and cap badges with the battalion's name, and crossed kookerie badges of rank for Native officers, *i.e.* Subadars two crossed kookeries on each shoulder strap, Jemadars only one. The cap badge was of silver with crossed kookeries and the initials of the unit's name. In the case of the Naga Hills M.P., red piping was worn round cuffs and collars and down the trouser seams until about 1904, and a winter uniform of khaki serge was retained by all battalions for many years, when owing to expense this was given up, thick underclothing being given instead. The whole force was directly under the Inspector-General of Police, at this time Captain Williamson, but he was followed before long by Mr. Driberg and a succession of Civil Police officials who, naturally not being conversant with military matters and needs, left everything in the hands of the commandants. All posts were revised and put in a proper state of defence, rifle ranges and parade grounds were made where possible, and Commandants were ordered to inspect their posts not less than twice a year. For the larger posts it was ordered that each year two-thirds of the garrison should be taken on a rough outing lasting some days, so as to train the men in work they would have to do when on active service. Proper barrack accommodation, or what was regarded as such according to the easy-going ideas of those days, was also put in hand, and recruiting for some time was tried with Sikhs, Punjabis, Dogras, and to a small extent with Mahommedans. The two former classes not answering so well in Assam as they have done in Burma, recruiting in their case was stopped after a few years, but Dogras until about 1912 continued to be enlisted by the Naga Hills M.P. Eventually the composition of each battalion came to be three-fourths the strength of Goorkhas, and one-fourth of Jaruas, or as near that as possible.

Of course the advantages accruing from this reorganisation of the force were not long in making themselves apparent, and an all-round improvement of discipline and efficiency soon became noticeable, followed in a few years by an admirable feeling of *esprit de corps* in each unit, and a proper emulation in inter-battalion sports, and in work when on active service together.

We can now trace the individual histories of the units of the old Frontier Police force, from the time that each became a separate body with a life and records of its own, and follow them into varied fields of activity.

CHAPTER V

1863 to 1869. The Surma Valley Frontier Police raised, 1863—General Nuthall's expedition into Lushai Hills, 1868—The Chittagong border and armed Civil Police—Exploration of the Koladyne river, 1848—The Mutiny, 1857—Proposed road connecting with Burma—Early expeditions in the Chittagong Hill Tracts—Lewin and the Arrakan Police on the Koladyne river, 1865—Chittagong Frontier Police organised, 1866—Its frontier posts.

To trace the history of the force which at the present time is known as the 1st Battalion Assam Rifles, it is necessary to go back to 1862, when a revision was made of protective measures for the southern and eastern borders of Cachar and Sylhet, and still further south to the Chittagong district, as the Bengal Frontier Police on that border were transferred, together with the Lushai hills district, to Assam in 1897. Hitherto, as has been shown, these protective duties had been carried out partly with the aid of Regular troops and partly by the armed Civil Police of Bengal, together with a small Kuki Levy (200) raised some ten years earlier by Major Lister and Captain Stewart, the latter being then Superintendent of the Cachar District. It was now decided to form a new body of Frontier Police for these borders on the lines of the old Cachar Levy, on whom in a large measure border protection should fall. This Kuki Levy and the North Cachar Hills Frontier Police in early 1863 were now amalgamated, brought up to a strength of 650 men by recruitment, commanded by a Civil Police officer, were clothed and armed as the Nowgong and Lakhimpur units, and had their headquarters at Silchar. At first designated the Cachar Frontier Police, ten years later this title was changed to that of the Surma Valley Frontier Police, and it was not long before the men of this new force were called out on active service across this southern border.

From 1865 to 1868 raids by Kukis, aided in some cases, it was found, by Lushais occupying the hills many days' journey south of the Cachar border, brought about several minor punitive outings in which men of the new Frontier Police Battalion took part, but in no case did they penetrate far afield. Towards the end of the latter year, after raids had taken place in which the tribesmen, with Sookpilal, a powerful Lushai chief, as instigator, destroyed the tea gardens of Doarband and Monierkhal, causing great loss of life, Brigadier-General Nuthall was ordered to conduct punitive operations with a force consisting of the Sylhet Light Infantry, the 7th Native Infantry, a Eurasian battery and strong detachments of the Cachar Frontier Police. Two columns were formed, one under the Brigadier, which advanced up the Dalesari river as far as Pakwamukh, an affluent of the right bank, while the other, under Major Stevenson, proceeded up the Sonai valley, reaching Bazaarghat. In addition to these, Messrs. Baker and Kemble (Civil Police) were directed to move with detachments of the Frontier Police and the 7th N.I. along the eastern border of the Tippera State (now known under its old name of "Tripura") to Koilashur, whence they reached and visited Rangboon and one or two other villages of Sookpilal's on the Gootur river (now called the "Tūth"), a left bank affluent of the Dalesari which it joins a little south of Jalnacherra. The whole expedition was, however, a failure; there was slight opposition and a few casualties. The Brigadier's column got within sight of Sookpilal's main village, but want of supplies, continuance of much bad weather, and a great deal of sickness obliged the columns to withdraw from the hills without having really effected anything.

We must now turn to a locality still further south, *viz.* the Chittagong Hill Tracts, which district belonged to Bengal, but the "hinterland" of which, *viz.* the south

Lushai hills, taken over by Bengal in 1890, was seven years later transferred, together with its Military Police Battalion, to the Province of Assam, this unit thus becoming a part of the 1st Assam Rifles (Sketch Maps 1 and 2).

For some time after the conquest of Bengal by the British little or nothing was known of the country about Chittagong, which came under British rule in 1761. What was known showed that this part of the coast and the neighbouring country of Arrakan had in early days been held by the Portuguese, who made themselves notorious for piracy in the Bay of Bengal during Shah Jehan's reign in the middle of the 17th century. Many traces are still to be seen of their occupancy, not only near the coast, but even far inland, as evidenced by ancient masonry tanks, ruined walls, and plinths, up the Myari river, an affluent of the Kassalong, and more than 150 miles to the east of the coast, a locality now covered by dense forests. Indeed, Chittagong with its hills and seaboard, until the rise of British power, had seen several races struggling for supremacy—indigenous tribes, Mahommedans, Portuguese, Burmese, all had preceded us as masters and left traces of their rule. An early writer describes Chittagong as being "a picturesque place; behind the native town and the port rise small grassy knolls on which Government officials, planters, and merchants had built their bungalows, as the lower levels were unhealthy and liable to be flooded." So Chittagong remains, except for vast improvements in roads, in houses, and in the extensive increase to the port since 1898 due to the advent of the railway.

It was in 1767 that Mr. Verelst, the first Chief of Chittagong, as that official was then styled, began to have his attention drawn to the area now known as the Hill Tracts and its people, and to express his desire to extend his border at Chandragona up the Kornaphuli river, so as to include the country to the foot of the Lushai hills. Such action, however, did not commend itself to the Bengal Government. About 1775, owing to the establishment of "kheddas" for elephant catching which took the operators further inland, the country began to be a little more known, and these men coming in contact with hostile people led to the first military expedition recorded, when in 1777 Captain Ellester with a wing of the 22nd N.I., then stationed at Chittagong, went into the interior to restore order. How far they got or any details are not known, but shortly after this Mr. Irwin, who succeeded Mr. Verelst, begins to report raids, as if the expedition had stirred up a hornets' nest; and he urged the taking over of the country and its administration to the foot of the main ranges. This again was not sanctioned by the Bengal Government, but Irwin was able favourably to influence certain distant tribal chiefs, who offered tribute for the privilege of being able to trade freely in our markets, which offer was accepted and all went well for some years.

Between 1787 and 1795 Bengal was constrained to pay some attention to outlying areas of Chittagong, owing, during this period, to the large numbers of refugees crossing our border in flight from the oppression and cruelty of the Arrakan King, who on one occasion actually followed them into British territory with an armed force. The Chittagong boundary was then extended from Chandragona to the line of the Kassalong and the Fenny rivers, but the new area was left unprotected, only political notice being taken of any aggression on the part of Arrakan, and the refugees were allowed to settle within our limits, but numbers of these unfortunates perished in the pathless forests they had to pass through.

The first visit of an English official to the south Lushai hills border was made, it appears, in 1800 by Mr. Rennell, Chief Engineer in Bengal, who published the earliest account of the peoples in those parts. Thereafter followed the Naaf River Expedition to turn the Burmese out of an island, Shapuri, which they had seized and stockaded between Chittagong and Akyab in September 1823, and which formed a prelude, together with other events, leading up to the first Burmese war, 1824–25, the results of which broke the power of Arrakan and Burma, and we hear of no further trouble concerning the Chittagong side till about 1860. Of this war and with reference to the fighting against the Burmese General, Maha Bandula at Ramu (Sketch Map 1), who in May 1825 was advancing on Chittagong with 8000 picked troops, it is interesting to quote an extract from the letter of an English officer who was present in the attack on Ramu, and who wrote to Lord Amherst as follows: "The country being more open round Ramu (now Cox's Bazaar), it was with astonishment that our men saw the Burmese advance and then their leading lines would disappear; while still at a distance we saw them advancing in a regular line, but presently the men forming that line were prostrate on the ground and in a very short time were comfortably ensconced in couples in small excavations made with a tool they carried, and from which they fired until a further forward move was decided on. They took careful aim, though their weapons were wretched, but they had excellent guns and gunners, for which we were unprepared." In his "Romance of India" Mr. Surridge also alludes to this method of the Burmese, whose soldiery, he says, usually carried a hoe or a spade in addition to weapons.

It is curious to read of the Burmese troops of those days being trained to advance to an attack on such modern lines, which were then novel in Europe! In this attack on Ramu and rout of Captain Noton's force after five days' fighting the Burmese were successful, and but for the recall of Maha Bandula for the defence of Lower Burma Chittagong might well have been taken, being undefended. Noton and five officers, with most of his force of 1000 troops and levies, were killed or wounded, and the rest scattered.

An attempt at survey and exploration into the extreme south of the Lushai hills was made by Captain Hodgkinson and Lieut. Sandes in the winter of 1848–49, who with an escort of native troops and police went up the Koladyne river from Akyab, ascended the Raletkhang, reaching the vicinity of Sherkor and the present post at Tuipang. A prominent hill seen from this village the Lushais (Lakher clan) call the "Tal Thla," and when the author was in those parts some years ago and inquired what the name meant he was told "the hill of the flag," and the aged chief said that in his boyhood he remembered how a party of sahibs and sepoys came to that hill, camped there, and set up a flag. They went away after a day or two, leaving the flag there (probably for survey purposes and forgotten). Hence the name, and as the old chief was over eighty years of age it must have been Hodgkinson's party he had seen. Both officers had to retire from this point owing to much hostility from the Shendus and some fighting, and returned to Paletwa, then the furthest military post up the Koladyne river.

It is interesting to note from the "History of Indian Railways and Communications" that in 1850 the subject of linking Chittagong, Akyab, and Lower Burma by road was for the first time put forward, and in that year Lieut. Forlong, R.E., reconnoitred and cut a road through the Arrakan Yomas east of Akyab to Minbu on the Irrawadi river. This route, however, lay through such unhealthy tracts and was so little used in consequence that it was abandoned in a few years. In the present day this subject of through communication but by railway, from Chittagong to Burma has come to the fore again, resulting in a reconnaissance of the Aeng Pass in the Yomas, followed by a short stretch of line from Maungdaw, a little north of Akyab, to Butidaung, of 36 miles. This railway project has, however, got no further.

The chief disturbance in the 'fifties which touched Chittagong and the Surma valley was connected with the Indian Mutiny, though fortunately only to a small extent, *viz.* when the 34th N.I. mutinied at Chittagong in November 1857, and marched northwards through Sylhet and Cachar, hoping to raise those district against the

British, in which they failed. Engaged and defeated at Latoo in Sylhet by the Sylhet Light Infantry, they were pursued through Cachar, where the S.L.I., joined by a detachment of the North Cachar Hills F.P., broke up the mutineers in an action near Lakhimpur, whence they fled into the hills across the Barak river, where Manipuri troops rounded most of them up and handed them over to the civil authorities at Silchar. It is said, though the authority is not definite, that the Tangal General, an old man who with the Senapatti was hanged for the Manipur Rebellion in 1891, was one of the 34th N.I. mutineers who escaped and took service in that State. It happened that a small sloop of war was lying in Chittagong port undergoing repairs at the time the 34th N.I. mutinied, and in fear of its being captured her four brass cannons were dropped into the river. Later three were recovered, and in 1891–92, when the rising took place in the Lushai hills, two of them were put in order and sent up to Lung Leh as being likely to be of use in defending the place. These two guns, dating from 1812, were later moved to Aijal, and now flank the Queen's Memorial in front of the 1st Assam Rifles' Quarter Guard.

It seems that, as in Cachar, the early troubles and raids were caused mostly by the nomadic Kukis of the outer ranges, who, as before stated, have moved gradually northwards under pressure of their relations the Lushai clans occupying the higher ranges in the interior. To these Captain Pemberton ascribed a Malay descent, in which he was later supported by Colonel Sir A. Phayre, for some years in charge of Arrakan, who in 1853 stated all these hill tribes to be slowly in motion trending north and eastwards from the south.

From 1860 on we get more succinct accounts of progress and action in the Chittagong Hill Tracts owing to repeated outrages by the hill tribes, which in January 1861 necessitated a military expedition, under Major Raban, of 230 rifles from the Native Regiment at Chittagong with 450 carriers. These, proceeding in small country boats, assembled at Burkul on the Kornaphuli river, whence they marched to Ruttunpoia's village—the offending chief, who submitted at once. No opposition was offered, only great difficulty is recorded in having practically to cut their way for five days through thick forest. Succeeding raids again disturbing these border lands, Government at last sanctioned in 1862 the definite taking over of the entire area now known as the Hill Tracts, and the placing of the same under the care of a British officer with the title of Hill Superintendent, whose headquarters were at first at Chandragona, 50 odd miles up river from Chittagong. A body of armed Civil Police fully equipped and 375 strong, mostly Bengalis, and of little use in the hills, was also given him with which to control the district and guard the frontier, the line of which was still that of the Kassalong and the Fenny rivers, beyond which east and south all was *terra incognita*. This, then, marks the starting-point of a unit in later years to form part of the Lushai Hills Military Police Battalion (1st A.R.).

The earliest bit of active service of this body was in 1865, when Captain T. Lewin, who the previous year had been appointed Hill Superintendent, was deputed to conduct a boundary settlement between the Chittagong and Arrakan districts. With 50 of his police he made a most difficult march to the south-east through unknown country, and met the Arrakan party near Daletmie on the Koladyne river, where some tribal opposition was experienced. Proceeding up this river, a large body of Shendus was encountered near the mouth of the Sulla river, and in the ensuing fight Lewin was wounded, as also were several of his men, which together with sickness brought boundary work to an end. The following year the Lushais raided over the border necessitating a fruitless punitive outing by Lewin, but during which friendly relations were established with Ruttunpoia, a chief whose village lay in the hills east of Demagiri, and to which he held true. Further raids by other tribal sections obliged the frontier post at Kassalong to be strengthened, and in order to be nearer the borderland and its troubles a site for a new post was selected by Lewin at Rangamatti (Sketch Map 2) in 1867, whither, when ready, the headquarters of the Hill Tracts was moved from Chandragona.

In this year also the armed Civil Police were turned into a body entirely distinct from the Civil Police and were styled the "Frontier Police of Bengal," for watch and ward of the border and Hill Tracts only. Cacharis and Nepalese now replaced the useless Bengalis, and the frontier posts in Lewin's day were established at Ruma, Bandarban on the Sungoo river, Politai at the foot of the hills east of Ruma, Kassalong, Burkul, and one up the Myari river, remaining so for many years.

CHAPTER VI

1869 to 1872. Surma Valley F.P. and Chittagong F.P., *continued*—The expeditions of 1871 and 1872—Chittagong frontier advanced to Demagiri—New arrangement of border posts—Old firearms of Lushais and Naga tribes—Primitive methods of making gun-powder—Difficulty of the country—Rebellion in North Cachar Hills district, 1882.

WE now come to the first of the extensive military operations necessary to subjugate the Lushai tribes. During January and February 1871 a series of raids took place on a large scale both along the Cachar and Chittagong borders, when in the former district the tribesmen destroyed the tea gardens of Monierkhal, Ainerkhal, Katlicherra, and Alexandrapur, massacring numbers of coolies and some Europeans, amongst whom was Mr. Winchester on a visit to the last-named garden, and whose little daughter they carried off. Some of these tea gardens had small Frontier Police posts in or near them, several of whom were cut up by the raiders, notably that at Monierkhal of 8 constables, who made a gallant defence, 6 being killed and 1 wounded. Mr. Daly (Civil Police), in charge of the Frontier Police at Silchar, with 40 of his men was first on the scene, and in a fight drove off the raiders, accounting for 57 of them. Other posts at Chargola and Alinagar on the Sylhet border were attacked at the same time, but managed to hold their own, the raiding parties here being smaller.

Government now decided to take punitive action in earnest, but owing to the lateness of the season this had to be deferred till the rains were over, when two strong columns were ordered to enter the Lushai hills at different points, *viz.* one from Silchar to reach and punish the villages of Lalbura and Vonolel as well as those of Lenkam and Poiboi, sons of Vonolel, who dwelt in the north and north-east portion of the hills, while the other was to enter from the Chittagong side to punish the Syloo and Howlong clans, in whose hands were many captives, including Mary Winchester, and who were more easily got at from that direction.

The Cachar Column under General Bourchier, C.B., consisted of the troops noted in the margin, assembled at Silchar in the beginning of December 1871 and advanced up the Barak river to Tipaimukh, where the advanced base was formed by the 15th of the month. In order to prevent the Lushais from escaping into the native States of Manipur and Tripura to the north and west respectively (Sketch Map 2), the Maharaja of the former State was asked to despatch a force to watch his south-west border from the neighbourhood of Chibu, while the O.C. 4th Native Infantry in garrison at Silchar was directed to occupy certain points on the Rengti and Moonvai ranges east of the Dalesari river.

22nd Punjab Infantry
42nd Assam Light Infantry
Detmt. 44th S.L.I.
300 Cachar Frontier Police
1 Eurasian Battery
1200 Transport coolies
157 Transport elephants

Colonel F. Roberts (later Lord Roberts, C.-in-C. India), who was Senior Staff Officer with the Cachar Column, records the difficulties of the advance up the Barak valley, the scenery of which he describes as "beautiful, with lofty wooded hills coming down to the water's edge, receding here and there to give glimpses of more distant ranges, and the river continually winding with occasionally sandy strips diversifying the character of its banks." Transport, none of the best, as usual in those days, obliged loads to be reduced to a minimum, *viz.* 80 lb. for a British officer, 12 lb. for a sepoy. The coolies were badly selected and of inferior physique, and easily succumbed to fatigue and sickness, while cholera broke out among them before the base was reached, which inadequate medical arrangements could hardly cope with. Elephants also, badly selected, felt the strain of continuous marching and climbing, the number soon being reduced to 33 effective beasts. From beyond Mynardhar, the last tea garden up the Barak, every bit of the road had to be cut and cleared, entailing endless labour, while in addition much bridging work had to be carried out. It is amusing to read in Lord Roberts' account of the expedition how, when it became necessary to construct the first bridge, he sent for the Sapper officer, who said he would arrange. It would take time, the officer said, as he first had to calculate the force of the current, weight to be borne by the bridge, strength of timber required, etc. He left to make his calculations and plans, and some of the Frontier Police came up to Lord Roberts to ask if he needed a bridge here. On hearing this was the case, the men, together with some Goorkhas of the 42nd A.L.I., set to at once, some felling bamboos and trees, others cutting them to required length, while others waded to their chests in the stream and drove the uprights into the river bed, to which the bamboo flooring was then rapidly attached. The bridge was completed in a rough but very efficient way, and was being tested by marching men over it before the Sapper returned with all his calculations ready to begin work. His surprise at seeing this unscientific but practical method of bridging can be imagined, and matters of this nature were henceforth left to those better acquainted with such work in this country.

On the 23rd December the advanced party ascended the Tipai river and were fired on while climbing the steep Senvong range on the way to certain Kholel villages. Skirmishing took place, causing the column 3 killed and 8 wounded, until the top of the range was reached and two villages were attacked and burnt, the enemy losing more than 40 men. On the 29th the Kholel villages 35 miles south of Tipaimukh submitted after slight opposition, and meanwhile the bulk of the force had been delayed on the lower Tuibum river by transport and supply troubles, which lasted some days. While Colonel Roberts was reconnoitring the country with parties of the 42nd A.L.I. and the Cachar F.P. on the Moortlang range (6000 feet), with many trying ascents and descents, they were suddenly fired into as they emerged from the forest on to an open "jhoom" (cultivation patch). The first shots badly wounded the Colonel's orderly, a Frontier Police constable named Panek a Kuki, who was acting as guide and had done several years' good service, while two sepoys were hit before the enemy was driven off with some loss. Kalhi's village and two others, all well defended, were then attacked and destroyed with 5 casualties to the column. At Chipowi on the 18th January, 1872, a halt was made as several villages in the vicinity, including an important one, Tingridong, came in to make submission, bringing captives taken in raids. The village of Kungnung (Sketch Map 2) was next proceeded against, where on the 25th January the Lushais made a stand, and in the ensuing fight the column lost 4 killed and 9 wounded, including the General, who was hit in the arm and hand, the enemy being dislodged with a loss of over 60 men by the 44th S.L.I. From here a portion of the force was detached under Colonel Roberts against Taikum village, while the main column continued the planned advance. Taikum was soon taken and destroyed, the guns being able to come into action effectively at 1200 yards as the country here was more open. A few shells into the stockade, seen to be crowded with armed Lushais, covered the attackers, who entered practically without fighting, the enemy having bolted, leaving a number of dead behind. This marked the last of any offensive action for the Cachar force, and on the 2nd February Chellam village was occupied. Here it was learnt that the Chief Vonolel had died, and that Lalbura had escaped far to the south-east. The Champhai valley, 110 miles from the base, where Vonolel's widow lived and where

A View in the Lushai Hills (Champhai Valley) showing Hill Sides denuded of Forest for "Jhooming" Purposes

Lalbura's headmen came in to submit, was reached by the 17th February. The object of General Bourchier's force was now attained, and with captives recovered, as also muskets and other loot taken in raids, though no meeting with the Chittagong column had been found possible, this force began returning, Tipaimukh being reached on the 6th March, where another outbreak of cholera hampered the retirement greatly.

At this period the Cachar or Surma Valley Frontier Police had a considerable number of Kukis in their ranks, who had been retained on disbandment of the old Levy for special duties such as trackers, sharpshooters, scouts, guides, collectors of tribal information, etc., most of whom formed the detachment under Mr. Daly with General Bourchier's force, and on whom Mr. Edgar, his Political Officer, animadverted strongly in his report. He found that though much individual bravery came to notice during the expedition, they were useless for the work expected of them, all aptitude for the essence of their tribal habits when at war having been drilled out of them by over-zealous Police officers in the past. "Those officers evidently had attached more importance to uniformity of action and the finish needed to produce smart soldiers, which the Frontier Police in general and certainly their Kuki elements were not supposed to attain to." "No attempt," he says, "had been made to keep up and foster those habits of the war trail which every Kuki and Lushai has learnt in his boyhood, consequently this expedition revealed the uselessness of these men with us." He recommended that, if they could not be trained for the specific purposes for which they were originally enlisted, and as soldiers they did not shine, they should be eliminated from the Frontier Police. This later was carried out, their places being filled by Goorkhas and Cacharis.

We can now turn and trace the progress of the column from Chittagong which entered the south Lushai hills under General Brownlow, to co-operate with the Cachar force. The troops of which it consisted were, as marginally noted, accompanied by boat and coolie transport. These began to assemble at Kassalong in mid-November 1871 with the object of moving against the Syloo and Howlong clans, with the latter of whom was Mr. Winchester's little daughter, whose release together with numerous other captives was to be effected.

2nd Goorkhas
4th Goorkhas
27th Punjab Infantry
1 Coy. Sappers and Miners
1 Mountain Battery
Chittagong Frontier Police

The Chittagong Frontier Police, at the earnest recommendation of Captain Lewin on whom signs of coming trouble had not been lost, had been allowed to increase the strength of his unit to 550 men during the hot weather of 1871, and he was also given the services of two Police officers, Messrs. Knyvett and Crouch, to assist in training and rearming the men with the Enfield rifle. A distinctive uniform of dark green serge with white metal buttons and bugle cap badge was issued at the same time.

A few years earlier, it will be remembered, a recruiting depot had been opened at Sylhet, where Lewin had obtained sanction to enlist his recruits, and when the trouble broke out this winter Captain Gordon and Mr. Bignell were sent him as additional assistants. The reorganisation of this Frontier Police unit was hardly completed when in October 1871 it received orders for all available trained men to join the coming operations. The duties expected of Frontier Police on both the Cachar and Chittagong sides were to act as scouts, keep open communications, collect information, and furnish baggage and various other guards. In early November the first forward move was made by Mr. Crouch with Inspector Mahomed Azim and 150 constables advancing up the Kornaphuli river in boats to Demagiri, where they cleared camp grounds and built a stockade to form the advanced base, in which work Ruttunpoia's men came down and rendered much assistance.

A Group of Lushais.

The line of advance into the hills was to be made up the river as far as possible, this being the most direct route through the Syloo country to Savunga's and Benkuia's villages, the two principal Chiefs known to have taken part in the raids and with whom was Mary Winchester. There was also strong presumptive evidence that the Syloos were guilty of raiding. Immediately above Demagiri begins a series of rapids and falls with long stretches of open water in between, and much hard work fell to the Frontier Police and the 2nd Goorkhas (the first troops to arrive) in preparing timber slides, up which to drag boats and stores over the many rocky falls to the open reaches above. On the 9th December the first skirmish with the Lushais occurred in which a Chief, Lengura, was captured, and this was followed on the 14th by an attack on Vanlula's village on the Belkai range (Sketch Map 2), which was made up a steep jungle-covered spur, the 2nd Goorkhas and Frontier Police doing the preliminary scouting work. Opposition did not last long and the village was taken and destroyed, several of the enemy being killed inside. The force had now left the river route, was well into the extremely difficult ranges, and as the line of communications lengthened out the tribesmen attacked it at one or two points, killing a few of the Frontier Police guards.

It was found the Lushais, like the Nagas, perch their villages high on the tops of spurs and ridges for the sake of health as well as for defence, and our troops found every village surrounded by one or more lines of heavy timber stockade work with rows of bamboo spikes outside, while each entrance was protected by a sort of block-house, and most villages met with contained about 400 houses, a few more important ones situated further into the country having upwards of 800.

During the rest of December the force successfully attacked Lal Hlira's and Vanoya's well-defended villages with slight casualties. The Towrang range overlooking the upper waters of the Dalesari river was reached on the last day of the year, and from here efforts were made to communicate with General Bourchier's force operating to the north, but these failed. Here, at a height which overlooked a sea of ranges and forest-covered valleys in every direction, Savunga's and Lal Gnoora's villages could be seen 8 and 10 miles off, respectively, and these were now proceeded against. The Frontier Police scouting up to Lal Gnoora's found the place very strongly defended, and in the assault of the 3rd January, 1872, 10 men were killed and wounded, amongst the latter being Captain Battye, 2nd Goorkhas.

On this the Syloos began to parley, but not coming to terms Savunga's village was attacked, and here the mountain guns got their chance, being able to cover the attackers from a point 900 yards from the stockade. The shells soon broke down the defences, scattering the enemy, who lost heavily, and the place was destroyed on the 21st. The Syloos now having had enough punishment came in and submitted, bringing some captives, and an effort was then made to get hold of and parley with the Howlong Chiefs, Ruttunpoia volunteering to visit them. Inspector Mahomed Azim and a small party of Lewin's men accompanied him, and by early February they returned, having been successful in their mission. With the party was Mary Winchester, and several other captives had also been given up by the Chief Benkuia, who by so doing hoped to obviate the likelihood of General Brownlow entering his country and punishing the Howlong clans, who really were more guilty of raiding than the Syloos. The latter so far had borne the brunt of punishment, had lost everything, and had submitted in a body by the end of January 1872.

As, however, the Howlong Chiefs did not come in themselves the force began a further advance across the upper Dalesari valley, Ruttunpoia being again sent forward to induce them to submit, as well as to try to gain information as to the whereabouts of the Cachar Column.

By mid-February General Brownlow had reached the vicinity of the present-day Thenjol Rest-house on the Aijal–Lung Leh road, where he halted not far from the Tuldung stream and awaited Ruttunpoia's return. A few nights after reaching this point, while Captain Lewin was asleep in his hut, a voice woke him, calling gently the name he was known by amongst the tribes, and their corruption of "Tom Lewin"—"Tangliena, Tangliena, is it peace?" It was evident a Howlong emissary had crept through the sentry line and found his way to where Lewin lay. On being answered, the man asked him to come alone with him to meet the Howlong Chiefs, to which Lewin consented, believing he could do more by his personal influence than if they were forced into formal conference with those of whom they knew nothing and whom they now feared. The Lushai led him by the way he had come; it was near dawn, and while descending the ravine through which runs the Lai Var stream Lewin suddenly became aware of two armed Lushais following him. On reaching the bottom he made out a large concourse of armed warriors quietly crowding the further bank, in the midst of which were the Howlong Chiefs. It was an anxious moment as he crossed the bridge of a single tree trunk and reached the centre of the hostile gathering, for none of these had actually met Lewin, knowing him only by reputation, while he was ignorant of the attitude they might adopt. However, the Chiefs met him quietly and a "pow-wow" followed, during which he was able to influence the Chiefs favourably, who at last agreed to come with him and tender their full submission. This was duly done, much to the General's surprise, who was not aware of the interview having taken place. The account of this episode in Lewin's book, "The Fly on the Wheel," is excellent reading, and shows the wonderful influence this officer had over these wild tribes, as well as his pluck and firm, tactful handling of them. Unfortunately, the Bengal Government disapproved of

Lewin's action in this case, as it led to the Howlongs escaping their rightful punishment.

It was found impossible to link up with the Cachar Column owing to distance and the high Maiphang and Hinglian ranges which intervened, so a month more was spent in flying columns being sent through the Howlong country, while some of the troops returned to Demagiri, whence they set out to visit the southern Howlongs, when Saipuia and Vandula submitted, whose villages lay near the present-day post of Lung Leh. With these flying columns went surveyors who mapped a good deal of the country, and with some 150 captives released, many looted guns given back, 20 villages burnt, the submission of all prominent Lushai Chiefs, and their fines paid up, General Brownlow's force broke up, returning to Chittagong by the end of March 1872, and for sixteen years the Lushais gave no further trouble.

The main Frontier Police post was now moved forward from Kassalong to Demagiri (Sketch Map 2), where Gordon and Crouch cleared the forest still further, building houses for Lewin and themselves, accommodation for their men, a bazaar, hospital, etc., so that during the following winter the place began to develop into a considerable trading centre. A new frontier line was demarcated along the Oiphum, Sirthay, and Saichel ranges to a point 40 miles from the Arrakan post at Daletmie, on which line for some time almost the whole of Lewin's Frontier Police were disposed in the following posts: Sirthay 50 men, Demagiri 200, Oiphum (1) 50, Oiphum (2) 50, Saichel 50, Sangu Valley (Ruma and Bandarban) 100, Politai 50. Before these were established it was thought desirable to locate a post in Ruttunpoia's village for a time to protect him from possible hostility by other tribal sections, owing to his having aided the expedition, while two other posts were placed in the Syloo country, all under Inspector Mahomed Azim, these keeping the peace between the Syloos and Howlongs, inter-tribal antagonism having been evinced.

RANGAMATTI IN 1888.

[From an old sketch.

COUNTRY BOATS ON THE KORNAPHULI RIVER USED FOR THE EXPEDITION, 1889–90.

During the early months of 1873 Gordon and Bignell, with an escort of their men and with surveyors, were employed in mapping the hills from Demagiri south of Arrakan along the south-west borders of the Shendu country (Lakhers and Pois), during which no hostility was displayed; and not long after this Major T. Lewin retired from the service, leaving a name behind him amongst the tribes which for many years was one to conjure with. In 1919 a monument to his memory was put up by his widow, to which Government gave a grant of money. It stands at Demagiri, near the spot where his house and garden had stood.

In these two expeditions it was found the Lushais were better armed than most other north-eastern tribes, as they possessed a considerable number of old percussion or flint-lock muskets, many of English make, Tower marked, some being stamped with the name "Alton," while others had French marks and stamps. Lewin states in 1869 that it was only some ten years earlier that the tribes had begun to learn the use of firearms and had begun to acquire some, also that they had learnt somehow, probably from the Burmese, to make a rough but still fairly useful powder. A regular trade in these weapons seems to have started in the early 'seventies from Burma, Bengal, and Cachar, until by the end of that decade Lushais, Kukis, and Angamis were in possession of considerable and increasing numbers. The Lushais and Kukis paint and varnish their musket stocks and butts in red, black, and yellow, while often their powder flasks of gayal (the mithun) horn are beautifully polished and inlaid with silver or ivory.

In his book on the Chin hills, which lie immediately east of the Lushai country (Sketch Map 2) between that area and the Chindwyn river, Sir Bertram Carey states that both Chins and Lushais began to acquire old firearms as early as the decade 1830–40 and that these came from Burma. After the annexation of Upper Burma in 1885 the country settled down, and disarmament was carried out amongst the people, but very many guns found their way to the various hill tribes, the Burmese often selling their weapons to these folk in preference to making them over to the British officials for nothing. The introduction of breech-loading rifles and the consequent discarding of old-time firearms, which were bought up by Native States and traders, diffused at first vast numbers throughout India, many finding their way into the hands of border tribes, such old weapons not being broken up in those days. Amongst them Carey found many of English, French, and American make with dates of issue and makers' names stamped on butt-plates, while some which were confiscated had belonged to the Guards in 1816. At first the local powder, Sir Bertram states, was made by the hill tribes from sulphur obtained from Burma, as there are very few sulphur springs in the hills, and when the export of this was stopped after 1885 that commodity was got by soaking and boiling the "aunglauk" bean, which contains much sulphur. Saltpetre and nitre also they obtained from heaps of manure collected in baskets and strongly impregnated with urine. The liquid drained into receptacles and was then boiled and evaporated, when crystals of saltpetre and nitre were produced.

The best charcoal they make by burning the stalks and pods of this bean. Such powder naturally is weak, but a tribesman's usual charge of 6 drachms will carry a bullet 300 yards, and even further, which for jungle fighting is far enough.

In this connection it would appear probable that the Nagas and those hill tribes in the neighbourhood of Assam might have got some knowledge of making gunpowder from the Ahoms, who certainly were making it themselves in the 17th century. Mr. Thomas Pennant, in his book on Hindustan (1798), quoting from the Mahommedan records, notes that "Mir Jumla in his invasion of Assam in 1665 found the Ahoms using cannon, the powder for which they made in vast quantities,

MAJOR T. LEWIN'S MEMORIAL AT DEMAGIRI.

CORNER IN THE FOREST NEAR DE GIRI—LUSHAI HILLS.

[From a sketch by L. W. S.

and stated that it was round and small in grain like European powder, and strong." Tavernier, the old-time French traveller, also alludes to their knowledge of powder-making, but whether the Ahoms derived it from China or from the Portuguese is a moot point. It is not unlikely they acquired it from the Mahommedans, of whom they captured large numbers in a war previous to that with Mir Jumla, and this knowledge retained by the Ahoms may in later generations have been picked up by the more warlike hill tribes, who constantly caused trouble with the plains people.

This was the first military expedition on a large scale across any of these north and eastern borders, and accounts are full of the extraordinary difficulty of getting into the hills owing to the thick forests through which, when once the rivers were left, the troops had to hack their way, and the like of which are not seen in India, except in the Terai at the foot of the Himalayas. More particularly is this the case in the outer ranges of the hills, which are but sparsely inhabited. In the operations of 1888–91 in the same country the Intelligence Officer describes it in his report as "difficult to find jungle and forest denser than in this area, which presents a net-work of forest-clad hills and valleys. Huge trees with great buttressed trunks raise their straight stems to a leafy roof, creepers of all kinds wind round these massive columns, hanging in festoons from tree to tree, or trail on the ground knotted and twisted together. Mixed up with this is a tangled mass of vegetation, thorny canes, and shrubs, so intertwined that it is only by dint of much cutting and clearing that a passage can be made through it. The pace at which this jungle grows is incredible; in spite of two clearings annually, paths are often impassable without more labour." As with the Lushai hills, so it is with the Cachar, Naga, Abor, and Mishmi countries, the same descriptions hold good; only in the higher ranges beyond the zone of tropical forests is anything approaching open country met with.

As a result of these operations a line of strongly manned posts, some held by the military, but most by the Frontier Police, was established and maintained along the Cachar, Sylhet, and Chittagong borders; but the Lushais, having had a severe lesson, did not disturb the peace of the frontier for many years. The year following the close of this expedition into the Lushai hills, the Surma Valley F.P. appear from an old Battalion Order Book to have sent a detachment to the Garo hills to take part in the tour of Captain Williamson and Mr. Davis through that country for survey and exploration purposes. Nothing of interest, however, is recorded of this tour.

They also furnished detachments with General Nation's and with Colonel Johnstone's forces to suppress the rising in the Naga hills, 1879–80. The first-named detachment does not appear to have been present at the assault of Khonoma, having been mostly employed in guarding posts on the line of communications.

Another portion of Cachar, *viz.* the north Cachar hills, had not been without trouble. In 1882 Sambudhan, a religious Cachari fanatic, started a minor insurrection to try to restore the old Cachari kingdom. A few years earlier (1879), the Frontier Police in this district having been moved to Silchar, they had been replaced by a body of Kuki Militia 200 strong, raised in these hills and stationed at Gunjong, then the civil headquarters, lying some 15 miles west of Haflong (Sketch Map 4), also holding posts on the south-west Angami border. Sambudhan took up his abode at Maibong, the old time capital of the Cacharis, whence he terrorised the people into following him.

Major Boyd, the Deputy-Commissioner, with 40 of the Militia, marched from Gunjong on the 13th January, 1882, to Maibong, 20 miles off, intending to capture the fanatic, who, leaving Maibong and evading Boyd, fell upon Gunjong, killing many and burning the place down. Sambudhan then turned back and hurried to

Maibong. Soon after dawn on the 16th Boyd's party, who had spent the night there, were roused by the shouts and drums of the fanatic's crowd returning exultant from their raid, and in the ensuing fight Boyd was mortally wounded, and the escort, who displayed but little fighting spirit, were dispersed with some loss. Detachments of Frontier Police from Silchar and Kohima were sent up at once, who scoured the district, hunting down the gangs until at last Sambudhan's main body of adherents were surrounded and he was shot down, which ended the insurrection. The Kuki Militia, having shown up badly in this episode were disbanded a few months later and the Surma Valley Military Police, as the Cachar Frontier Police were called on reorganisation in early 1883, took over all protective duties in this area.

CHAPTER VII

1872 to 1890. Surma Valley and Chittagong F.P., *continued*—Survey work on the Chittagong border—Lieut. Stewart's massacre, 1888—General Tregear's expedition—Lung Leh post established—Subadar Major Jitman Gurung—General Tregear's second expedition, 1889/90—Colonel Skinner's column—Flying Column to Haka.

AFTER the expedition of 1871–72, as mentioned before, the peace of the southern part of the Assam border and that of Chittagong was unbroken for sixteen years, save for brief trouble in the neighbouring Native State of Manipur during 1886, which necessitated the dispatch of a detachment of the 44th Sylhet Light Infantry and 150 of the Surma Valley Military Police to restore order. This was accomplished after slight skirmishes near Kala Naga on the Silchar-Imphal road.

About 1887, the results of the third Burmese war (1885–86) and the annexation of Upper Burma began to make themselves felt, when the British Government was brought into contact with the wild tribes of the Chin hills lying west of the Chindwyn river and close neighbours of the Lushais. For protection against their frequent depredations on Burmese villages and the enslaving of people captured, a military force had to enter the Chin country, where much fighting took place, and Fort White was established as a permanent post. In spite of the long quietude of the Lushais it was thought quite probable that, stirred by what was going on amongst their neighbours to the east, they too might break out again; in which case combined operations from Burma and Bengal seemed almost certain, and which would then mean the eventual occupation of the entire area from the Chindwyn river to the Chittagong border. The military authorities in Calcutta, on whom in the ordinary course would rest the preparations of plans for any operations from the west, therefore thought it advisable to bring their information as to lines of approach up to date. To this end it was decided that winter reconnaissances, which at that time were carried out in every command both to train officers as well as to collect information, should be conducted in the Chittagong Hill Tracts. Mr. D. Lyall, Commissioner of Chittagong, welcomed the suggestion, promising all assistance, and asking in return that the reconnaissance parties might be allowed to help the frontier authorities by improving the alignment of the patrol paths.

Accordingly in January 1888 two such reconnaissance parties were dispatched from Calcutta to Rangamatti, whence the foothills were to be entered, both parties working separately and some distance apart. The first party, consisting of Lieut. Stewart and two Corporals of the 1st P.W.O. Leinster Regiment with 10 men of the Chittagong Frontier Police as escort, left to work along the Belaisari range, while the second, with Lieut. Baird and one Corporal of the Derbyshire Regiment with a similar escort, went up the Kornaphuli river to Demagiri, whence it would work southwards along the Oiphum range until both parties met somewhere on the Rang Khyong river. Captain J. Shakespear, Leinster Regiment, in charge of the whole reconnaissance, went with Baird's party to see it start work.

As no hostility on the part of the Lushais was anticipated and as both parties were to work well within our boundary, in the opinion of the Civil Authorities any danger of their being attacked was negligible, so only very small escorts of 10 Frontier Police were told off to each, more to aid them in the work of jungle clearing, hut building, and to control the coolies, than to guard them against attack.

Shortly after the parties had commenced work a message reached Rangamatti from Saipuia, a friendly

Chief, to the effect that Howsata, Vantura, and Dakola, three brothers of the Poi clan who had villages some days' marching south of him, were intending to raid into British territory.

This information was passed on to both survey parties, but as little importance was attached to the message, nothing was done to increase the strength of the escorts. After some days Stewart found the elephant which had been supplied him to carry part of the baggage could go no further until the track had been improved, so he left the animal with certain stores in charge of three of his escort, going on a day's march up the Saichel range with the rest of the party. From here he sent back two men, so that on the 2nd February he had only five sepoys with him. During the night one of these was on sentry duty, but after dawn he was taken off and not replaced, no danger being thought of. Stewart was standing partially dressed outside his little hut, his servant handing him a cup of tea; both the Corporals and most of the others were still asleep rolled in their blankets, the sentry had finished his duty, and the whole hill-side was shrouded in dense white mist, which at that season of the year hangs about till near midday. Suddenly there was a volley from the jungle, followed by a rush of shouting savages. Exactly what occurred is not known, but the first shots broke the thigh of one sepoy and killed another. All was at once confusion, the two Corporals were stabbed to death as they lay and the Police havildar fell, a Naick and one sepoy managed to get at their rifles and returned the fire. Stewart is said to have reached back into his hut and got out his revolver and gun, but these three were, however, not able to fire for long and had no chance of beating off the attack of some 200 to 300 savages armed with spears, daos, and some muskets. Stewart retired up the hill-side firing, but was shot at the edge of a ravine, down which he fell, his body being found some days later so tightly wedged in the bamboos that the Lushais could not strip it, but they took his head and weapons. Having expended their rounds the Naick and sepoy retreated towards the last supply camp from which the other five sepoys were bringing up stores. With these they returned to the scene of the tragedy, now vacated by the raiders, and where many decapitated bodies were found; several of the coolies and servants, having been on the further side of the camp from which the attack started, had managed to escape.

News of the disaster reached Mr. S. Walker, Assistant Superintendent of Police at Demagiri, at midnight on the 4th, and within an hour he was off with as many of the Frontier Police as he could collect at the moment, and by 9 a.m. reached Baird's camp on the Oiphum range, whence, taking on the Europeans of the party, they pushed on in the hope of cutting off the raiders. However, coming across the fresh trail of the returning savages and realising they were too late, a return to Demagiri was obligatory as they had no spare food with them. Had Walker only received the news a little earlier his spirited dash might have been successful, but in those days there was no telegraph line east of Rangamatti and communication between posts was slow. As soon as the news reached Rangamatti Mr. Murray, D.S. Police, with an escort, proceeded to the spot and buried the bodies, the camp being found thoroughly looted, heads, weapons, ammunition, and personal belongings having been carried off.

The season during which military operations are possible in these unhealthy regions was now too far advanced to permit of Stewart's murderers being punished at once, but a plan was drawn up for a small expedition to enter the hills early the following cold weather. This, however, the Council at Simla decided to postpone, as operations on the Burma side of these marauding tribes had not progressed far enough to admit of a combined move in the winter of 1888–89. But in order to prevent a recurrence of raids, 250 rifles of the 9th Bengal Infantry under Major Woodhouse were sent to assist the Commissioner in guarding his frontier. The Frontier Police were moved forward to occupy a line of posts nearer the border, detachments of the 9th B.I. taking their places at Rangamatti and Demagiri, Lieut. Widdicombe being in command at the latter place, where it was soon found even their presence was insufficient to check outrages.

Hardly had these arrangements been given effect to when a large raiding party from the north of the Lushai hills, led by three Chiefs, Nikama, Kairuma, and Lungliena, suddenly arrived on the border and cut up with unusual ferocity the village of the Pakumi Rani, a bare 4 miles from Demagiri, killing the Chieftainess with more than 20 of her people and carrying off 15 persons. Directly this outrage was heard of Lieut. Widdicombe with parties of his own men and Frontier Police started for the scene, but the raiders had rapidly retreated into their own hills, and pursuit without any kind of transport was impossible.

The Council at Simla now definitely decided on military action, and a column (called the "Lushai Expeditionary Force"), under command of Brigadier-General Tregear, was ordered into the south Lushai hills and began to rendezvous at Rangamatti, its strength being 1250 of all ranks and its composition as in the margin.

400 2/2nd Goorkhas
250 9th B.I.
250 2nd B.I.
200 Madras Pioneers
½ Coy. Sappers and Miners
4 guns 2nd Bombay M.B.
Signallers
Coolie Corps and Elephants

The policy hitherto obtaining of punitive expeditions attacking and burning villages and retiring out of the country was now abandoned in view of permanent occupancy, the orders given to General Tregear being (1) to make a road through to the Chin hills; (2) to build and stock a permanent post at some suitable spot well into the country; (3) when this was done, then to move and punish Howsata and Co. (Sketch Map 2).

As soon as it was learnt that the troops were *en route* Messrs. Walker, Murray, and Taylor, of the Police, set to work with their men, and had erected rough barracks

Bamboo Huts built at Demagiri by the Frontier Police.

and store sheds at Demagiri by the time the first troops arrived. These were sent by river steamer from Chittagong to Rangamatti, whence, some in country boats and others marching, the Base at Demagiri was duly reached in late December. First arrivals at once took up the work of cutting a road eastwards through the lower bamboo-covered hills with Haka in the Chin hills as the ultimate goal, and by the 6th January, 1889, 5 miles had been opened.

Before the whole force had assembled, Rangamatti was startled by news of another serious and extensive raid into the upper Chengri valley, 43 miles to the north-east, where 23 villages were completely destroyed, over 100 people being killed, and 91 were carried off captive. These raiders, it was ascertained, were of the Syloo clan belonging to a Chief Lienpunga.

Reconnaissances of the neighbouring country were carried out during January and February by Captain J. Shakespear with an escort of 40 Frontier Police sepoys. This officer, having been in this region on survey duty and having some knowledge of the people, had been appointed Field Intelligence Officer to the expedition. He visited Saipuia's village (Howlong clan), 47 miles east of the Base, when that Chief's friendliness, together with that of his aged brother, was confirmed.

Mr. Murray, also with 50 F.P. men, made an extended reconnaissance over Teriat and the Bolpui range down into the valleys of the Mat and Koladyne rivers, during which in one village passed through, he was told of the death of Howsata, also that Stewart's gun had been buried with him, and that all heads had been sent to a Chin Chief named Paona, living far to the east. Certain Lushai notables finding their hills being entered from the west, and knowing of the military activity in the Chin hills, hastened now to submit and make their peace with the "Sirkar."

Meanwhile work on the new road was progressing slowly, having to be laboriously cut through dense bamboo jungle in the lower ranges and thick forest in the higher ones. There was no opposition, but sickness took a heavy toll of the coolie corps and numbers of elephants were lost from disease or by falling down hill-sides and injuring themselves. Camps were formed at the Phyrang river and at Sailingret, where prolonged halts were made until the road had been opened a few miles ahead, so that it was not till mid March that Lung Leh was reached, a distance of 47 miles from the Base. The country passed through was so far uninhabited, and here at a pleasant altitude of 3300 feet, on a long open saddle not far from Lalruma's and Saipuia's villages, a large timber stockade was constructed with accommodation for 3 officers and 250 rifles, as it was decided to locate a strong post in this area by means of which it was hoped to dominate the southern hills.

As soon as this post approached completion a flying column set out to visit and punish Howsata's and another village, which lay 30 odd miles to the south-east across the Koladyne river, for their share in Stewart's massacre, detachments from all units forming the Column. Cutting their way over the Bolpui range (5200 feet) they descended into the low hills between the Mat and Koladyne rivers, and it was at the crossing of the latter that opposition was expected, but none occurred. A shot or two only were fired by the advanced guard, who stumbled on a Lushai picquet, which hastily disappeared. On approaching Howsata's village it was set on fire by the people, but two or three rounds from a mountain gun cleared out the inhabitants and the Column entered. Part of the place was blazing, but the Chief's grave in the centre of it was pointed out and opened, when Stewart's gun was found under the body, thus proving his complicity in the outrage. The village being now destroyed together with that of its neighbour Jahoota and the people having all fled, nothing more could be done here, so the force returned to Lung Leh. Here in mid April a number of prominent Lushai Chiefs paid a visit to the General, who

FRONTIER POLICE LEAVING THE LUNG LEH STOCKADE, CARRYING THEIR OWN KITS, 1889.

THE OLD STOCKADE AT LUNG LEH, 1890.

[From a sketch by L. W. S

held a Durbar at which the intentions of the British Government were explained to them.

The stockade and barracks being now completed and the 250 men of the Chittagong Frontier Police who were to form its garrison having arrived, the force withdrew from the hills in late April 1889. Certain Goorkha officers had been recently appointed from the Indian Army to this Frontier Police unit, one of whom, *viz.* Subadar Major Jitman Gurung, deserves mention as being a link with a stirring past. He had been one in Jang Bahadur's Nepalese army which assisted the British during the Indian Mutiny and took a large part in the Oudh campaign, 1857–58. Later he entered our service, joining the 44th S.L.I., and had seen a very considerable amount of campaigning on the wild eastern borders and in Burma, eventually retiring with the title of "Rai Bahadur" in 1895 after thirty-eight years' army service, the last seven of which had been spent with the Chittagong Frontier Police. The loss of his valuable services was much felt and a great entertainment was given him at Lung Leh before he left for Shillong, where he lived some years longer.

During 1889 frequent raids by the Chins necessitated a large force from Burma being again sent into their hills under General Penn Symonds, to co-operate with whom and to complete the road linking Chittagong with Burma, General Tregear was given command of a larger force totalling 53 British officers and 3924 men (units composing the force as per margin), which he led into the south Lushai hills again in November 1889. His orders also were to dispatch a column northwards from Lung Leh to punish Lienpunga and other Chiefs concerned in the Chengri valley raid, a force of the Surma Valley Military Police 400 strong under Mr. Daly co-operating from Silchar at the same time with his

3rd B.I.
2/2nd Goorkhas
28th Bombay Pioneers
½ Coy. Sappers and Miners
Wing 9th B.I.
Wing 2/4th Goorkhas
Signalling Company
200 Chittagong F.P.

advanced Base at Jalnacherra. The S.V.M.P. posts on this border were held by the 40th B.I. to release more men for Daly's advance.

Cholera broke out at Rangamatti, spreading up river to Demagiri, and greatly delayed the assembly of the force, which did not reach Lung Leh till well into January 1890. Here the northern Column, as it was styled, was formed under Colonel Skinner, 3rd B.I., consisting of 300 rifles 2/2nd Goorkhas, 250 of the 3rd B.I., 50 Bombay Pioneers, and 100 Chittagong F.P., and these left for the northern Lushai hills and Lienpunga's village.

Their route lay down the Klong valley (upper waters of the Dalesari river, Sketch Map 2), and progress was mainly carried out by means of rafts, large numbers of which were constructed by the Frontier Police, to whom the river work mostly fell. This method of progression went smoothly often for miles, till rapids obliged the old rafts to be abandoned and fresh ones were put together again on the open water below.

About the middle of February Colonel Skinner's Column reached a point on the river in the near neighbourhood of Lienpunga's village, so water progress was given up and the hills were climbed to the place, which lay 18 miles south of Aijal, not far from the present-day stage of Sibutilang. Here they joined hands with Mr. Daly's force from Silchar, with whom were also Mr. Broderick and Mr. Walker (Civil Police), and the two different Police units (Surma Valley Military Police and Chittagong Frontier Police), which later were to be amalgamated into one force, met for the first time. Mr. Daly just before this meeting had, contrary to instructions, received the submission of Lienpunga, which, it was intended should have been only received by Colonel Skinner; and it was also learnt that that notable, probably in fear of a meeting with the leader of the bigger force, had managed to escape.

This brought about the first hostility on the Lushais'

side, who after intermittent firing from the surrounding jungle attacked the village in which the Column had established itself, causing casualties to the extent of 1 sepoy killed and Captain Brownrigg and a few men wounded. The attack was beaten off and the village with its granaries was destroyed, its cattle also being confiscated.

A small force of the 2/2nd Goorkhas and the Chittagong F.P. under Major Begbie then moved eastwards and punished with slight opposition the villages of Lungliena and Nikama for their raid on the Pakumi Rani, after which the whole force proceeded against Thanruma's village also for punishment. In this affair at Nikama's village Jemadar Mallo Rai, of the S.V.M.P., was "mentioned" for gallantry in capturing single-handed two armed Lushais who were firing, though he at the moment happened to be without a revolver. This being accomplished, Colonel Skinner selected a site near by for the location of the permanent post in the north Lushai hills. Work on this was commenced at once, and when completed and rationed the force withdrew to Silchar and India, leaving a garrison of 200 rifles of the Surma Valley Military Police Battalion at Aijal, as the new post had been christened, and 50 at Changsil on the Dalesari river, the furthest point to which boats from Silchar could reach with supplies.

While the Northern Column was employed thus General Tregear's main force had advanced from Lung Leh eastwards, a road being cut across the Bolpui range down into the Mat and Koladyne valleys, after which came the ascent of the Darjow Klang (5700 feet). These valleys were full of bird and wild animal life; but work, denseness of the forests, and very few officers with sporting guns made shikar impossible. The beautiful Polipectron or peacock pheasant is found here, jungle fowl abound in swarms, though only heard and but rarely seen, the greater hornbill with its enormous beak and handsome black and white plumage, and many other varieties of bird life. The author remembers while the stockaded post at Lung Leh was in course of construction a two-horned rhinoceros, a couple of tigers, and a Malayan sun bear were shot on different occasions by men of the escort to wood-cutting parties in the valley below. While the Bombay Pioneers were at road work some way up the Darjow Klang with their rifles piled along the narrow track, a great disturbance was heard above them, and suddenly a large rhino burst out of the jungle, charged down the path, scattering men and rifles, and before anything could be done had disappeared far down the hill.

On an open spur of the Darjow Klang in helio communication with Lung Leh and commanding extensive views over a sea of hills away to the Tao Peak in the Chin country, a strong defensive post for 200 rifles was now constructed. While this work was in progress a small flying Column of 60 rifles 2/2nd Goorkhas and 25 of the Chittagong Frontier Police under Captain L. M. Hall, 2nd Goorkhas, with whom went Captain J. Shakespear (now Assistant Political Officer to the force) and Lieut. Bythell, R.E., started off for Haka in early March 1890 to link with General Penn Symonds' troops, and to assist in recovering the heads and loot carried off in the raid on Stewart's camp.

A rapid and most arduous march with few coolies, the sepoys carrying their own loads in addition to arms, equipment, and ammunition, and Tao village was reached, a few miles beyond the upper Koladyne river (or the "Boinu," as it is called here), which forms the boundary between the Chin hills and Lushai districts. Here they were joined by a small Column of the Burma force under Captain Rundall and Lieut. Stevenson, who, it was learnt, had passed the previous night in Paona's village, ignorant of the fact that that Chief held Stewart's head and some of the loot, and Rundall had received his submission. At Hmunlipi village, on a stern message being sent next day, the Chief duly sent in Stewart's head or what remained of it, together with two other heads and certain articles carried off by the raiders, and visits were paid to Twalam and Tlan Tlang, where, under show of force, the people promised submission and gave up all remaining loot.

Haka, 18 miles east of Tlan Tlang, was reached, where the heads were given burial, and consultations were held with General Penn Symonds as to the punishment of these Chiefs, they dwelling within his area of operations; after which Captain Hall's party returned to the Darjow Klang.

Contrary to expectation, the Chittagong main force had no fighting such as was experienced in the Chin hills, and work on the military road through the hills went on steadily. Once beyond the Tao range the country was found much easier and very different from the densely forested country west of the Koladyne river. It was far more open with oak, pine, rhododendrons, and far less undergrowth. Unlike their neighbours the Lushais with their nomadic tendencies, the Chins, it was found, built substantial permanent villages of fine large timber houses, in many cases with shingled roofs of wood slabs.

The road through to Haka was completed by mid April, and the new post on the Darjow Klang named Fort Tregear being ready and garrisoned by 200 rifles 2/2nd Goorkhas under Captain Hutchinson and Lieut. P. Boileau of that regiment, with whom also were Captain J. Shakespear and Captain Moir, I.M.S., as Political and Medical officers, respectively, the force began to leave this country, Chittagong being reached in the middle of May 1890. The award of the Indian General Service medal issued for these and following operations was participated in by both the Chittagong F.P. and the Surma Valley M.P. General Tregear's dispatch in complimenting both the Chittagong Frontier Police and the Surma Valley Military Police Battalion adds that "besides being keen soldiers they can build and roof huts, construct rafts, know all about river and jungle work, in fact can put their hands to anything and are accustomed to carry all their own kits."

A memento of the 1888–90 expeditions is kept in the bungalow of the Superintendent of the Hill Tracts at Rangamatti, in the deal table from the old stockade at Burkul, whereon practically every officer with Tregear's two expeditions had at one time or another carved their initials or names. Burkul was a Frontier Police post from Lewin's early days until about 1898, when it was given up, and a new Rest-house was built on the opposite bank at the top of the 3-mile stretch of rapids, which are now negotiated by a trolley line along the right bank.

Lung Leh was held by 150 men of the Chittagong Frontier Police under Messrs. Pugh and Taylor with a strong detachment of their men at Demagiri, and headquarters under Mr. Murray at Rangamatti, the south Lushai hills being for some years longer under the Commissioner of Chittagong.

RAFTS ON THE KLONG RIVER BEING LOADED FOR THE NORTHERN COLUMN.

PASSING BOATS BY HAND THROUGH THE BURKUL RAPIDS, KORNAPHULI RIVER.

CHAPTER VIII

1890 to 1924. Surma Valley M.P. and South Lushai Hills M.P., *continued* —North Lushai Hills rising, 1890—Its suppression—South Lushai Hills formed into a district, 1891—Composition of Chittagong M.P. —Troubles in the southern hills—Fort Tregear burnt down—Aijal under Colonel Loch—Missionary enterprise.

All seemed now to point to a state of comparative peace in these hills, though it was realised the clans round Aijal were not exactly in a submissive state of mind, and in early September 1890 disturbing news reached Lung Leh from the north. It has been shown that a strong permanent post had been built at Aijal to control that region, under Captain Browne and Lieut. H. W. G. Cole, 2/2nd Goorkhas, the former officer having political powers. On the 9th September, 1890, Captain Browne with an escort, *en route* to visit the Changsil post and supply depot, was ambuscaded by a large gathering of Thanruma's men, and in the fight 17 sepoys were killed or wounded, Browne being mortally wounded and dying in Changsil, which the rest of the escort managed to reach, and where he was buried. The Lushais in considerable strength at once attacked both posts. At Aijal a second stockade was in process of being built for the better storage of supplies, and the men were at work on this when the unexpected attack opened. Driven out into the main stockade, this was soon surrounded by large numbers, who attacked boldly for several hours, in which the Military Police had more casualties, but the enemy was beaten off with heavy loss. From the dead Lushais, it was found, many other villages further afield besides Thanruma's were concerned, and it seemed the country-side was badly in revolt. A messenger got through to

Silchar with the news and a detachment of the 44th S.L.I. with another of the Surma Valley M.P., followed later by other detachments, including one from the Lakhimpur M.P., were dispatched in boats up the Dalesari river to the relief of Aijal and Changsil. The first-named detachments before reaching the latter post were attacked in their boats, Lieut. Swinton being killed and several men wounded, but they got through. Mr. R. McCabe, who had established a great name in the Naga hills for dealing with rebellious hill tribes, was sent up at the same time, and in a short but vigorous campaign, in which the 40th B.I. arrived to assist, he restored the situation and enforced the surrender of the guilty Chiefs, including Lienpunga, who were deported. Hardly had these troubles been brought to a close than the Manipur Rebellion broke out in March 1891, claiming the services of the Surma Valley M.P., which, sending a strong detachment with Colonel Rennick's Column, advanced into that Native State from Silchar, and remained some months holding posts on the road and in the Manipur valley.

A few months later trouble arose in the southern hills as a result of injudicious action on the part of Mr. Murray (Civil Police), who was on tour with an escort of F.P. and visiting Jacopa's village, a Chief who had submitted but whose people were still restive and unsettled, and who lived some distance north of Fort Tregear across the Koladyne river (Sketch Map 2). Here, having stirred the people to anger, his party were suddenly attacked and driven out with loss. It was an unfortunate episode and had to be dealt with by a detachment of the 2/2nd Goorkhas under Captain Hutchinson from Fort Tregear, who, however, failed to catch Jacopa. In this affair at Jacopa's village Subadar Sangram Sing and Havildar Chandra Sing Thapa of the Chittagong F.P. distinguished themselves by their gallantry, both being badly wounded, the former losing an arm, for which they were rewarded by the presentation of the

Indian Order of Merit, 2nd Class, at a Durbar held at Lung Leh by the Commissioner of Chittagong.

The detachment of 2/2nd Goorkhas left Fort Tregear for India in April 1891, being replaced by one of 150 Frontier Police, having lost Lieut. Boileau by drowning, and both the north and south Lushai hills were again seemingly more settled. On the 1st of this month the south Lushai hills area was constituted a district of the Chittagong Division and placed under the charge of Captain J. Shakespear with the title of "Superintendent." At the same time the Chittagong Frontier Police unit was renamed the "South Lushai Hills Military Police Battalion" and its headquarters was moved from Rangamatti to Lung Leh, which was from now on also the centre for administration of the new district. Mr. Pugh became the Commandant with Messrs. Sneyd Hutchinson, Taylor, and Thomas, all of the Civil Police, as Assistants.

Up to this time the Chittagong F.P. had been wearing their old dark-green serge uniform, which was now replaced by khaki drill with thick underclothing for winter wear, and the old Enfield gave place to the Snider rifle. Its composition prior to this period was decidedly of the "mixed pickle" description, containing as it did Nepalese, Jaruas, Chakmas from the Kornaphuli valley, and even some Mahommedans; a useful and serviceable lot all the same. A little later recruiting was confined to the enlistment of Goorkhas and Jaruas only. Their first Subadar Major was a man named Stevens, a buck nigger who had served in the Calcutta Police and who became a well-known and respected character in the Hill Tracts. He was ever ready to help anyone, and with his wife, a quaint little half-caste woman named "Pussie," they formed a source of considerable amusement and interest to all who had dealings with this worthy couple.

Interest during 1891 centred itself in visits to all the principal villages and generally in exploring and pacifying the country, not forgetting efforts to capture various Chiefs "wanted" over the earlier raids, and who were

H

still at large. The successful capture of one of these named Dokola may be mentioned as showing the kind of work the F.P. were frequently called on to carry out. At the close of 1891 Mr. Hutchinson had suddenly to take 50 rifles to stop the fighting between the people of Sherkor far down the Koladyne valley and those of Vantura and Dokola, who also had both been concerned in the raid on Stewart's camp. Before they got to the scene Vantura had been killed in the fighting, and Dokola withdrew, taking a number of Sherkor heads. His whereabouts being reported, arrangements were made for his capture. The Superintendent, then *en route* to Tao to confer with the Chin Hills officials, let Dokola know he should visit him on his return, at the same time sending a message to Hutchinson to leave Sherkor at once and move to surprise the village where Dokola was. A long and most difficult night march brought him to the neighbourhood of the place, and on gaining the top of a hill about 4 a.m. a cock crowing showed the village was near and all crept cautiously on, soon sighting it where fires were being lighted. On nearing the entrance the sepoys charged in, Lushais with guns came rushing out of the houses, shots were exchanged and two or three Lushais were killed. Many were captured, amongst them being Dokola, the surprise having been complete. Certain articles belonging to Stewart confirmed Dokola's implication in that raid, and he was transported for life to the Andamans. The hard work done and general handiness of the F.P. are also illustrated by the Superintendent's first exploration of the Koladyne river southwards on rafts, and which proved most laborious. Rafting material had to be cut from the bamboo jungle and fresh rafts made up after each of the many rapids, over which supplies, ammunition, baggage, etc., had to be man-handled; all forming a fatiguing experience, in which the 40 Jaruas with the escort proved the most expert of all, consequently the bulk of the toil fell to them, and none grumbled or shirked. Occasionally,

,Fort Tregear on the Lung Leh—Haka Road.

when on visits to new villages uncertain of temper, it would fall to the F.P. sepoys to lubricate the wheels of diplomacy as it were, by giving a "tamasha" of the "song and dance" type, to humour the tribesmen and show friendliness. Half the escort would perform thus while the remainder were under arms, until the people were in a happy mood and would listen attentively to the Superintendent—and this often after a long and fatiguing march!

In January 1892, after the administrative centre had been moved to Lung Leh, a serious fire occurred at Fort Tregear which destroyed the entire post and in which Dr. Antonio lost his life, in spite of every effort to save the place. A party of the M.P. did gallant work in saving the treasury and ammunition, entering the magazine while it was blazing and carrying out the ammunition boxes, the last one to be conveyed outside actually having two holes burnt in it.

Meanwhile in the north Lushai hills Captain Loch, 3rd Goorkhas, had come late in 1891 to command the detachment of the Surma Valley M.P. garrisoning Aijal, and which at the end of 1893 was made into a separate unit, styled the "North Lushai Military Police Battalion." It began at once recruiting Goorkhas and Jaruas; the old parent Battalion at Silchar having sent the bulk of its men to Aijal, then dropped to the level of a small unit of 350 rifles under a British officer, and remained so till finally incorporated into the Dacca M.P. Battalion some years later, when Eastern Bengal was joined to the Assam Province.

It may here be mentioned that Captain Loch, being an engineer by inclination though a soldier by profession, soon started on improving the station of Aijal. He trained some of his men in quarrying and shaping stone, and as an experiment built himself a "pucca" house. This proving a success he instructed greater numbers of the sepoys in stone work, carpentering, and road-making, gradually developing his Battalion more on the lines of a

Pioneer than of an ordinary Infantry unit. In a few years' time the old stockade and "wattle and daub" houses and barracks had disappeared, and he had rebuilt the entire station of well-constructed stone houses, with corrugated iron roofs, proper doors and windows, and had generally laid out the charming little place as one finds it nowadays—a pleasant surprise to all who see it for the first time after 8 days' marching from Silchar through a forested wilderness. The present-day parade ground—a stupendous piece of work—was achieved by Loch cutting away a spur jutting out from one of the central knolls. It took nearly 5 years to complete and when done he had a sheer cliff of 60 feet or more on one side, and 150 feet of filling in on the other. This work cost Government nothing, the men having received working pay out of the Battalion Canteen profits, rendered large through thirst engendered by toil. A good rifle range and most of the older district roads stand to the credit of the Battalion under this Commandant, who also about 1893 introduced pipes and drums, the men being sent for instruction in the instruments to his old Regiment, the 3rd Goorkhas.

As mentioned before, Assam now controlled the North and Bengal the South Lushai hills, Mr. McCabe and Captain Shakespear being the respective Superintendents, and though outwardly matters seemed quiet, neither officer was very hopeful of a rapid and peaceful settlement among clans known to be chafing under new restraints. Conditions below the surface were not long in coming to a head, for in March 1892 trouble arose in the northern area where a coalition of Lushai Chiefs objecting to requisitions for labour which they flatly refused to supply, attacked Mr. McCabe while on tour with an escort. A large force of Lushais surrounded them near Lalbura's village and for several days made persistent attacks in which Jemadar Bhudai Sing, 3 sepoys, and a Havildar of the S.V.M.P. were wounded (1 sepoy mortally) and a ration convoy *en route* to McCabe was attacked and had 2 sepoys killed. Various escorting parties were at different times attacked, each occasion causing one or two casualties, and the rising becoming widespread the 18th B.I. were sent up to Aijal to reinforce the Military Police. The Commandant at Aijal wired the news to Lung Leh, as the trouble connected itself also with certain villages in the jurisdiction of the southern hills, and Captain Shakespear set out at once with Lieuts. Towsey and Boileau, R.E., and 150 rifles of his Military Police. At Lalhuova's village they received warning of a probable attack and it was said that further on the country was "up." Moving further north on the 16th March the Column was attacked near Vansanga's village. The enemy was beaten off, the place occupied, and the force stockaded itself close by. On the 18th the strongly defended village of Zaote was taken and burnt, 2 sepoys being wounded here, and by a night march Lungrang was reached by dawn on the 20th. This village stood on the top of a line of cliff, the approach guarded by stockades full of armed Lushais. With a small party Boileau made a flank attack, and after firing three volleys charged uphill at a small gate seen to be open, the main body slowly firing to occupy the enemy's attention. Boileau got in with 1 sepoy killed and 1 wounded, when the Lushais bolted, leaving several dead behind.

Lungrang was then destroyed, but as no position there was found suitable for defence and hostility all round was most determined, the Column returned to Vansanga, unable at that time to reach McCabe near Lalbura's village (Sketch Map 2). Here they remained till the 28th, beating off attacks and pursuing hostile parties, until reinforcements could be sent. On one of these occasions Boileau with 90 sepoys, making a rapid night march, attacked a new stockade at Lalthana's village. Here the precipitous nature of the ground made flanking movements hopeless, but a charge by one portion of the party under covering fire from the rest was successful, and they got in, losing only 1 sepoy killed, while several had narrow escapes with bullets through their clothing. The defenders as usual bolted, to keep up a desultory fire from the surrounding jungle, causing a few slight casualties before the Vansanga stockade was reached. In these actions Subadar Man Sing, Bugler Daloo Sing, and sepoys Bakhtabir Thapa and Subhan Sing distinguished themselves in leading and in keeping their men together.

It was evident the rising could not be put down with the 100 odd men, which was all that could be spared after providing for the safety of Lung Leh and Fort Tregear, as well as guards for the long stretch of road from Demagiri up, over which convoys were moving bringing the annual supply of stores. Therefore reinforcements of 300 rifles of the 3rd B.I. under Major Anderson were hurried up from Calcutta, followed later by a detachment of the armed Civil Police from Dacca under Mr. Savi. These took over the defence of Demagiri and the road posts as far as Lung Leh, while 50 rifles 3rd B.I. increased the garrison of the latter place.

During the first half of April the Lushais persistently attacked ration convoys *en route* to Lung Leh, killing a number of coolies and now and then dropping a sepoy, also wounding an Indian officer. On the road to Fort Tregear the same thing was occurring, where both coolies and sepoys suffered casualties. Lung Leh itself also experienced attacks, and the recently erected telegraph lines were destroyed in many places.

Meanwhile McCabe in the northern hills, after repelling many attacks, had been obliged to return to Aijal to refit and start out again with Captain Loch in greater strength. Early news of the rising had been sent to Silchar, and by the beginning of April detachments of Regulars were holding Aijal and Changsil, releasing the North Lushai M.P. for the suppression of the revolt, now widespread. Burma was also stirring, as the disturbances touched the border, threatening trouble amongst the Chins, and a Column under Captain H.

A CHIEF OF THE SOUTH LUSHAI HILLS (MĀMTE).

Rose, 3rd Goorkhas, was ordered from Fort White to co-operate with those under Loch and Shakespear.

In mid April McCabe and Loch, with 400 M.P., left Aijal and moved against the villages of Kairuma and Poiboi, while Shakespear, with 200 of his men, advanced northwards. On the 10th May Captain Rose's Column, consisting of detachments from the 60th Rifles and 39th Garhwalis with 2 mountain guns, accompanied by Mr. (later Sir Bertram) Cary, joined hands with Shakespear after a most trying march in great heat and not without some skirmishes, near Daokoma's village. Here plans were made for a number of strong parties to overrun the central and southern regions while Loch and McCabe dealt with the northern clans. This was duly carried out; many offending villages were attacked and destroyed including those of Lalbura, Bungteya, and Maite, where opposition was encountered and a few casualties were sustained. Before the rains broke the revolt had been suppressed, entailing the destruction of 20 villages and their stockades, numbers of Lushais killed or wounded, grain and cattle confiscated, while only slight casualties were caused amongst the rapidly operating detachments. The Indian General Service Medal was issued later to the troops and Military Police who took part in these operations.

It was found that the sudden appearance of Rose's Column from the east had vastly impressed the Lushais, showing them the futility of further resistance and causing their offensive action to slack off. Although the principal revolting Chiefs evaded capture for some time longer, the clans submitted and the trouble ceased. After the rains a wing of the 3rd Goorkhas who had relieved a regiment at Demagiri was sent up to Lung Leh under Major Pulley and Captains Tillard and Browne, whence they made a tour of the southern hills that winter before returning to India.

During the hot weather of 1893 it was learnt that the Chief Lalthuama and his mother, widow of Vandula, living in neighbouring villages between the Mat and the Koladyne rivers, were still a centre of disaffection and were intriguing with Daokoma, a northern Chief, for a fresh revolt. The cutting up by them of some coolies and an interpreter took place, and matters had to be taken in hand before trouble could spread to Kairuma and other Chiefs, wanted but still at large. So in August, at the height of the rainy season, Captain Shakespear, with Messrs. Pugh and Hutchinson and 80 rifles, left Lung Leh to surprise the widow's village, and this incident is also typical of what the Military Police were frequently called on to carry out. The last march was made in pelting rain, floods had broken down parts of the road, and the Mat river was reached at nightfall, where the road was left. Through the night the party waded up streams often waist deep, and climbed with extreme difficulty through dense and dripping jungle alive with leeches. Just after dawn the village was reached and rushed. Surprise was complete, Lalthuama and his intriguing old mother were captured and their people rapidly disarmed, the weapons being confiscated. At the same time messages were sent to all neighbouring villages to come in at once with all their guns, to which they complied. Nothing impresses these wild folk more than a surprise show of force, and they responded readily to avoid the "Sirkar's" further wrath. The village of Tulthang also had a rapid visitation and its teeth drawn by the seizure of all weapons. It was found that Daokoma had been with Lalthuama and had only left the village the day before Shakespear's visit, where he had been arranging for another rising. The party returned to Lung Leh after a very successful outing in which it had by initiative and well-timed surprise nipped in the bud what undoubtedly would have developed into another serious effort to force the British out of the hills. Lalthuama and his mother were deported, and their villages duly paid up the fines levied on them.

The year 1894 was chiefly noticeable for much touring

through both the northern and southern hills, disarming important villages and enforcing the payment of fines for former offences against law and order. The results of these labours were excellent, as village elders declared they " could now do nothing, their communities were destitute, their women even having sold their petticoats (scanty at the best of times) to help pay up their fines."

At this time the posts held in the south Lushai hills by the M.P. were Demagiri, Lungsin, Lalthuama, and Fort Tregear, while those in the north were Sherchip, Changsil, Kolosib, and various small ones, the headquarters of both Battalions being at Lung Leh and Aijal, respectively. The Sherchip post in 1898 was moved to Thenjol on the Aijal–Lung Leh road.

Gradually, one after another, the outlawed Chiefs were captured, Vansanga in March 1895 after a smart piece of night work entailing a long march of 26 miles on the part of Mr. Plowden and his M.P. men. This rapid seizure of a noted outlaw impressed all neighbouring clans greatly, but Kairuma, Jacopa, and his brother Jaduna still evaded us. To effect their being rounded up Mr. Porteous, now in charge of the north Lushai hills, with Captain Loch and 100 of his men, Shakespear with 150 M.P. from Lung Leh, and a similar force from the Chin hills, co-operated together and scoured the country. Finding further resistance useless, Kairuma surrendered himself, and M.P. posts were located in his principal villages till all fines were paid up.

Before the winter was over Jacopa and Jaduna were taken. Information showed the former to be in a certain village, for which two parties of the M.P. set out. After a long night march and towards midnight on the 3rd January, 1896, one party in bare feet crept into the place at different points, while the other one quietly surrounded it. The principal houses were entered and searched, all being at once in a state of confusion. The sepoys emptied each house of its occupants, who were collected in the centre of the village under a guard, but none would divulge which was the outlawed Chief. At last a sepoy, noticing a man in the crowd whose long hair was hanging over his face, pulled it roughly back, when Jacopa was at once recognised, made prisoner, and transported to the Andamans with the other Chiefs. The village was then destroyed as a lesson to the people not to shelter enemies of the British Government. Two nights later, after a 10-hour march, Captain Shakespear and Lieut. Drage were successful in rounding up Jaduna and some of his following who were hiding in the Lonlair forest across the Tyao river. Both Chiefs were sentenced to five years' imprisonment, but were released earlier and did good service on return to their homes. These last captures removed all the most troublesome elements, and completed the pacification of the Lushai hills both north and south.

During these disturbed years the North Lushai M.P. had been allowed to enlist up to 1000 men, while the strength of the southern Battalion stood at 540. Both were dressed in khaki, with the small round rifle cap and bronze badges and buttons. They were armed with the Snider rifle till 1901, when the Martini was issued, and their equipment was the Mackenzie pattern of brown leather.

In the intervals of quietude and from now on an immense amount of road work through the entire hills was accomplished, also a rough cart-road had been cut from the Phyrang river to Lower Lung Leh, 4 miles below the H.Q. Station, to facilitate the carriage of supplies. It often happened at certain seasons for crops when village labour was not available that the M.P. sepoys were called on to carry up loads of a maund (80 lb.) each from the end of the cart track, and heartily they responded, doing two trips a day, *viz.* 16 miles, and of which they thought nothing. By the end of 1895 almost all roads and bridges as at present existing had been completed, though the very comfortable Rest-houses at all stages north of Lung Leh did not come

ONE OF COLONEL LOCH'S REST HOUSES (NEIDAWN) IN THE NORTHERN LUSHAI HILLS.

TUIPANG STOCKADE AND DETACHMENT 1ST ASSAM RIFLES.

into existence till later, through the efforts of Major Loch and Captain H. W. Cole.

A large tract of hill country which was "unadministered" lay between the settled areas of the Chin, Lushai and Arrakan hills, and Lower Burma, which even in these early days, as in later years, proved a thorn in the flesh of the surrounding administered districts, as it harboured their bad characters, large numbers of guns, and became a perfect "Alsatia." These people raided at will, and as it was a long and expensive business to march troops down amongst them, we first hear of proposals in 1896 to establish a strong post in the vicinity of Sherkor, 70 miles down the Koladyne from Lung Leh, and to supply it with rations from Arrakan. This, however, was not sanctioned for many years, the present post at Tuipang not being located till 1907, though for a time it was found desirable to place a temporary one at Sherkor.

The route from Silchar up the Dalesari river was now improved by men of the North Lushai M.P., who, under Major Loch's supervision, blasted away the numerous huge boulders which obstructed the river traffic above Changsil. This opened the river to boats as far as the present Sairang Ghat, 14 miles from Aijal, between which points a cart road was made, thus lessening the cost of transporting rations and stores into Aijal, and Changsil ceased to exist as a post.

This brings us to the year 1898 and the great change affecting the administration of these hills and the lives of the two separate Military Police Battalions controlling the two areas, by which the whole of the Lushai hills was made into one district under one Civil head. The South Lushai hills were joined to those of the north and came under the Assam Government, Bengal thereafter only concerning itself with the country up to, but not including, Demagiri. With this change the centre of administration became Aijal as it is at present, and the South Lushai M.P. Battalion, which had been an entirely distinct force, was amalgamated on the 13th April, 1898, with the sister Battalion in the north, the whole from now on being designated the "Lushai Hills Military Police Battalion."

In 1898 Fort Tregear was given up, chiefly owing to scarcity of water, and another position for the post was selected some 9 miles further east at what was known as South Vonlaiphai. The post at North Vonlaiphai had been established by Mr. Porteous in 1896, and two years later another post was placed at Champhai 8 marches east of Aijal, where, at an elevation of close on 6000 feet, it became the favourite post in the hills. Champhai was before long linked by a good bridle path, *via* the charming little Ri Lake and the Aikon Klang range, to Falam, the H.Q. Station in the Chin hills and 7 marches further south-east. These posts were finally given up, South Vonlaiphai in 1900, North Vonlaiphai in 1922, Champhai in 1923. The only posts remaining in the Lushai hills at present are Lung Leh, Tuipang, and a detachment at Silchar.

By 1900 the parade ground at Aijal, alluded to before, gave ample flat space for drill and amusements generally, such as football and hockey, while Polo for long was played on it by officers in the Station and any Goorkhas who could ride, the mounts being chiefly mules, of which a number were kept for transport purposes. This latter game became very popular, the sepoys striving to attain the art of riding, not easy for short thick-limbed mountaineers, so as to be able to take part in what was distinctly unusual Polo but none the less great fun and good exercise for all that.

With the amalgamation of the two Battalions Lung Leh lost its former importance, becoming an ordinary post of 100, later reduced to 50 rifles, and in 1901, owing to the generally peaceful attitude of all the clans, the Lushai Hills M.P. Battalion was reduced in strength from 10 to 8 companies, or a total of 850 rifles.

In regard to the settled quietude of the people, a word

Lung Leh Ridge from the Civil Officer's House.

The Civil Officer's House at Lung Leh.

may here be said of the missionary enterprise which has largely helped to bring about this desirable state of affairs. Messrs. Lorraine and Savidge, belonging to a private mission and who only retired from the scenes of their labours in 1925, were the pioneers in this field of usefulness, coming, as they did, from Sadiya to Aijal in 1891. For the next few years, owing to revolts and the unsettled state of the tribesmen, they obtained but small results from their unceasing labours. Later, their medical knowledge and assistance appealing to the people, they were listened to and obtained many converts, thus paving the way for the members of the Welsh Mission who followed, on Lorraine and Savidge moving into the southern hills. Here the excellent couple settled themselves near the site of Saipuia's old village overlooking and 2 miles from Lung Leh, where in course of time they established a school, hospital, and pleasant bungalows. They were joined by Lorraine's brother and his wife, who eventually moved to Sherkor, starting a branch of the mission there. The long years of unselfish efforts on their part and on those of the Welsh Mission at Aijal have had a remarkable effect on the Lushais, who, once their dislike of foreigners was overcome, gave way to conversion in vast numbers. The Christianised Lushais now run into many thousands, these people having accepted our religion in a way no other of our wild north-eastern tribes have done, with the exception of the Khasias.

It was years before the Lushai Hills M.P. saw expeditionary work again, when in 1911 detachments took part in General Bower's expedition, and in 1912–13 in the Mishmi Survey escorts, accounts of which will be found in the chapters dealing with the Sadiya side of the province and the Lakhimpur M.P. Then followed their employment with Goorkha regiments in the Great War, and their part in the suppression of the Kuki Rebellion, 1917–19, and in the suppression of the Rampa State revolt, 1924, all of which are narrated in separate chapters. The present senior Indian officer, Subadar Major Mansur Rai, has served long years with the Battalion, has a distinguished record, and is a first-rate officer, looked up to by all ranks. He served throughout the Great War with the 2/2nd Goorkhas in France and then with the 1/2nd Goorkhas in Mesopotamia, with both of whom his usefulness and gallantry were acclaimed, and he won honour and distinction. From 1906 onwards the Battalion was also called on at varying intervals of time to assist the Civil power in the suppression of seditious disorders and riots, which, being alluded to elsewhere, this individual life of the Lushai Hills M.P. Battalion, now the 1st Assam Rifles, can be brought to a close.

The 1st Assam Rifles Quarter Guard at Aijal.

The Parade Ground at Aijal, dug out by Major Loch and his Men.

CHAPTER IX

1859 to 1910. The Lakhimpur F.P., 1864—Lakhimpur Military Police Battalion—Sadiya—Holcombe's disaster, 1875—Aka expedition, 1883—Lushai expedition, 1891—Abor expedition, 1894—Railway surveys and escorts—Mishmi expedition, 1899—New posts—Strikes.

It was after the Abor and Mishmi troubles of 1855 and 1859 that proposals were made to Government for the raising of a special Frontier Police force for service in and along the borders of the Sadiya and Lakhimpur districts, the detachment from the Nowgong unit doing duty at Dibrugarh being insufficient for the purposes now required. At first sanction was refused, but in the winter of 1864–65 the matter was reconsidered and acceded to, and with the title of "Lakhimpur Armed Police Battalion" the new unit came into existence at Dibrugarh, many Cacharis, Shans, and Nepalese being transferred as a nucleus from the Civil Police and the Nowgong F.P., after which the methods of ordinary recruiting filled its ranks to a strength of 500 men.

Their first taste of active service took place in the winter of 1865, when a detachment formed part of the punitive Column under Colonel Garstin which entered the Abor hills to proceed against Runkang village. The people, however, submitted at once and paid the fines, the Column returning without having had any active opposition. Shortly after this another detachment with a party of the 2nd A.L.I. had to pursue a raiding gang of Mishmis, whom they successfully rounded up, capturing the leaders. This last-named tribe later, again showing signs of unrest, led to the placing of military posts, at first temporary but permanent from 1881 on, at Nizamghat on the Dibong river and at Bishemnagar further south-east, which for many years were held by the 2nd A.L.I. at Sadiya. Nizamghat only is kept up at the present time and has been held by the Lakhimpur Military Police Battalion since 1900 (Sketch Map 3).

In the winter of 1874–75 survey operations were undertaken in the Naga hills by Captain Butler, working eastwards through the Lhota and Ao country. To co-operate with him and to define the boundaries of administration between the Sibsagor and Naga hills districts a survey party with Captain Badgely and Lieut. Holcombe, Assistant Commissioner of Sibsagor, escorted by 40 men of the 2nd A.L.I. and 60 of the Lakhimpur F.P. Battalion (which had dropped its old title in 1873) with a large number of carriers, crossed the border near Jaipur and entered the hills in mid January 1875, the intention being to work gradually westwards and meet Butler's party somewhere on the Dikkoo river. Badgely, after a fortnight's march, with halts for surveying, reached Ninu village of the Banfera clan on the evening of the 2nd February without experiencing any hostility. Early the following morning a large body of Nagas arrived at the camp ostensibly to sell provisions, some of whom approached Holcombe, who was strolling about. The constables, sepoys, and others were cooking their food; one sentry only was posted over the front of the camp, and Badgely was still dressing in his tent. Through an interpreter Holcombe chatted with the Naga headmen, one of whom asked to be shown a rifle. The nearest one happened to be the sentry's, which Holcombe, not suspecting treachery, took and showed. This was evidently the signal, for the next moment the Nagas threw off their shawls, under which each had his "dao." Holcombe and the sentry were cut down dead at once, and the enemy rushed through the camp, cutting up the sepoys and all within their reach before any could get to their weapons.

Badgely was cut at and wounded as he left his tent on hearing the tumult, but succeeded in collecting a few sepoys and making a stand while rifles were got out. The stand, however, was of short duration and a retreat had to be made, fortunately well conducted, or none would have returned at all. The affair was over in a very short time and the camp swarming with exultant savages, who had accounted for Holcombe and 80 men killed, Badgely and 51 wounded, and were now busy making their bag of heads. Badgely with the remains of the party effected a retirement out of the hills *via* Bor Mutan with such of the badly wounded as they could carry along.

A military expedition totalling 400 rifles drawn from the 42nd A.L.I., the 44th S.L.I., the Lakhimpur, and the Naga Hills F.P. followed at once to exact reparation for this gross and unprovoked outrage, and was commanded by Brigadier-General Nuthall, with whom Butler was sent from the Naga hills to assist with his knowledge of the tribes. Seven villages had to be visited and punished, of which the principal ones were Senua, Ninu, and Kaimoi. The force assembled at Jaipur on the 10th March, 1875, and marched through the hills *via* Bor Mutan. Slight hostility was met with at the Dilli (Tisai) river below Senua, which was in flood, offering great difficulties to a crossing. Three of the F.P. men and two of the 44th made a gallant but unsuccessful attempt to swim across and bring over boats which were on the other bank, in which one man lost his life. A crossing elsewhere was effected and Senua was taken without opposition and destroyed. From here the force moved in two columns, one on Ninu and Nisa, the other on Lonkai, which were burnt without resistance on the part of the tribe. At Ninu 71 heads of those massacred were recovered and with the remains of the bodies were burnt, the ashes being buried. The Nisa Column split up into small parties to scour the country and destroy grain and property hidden in the jungles. Three more villages were visited and punished, but as the offending community had scattered and the real culprits had by now fled into the Patkoi range, the force returned to Jaipur in the beginning of April and dispersed.

The foregoing is taken from Butler's diary, but another official account seems to show that nothing like adequate punishment for such gross treachery was inflicted, that although the force certainly burnt Ninu and certain other villages, being opposed nowhere, it was a futile effort, and that the force left the hills far too quickly to have made any real impression on the tribe. That this somewhat scathing judgment was based on reality seems proved by the fact that before the year was out another Column had to be sent into these hills to complete the work of the first one, as the tribesmen would not surrender those mainly responsible for the massacre. This was only done after Ninu, which had been rebuilt, was again destroyed, several other villages receiving drastic attention from the second force (Sketch Map 3).

By 1880 the Lakhimpur F.P. Battalion was holding a series of posts extending from the Darrang border, round that of Sadiya, to Geleki at the foot of the Naga hills in Sibsagor district, the posts at Borhat, Jaipur, and Rangarora being also held by its men. The Battalion was therefore much split up, was never together for drill, etc., and suffered somewhat in consequence; a condition which continued till 1883, when, under the new scheme of reorganisation of the whole of the F.P. into Military Police Battalions as set forth in Chapter IV, this unit became the Lakhimpur Military Police Battalion, to which drafts from the Garo Hills and Nowgong F.P. were sent to raise its strength to 700 men, and from Battalion records it appears to have retained its old title till 1888. Raised as a Military Police Battalion by Captain E. Molesworth (44th S.L.I.), its headquarters continued to be at Dibrugarh, where a Native Infantry Regiment was also stationed up to 1907, and its strongest detachment was at Sadiya.

THE STOCKADE AND PICQUET POST AT GELEKI.

[From a sketch by L. W. S., 1880

GROUP OF THE LAKHIMPUR FRONTIER POLICE, 1887.

Its many other posts were of varying strengths, some with only 1 N.C.O. and 8 sepoys (the old Civil Police titles now gave way to military ones), others with 1 Native officer and 20 sepoys, others again with greater strengths. Of course the very small posts were practically useless and were gradually abolished, and the total number to be furnished at this period were 15, *viz.* Barapathar, Laluk Doloni, Bhebelesuk, Lakhimpur, Makum, Dijmur, Pobo, Sissi, Dibong, Dikrang, Disoi, Diphoo, Hajul, Sonpura, and Rangarora, making a total of 468 men on post duty out of the full strength of 682 of all ranks (Sketch Map 3). Most of these posts vanished during the next ten years, the need for their upkeep ceasing with border quietude, and the Battalion benefited by its companies being more together for training and discipline. Sniders now replaced the old muzzle-loading Enfield rifle, but until about 1887, when khaki and the Mackenzie equipment were adopted, the old blue serge uniform and equipment were worn.

With regard to Sadiya, where the Battalion's strongest detachment was on duty, an old map of 1869–70 shows the lines for troops (the Assam Light Infantry) to have been practically on the site now occupied by the new A.R. Barracks built in 1919–20, while the F.P. lines then and for many years stood east of the racecourse made many years earlier and a little to the north of the present Political Officer's house. The masonry blockhouses at Selim to the west and at Dikrang to the north were then the nearest to the station, of which only the latter exists to this day, though unoccupied since 1900.

Of the activities of this new Battalion the following is gleaned from its records and other sources.

Shortly after the Battalion was complete, in December 1883, it was ordered to send a detachment of 2 British officers (lent by the Army temporarily) and 150 men to join General Sale Hill's expedition against the Akas. There was but little fighting, but the detachment was present with the main camp on the Bareli river when the tribesmen attacked it at night, causing several casualties, and a portion of it took part in the capture of Mehdi, the principal village, after which the Akas made submission, restoring the captives taken in raids, and paying the fines imposed. During this year Mr. Hughes, of the Civil Police, was appointed European Subadar Major to the Battalion, an absurd title obtaining for similar billets in the Naga Hills and Surma Valley M.P. units, and which continued up to 1904.

The next five years were without special interest save for a small punitive outing to Punia in 1884 and escort duty in 1888 to Mr. Needham, Political Officer at Sadiya, into the Hukong valley for the purposes of exploration and the gathering of information concerning that little-known tract.

In 1888 Lieut. Maxwell, 6th Jat Light Infantry, succeeded Captain Molesworth in command, and in early December that year he was ordered to take a detachment of 70 sepoys to join Captain Macintyre's punitive expedition against certain Trans Dikkoo Naga villages which had committed a serious raid on Mongsemdi village in the Ao Naga country. He marched from Dibrugarh *via* Geleki, reaching the rendezvous at the end of the month. An account of their doings will be found in Chapter XII on the Naga Hills M.P., the country operated in being in that Battalion's area. The force experienced a little scrapping, a few casualties, and much hard marching in mountainous country, returning to Dibrugarh in late February 1889.

The rising in 1890–91 in the North Lushai hills, an account of which is given in Chapter VIII, as it mainly concerns the Lushai M.P., obliged reinforcements to be called for, and a detachment of 2 Native officers and 120 sepoys under Captain Maxwell was dispatched to that district. Travelling by river steamer down the Brahmaputra and up the Surma river to Silchar, they reached the disturbed area and took over certain posts, releasing their garrisons for work further afield, until peace was restored in March 1891. Captain Maxwell had just received orders for the return of his men to Dibrugarh, when they were countermanded owing to the outbreak of the rebellion in Manipur, and he was directed to send 2 Native officers and 100 sepoys to join Colonel Rennick's Column assembled at Silchar (Sketch Map 2), and by making eleven forced marches they were able to join the Column on the Manipur border, the remainder returning to headquarters. Imphal, the capital of the State and the scene of the massacre of Mr. Quinton, Chief Commissioner and party, was reached without opposition; of the three punitive Columns that of General Graham from Burma being the only one which had any fighting, and after a few months of duty there the detachment rejoined at Dibrugarh.

The following years, 1892 and 1893, were uneventful save for the Mishmis attacking and cutting up a patrol of 3 sepoys near Bomjur, while another patrol lost 1 sepoy killed and 1 wounded in the same way, which outrages necessitated a blockade of their hills for a time.

During 1893 the Abors began stirring again, their Pasi and Minyong clans committing raids on Mishmi villages on our side of the border and carrying off numbers of captives. Negotiations were made for their restitution with the usual barren results, and as their offensive, truculent attitude seemed likely to affect other tribes it was decided to send an expedition into their country. A well-equipped force of 150 of the 44th Goorkha Rifles (now the 8th G.R.) with 300 of the Lakhimpur M.P. and 100 of the Naga Hills M.P. under Captain Little with 2 7-pounder guns and 1500 transport coolies, assembled at Sadiya in January 1894 under command of Captain Maxwell. The Political Officer with the force directed the political side of the expedition, and also seems to have been given a large measure of control in its general management, which, as was only to be expected, produced disagreement and friction between the military and civil heads.

The advance was made up the Dibong valley, Dambuk and Silluk villages being the earlier objectives (Sketch Map 3). The force crossed the river to Dambuk, a mile in front of which a strong stockade was encountered held in strength. The dense forest made any turning movement a matter of much difficulty and time, and as the first efforts of the advanced guard to rush the place failed and the guns also had no effect, a general assault followed.

The Abors fought well, standing to their defences and keeping up showers of arrows on the attackers, who had to hack away the *chevaux de frise* of bamboo stakes and long " panjis " which prevented the stockade being reached. At last the Abors gave way and the defences were carried, many dead being found inside, Maxwell's casualties being 25. Success occurred, however, too late in the evening to allow of any further move on the village, which next morning was found deserted. For gallantry in this affair Havildar Bhuta Sing, of the Lakhimpur M.P., was awarded the I.O.M. 2nd Class.

The advance continued to Mimasipu and Silluk, both being destroyed, with resistance only at the latter place in the valley of the Dihang river. Here the Political Officer learnt that Damroh, a large, influential village stated to be 4 long marches further into the hills, had also taken their share in the fighting, so an advance against it was decided on. Transport and supply difficulties now arose, and a halt had to be made until 20 days' rations could be collected at Bordak, just below the junction of the Yamne and Dihang rivers, to which place the force had advanced. This was now made an advance Base, while sick and wounded were sent back to Sadiya. The Political Officer, trusting to local information, declared a strong guard at Bordak to be unnecessary, to which Maxwell disagreed, but as the management of the expedition was mostly in the hands of the former, he gave in to the extent of leaving a small party of 17 sepoys composed of weakly men under a sick Native officer and 44 coolies. After nearly a month's delay here the requisite rations were collected and the force moved on towards Damroh high up the Yamne river, after having made arrangements that rations at stated times be sent forward by friendly Abors. The force was now in difficult country where the going was very slow. Dukku, 2 short marches on, was reached without incident and next day only 6 miles were covered owing to the nature of the country, during which the Column was fired on by unseen tribesmen. The following day an advance of only 2 miles was possible and further trouble was experienced owing to coolies deserting or falling sick. The Column was now in straits; it had been far longer on the way than had been anticipated, and as yet no rations had reached them from Bordak. An attempt was made to reach Damroh, now only some 4 miles off, with a flying Column of the fittest men, which was to destroy the village and return the same day. This, however, failed, the move being greatly delayed by having to turn the enemy out of several great stone "shoots" built far up the hill-side. So this flying Column returned without having reached its objective. The whole force had now to turn back, no rations having reached it, and on the way the Abors strongly opposed the retirement both at Silli and at Dukku, particularly at the former place, where a strong stockade had been erected and a sharp fight took place. In charging this stockade with some of his own and some of the Lakhimpur sepoys, Havildar Major Bakshi Ram Dogra, of the Naga Hills M.P. (later promoted to Jemadar), displayed great gallantry and was first into the stockade under showers of arrows and some bullets, for which he gained the Order of Merit. Bordak was at last reached and the reason for the non-dispatch of supplies was explained in the dreadful scene which presented itself to the Column. The camp was found completely gutted, dead and headless bodies littering the ground, and stores mostly destroyed.

It transpired from the one man who escaped the massacre by swimming the river and hiding, that the enemy had come into the camp in the guise of carriers, who were expected, and that while loads were being distributed to them they suddenly whipped out their "daos," which each had concealed under his cloth and set upon the guard, cutting down all in a very short time. In this condition and with hardly any food supplies left, the Political Officer decided to clear out of the country at once, but Maxwell persuaded him to stay long enough to punish the neighbouring villages of Padu and Membu, which must have been concerned in the destruction of the Bordak camp. Both villages were burnt with but little opposition and the force withdrew to Sadiya by the end of March 1894. The objectives of their expedition can only be said to have been half accomplished and at considerable loss to the force, *viz*. 49 killed and 45 wounded, including Lieut. East, R.A., badly hit by a poisoned arrow, while many died of disease due to hardships and lack of food. The monetary stipend, or "Posa," given by Government to the Abors hitherto for their good behaviour now ceased, their country was blockaded till 1901, and with one exception, that of a small raid in 1903, this tribe gave no trouble for many years.

In 1894 Captain G. Row, 44th G.R., succeeded Captain Maxwell in command of the Battalion, during whose five years' tenure of the billet only two outings of interest took place, one being in 1897 with Subadars Gopal Chandra and Anjab Ali, Jemadar Bhuta Sing, and 200 sepoys, who escorted Mr. McCabe, I.G. Police, into the Apa Tanang hills between the Mirris and the Daphlas, whose people had been showing signs of unrest, but which was made to effect the release of captives and as a demonstration of power. Although much hostility was displayed at first it did not come to actual fighting, thanks to the excellent discipline of the Lakhimpur M.P. The other one was the strong escort to the Hukong valley railway surveys in 1895–96.

It had for some time past been under discussion to

link the Burma railway system with that of Assam, thus giving through connection with India. Three routes were before the authorities—in the south a line from Chittagong to Akyab and over the Aeng Pass in the Arrakan Yomas to Prome, in the centre from Lumding *via* Berima in the Naga hills to the Mayankhong valley and so through Manipur to Tammoo and Monywa, in the north from Margherita over the Patkoi range down the Hukong valley and on through Maiankwan to Mogoung on the present Shwebo–Myitkhyina line (Sketch Map 1). At this time the Chittagong–Dibrugarh line (A. and B. Railway) had been surveyed and construction had been commenced in different sections of the line. Of the three propositions that of the Hukong valley was favoured by the military for strategic purposes, as it would run at no very great distance from the south-west border of China, while civilian views *re* trade and commerce favoured that *via* Akyab. The idea of the Berima route was definitely abandoned after a short survey, the great gorges of the Barak valley proving too difficult and costly from an engineering point of view. This first Hukong valley survey, under the direction of Mr. Way, was furnished with strong escorts of the Lakhimpur Battalion under Captain Row, while similar parties on the Burma side surveyed from Mogoung, both meeting at Nyngbin. However, nothing came of these projects save a short length of line from Maungdaw to Butidang of 36 miles in the Akyab district, and though further surveys were made again in 1920–21, nothing so far has materialised.

The Band of the Lakhimpur M.P. dates from Captain Maxwell's time, about 1893, when it began in a very small way on a Government grant of 50 rupees a month. As the musicians improved, funds were acquired by much playing out at tea garden gatherings and local functions, which enabled the Band in course of time to develop well and to be often employed to play at Shillong during the season.

In 1899 the Bebejiya Mishmi clan started on the war-path and raided a village 16 miles from Sadiya, killing several people and carrying off others as slaves. In punishment for this outrage an expedition under Colonel Molesworth, 44th Goorkha Rifles, was ordered to enter their hills, consisting of the troops in the margin.

1 Coy. Sappers and Miners
2 Coy. 10th Bengal Infantry
1 Coy. 43rd Goorkha Rifles
3 Coy. 42nd Goorkha Rifles
2 Coy. 44th Goorkha Rifles
200 of the Lakhimpur M.P.
2 Mountain guns

They left Sadiya in November 1899 and visited the chief villages of Hunli and Kaladoi (Sketch Map 3). No opposition was offered, but there was much exceedingly hard marching and climbing to considerable altitudes, notably over the difficult Makoo Pass at 8900 feet, all in bitter cold weather with snow in the higher ranges. The offending villages restored their captives, paid up their fines, and the expedition returned to Sadiya on the 8th February, 1900, having caused an expense to the local Government of over 2 Lakhs, when really the work could have been equally well carried out by a company of Military Police alone, at far less cost. As showing the vast difference in the expenses of military as compared with M.P. expeditions, it may be stated here that while Colonel Molesworth's was taking place in the Mishmi country, of which only 110 out of his 1200 men reached the Hunli valley, another expedition in the eastern Naga hills was in progress. This one, under the Deputy-Commissioner, the Commandant, and Mr. N. Williamson, consisted of 2 Goorkha officers and 100 rifles of the Naga Hills M.P. They were absent 2½ months and went through much hard marching, three weeks of which were spent in high unknown ranges where they experienced considerable active opposition at one place. The object of this outing was attained at an extra cost to Government of under 1800 rupees.

From 1899 to 1905 there appears nothing particular to record in the life of the Battalion beyond the furnishing of a Guard of Honour at Gauhati to Lord Curzon

AN ABOR CANE BRIDGE.

of 100 men under Subadars Karak Sing and Chandra Sing during the Viceregal visit to Assam, a small punitive outing to Yogli village in the Ranpang country, the attendance of Subadar Chandra Sing with 8 sepoys at Lord Curzon's Durbar held at Delhi in December 1902, the establishment of two new posts at Laimakuri and Lallimukh, and the rearmament in 1902 with Martini-Henry rifles. During 1904 the Battalion was called on to add to its line of posts by furnishing 3 Native officers and 130 sepoys, divided between posts at Udalguri, Gagrapara, Daimara, and Dikul, along the Kamrup and Darrang borders, with a reserve at Tezpur. During the rainy season these were withdrawn to Dibrugarh, only a post of 34 men remaining at Tezpur. This continued till 1915, when the stress of the Great War caused their abolition, and in 1920 the newly-raised 5th Battalion Assam Rifles took over these border duties.

In 1905 occurred the first serious acts of sedition and strikes in the Surma valley and Eastern Bengal necessitating the dispatch of two companies of the Battalion to aid the Civil power, one under Major Chatterton (who had succeeded Captain Row as Commandant) with Subadars Jitman Lama and Mohun Sing Chettrie being sent to Silchar, the other under Lieut. Lyall with Subadar Gopal Chandra and Jemadar Birbhan Gharti going to Barisal, where their exceedingly unpleasant duties of suppressing the state of disorder were well carried out. Mr. Hughes retired this year, his place in the Battalion being filled by Sergeant Dorward, R.A.

Two years later, civil disorder arising in Dacca, it became necessary to call on the Battalion to assist in its suppression, to which place Subadar Gopal Chandra with 90 sepoys was dispatched, and in May the same year (1907) Lieut. Lyall with 82 men was sent to Goalpara for guard duties on the Viceregal camp.

The Partition of Bengal had taken place in 1903 by which Eastern Bengal with Dacca had been added to Assam, and the Dacca Military Police unit was shortly afterwards found too small for its duties, which had increased through its headquarters having become the seat of Government. Drafts from other Assam Battalions were therefore sent to increase its strength, the Lakhimpur Battalion transferring Subadar Gopal Chandra and 30 men in 1908. October this year saw a punitive expedition under Captain C. Bliss (temporary Commandant), with Subadars Jitman Lama, Jemadars Jasbir Gurung, and Sarabjit Thapa, and 150 sepoys, enter the Ranpang country to punish the village of Rashi for raiding. The object was duly achieved and Subadar Jitman Lama, Jemadar Sarabjit Thapa, and Lance Naik Kalu Konwar were specially brought to the notice of the I.G.P. for excellent work. This year also saw a considerable reduction in the number of the smaller posts held by the Battalion, and on the abolition of those at Dikrang, Sissi, and Gagrapara in 1910, its strength was reduced from 848 to 673 of all ranks.

In the cold weather of this year (1910), owing to threatened trouble with the Daphlas, the Battalion was ordered to send 100 sepoys under Subadar Gan Sing Cachari to make a military promenade through their hills, and to enforce payment of fines due for various offences. With them went Captain Sir G. S. Dunbar, now Commandant, Captain Hutchins, and Mr. Noel Williamson, the Political Officer at Sadiya, and the party returned to headquarters after a six weeks' tour, in which it appeared a better system of training in hill and jungle warfare was desirable. To this end a selected party of 100 N.C.O.'s and men under Captain Hutchins and Mr. Dorward were sent from Dibrugarh to Sadiya and thence to Pasighat at the foot of the hills. A month of hard, systematic work here gave such good results that the whole party were transferred to Sadiya to be retained there as a Movable Column, and a few months later were employed on active service, proving themselves of great value.

CHAPTER X

1910 to 1924. The Lakhimpur M.P., *continued*—Abor expedition, 1911/12—Lohit Valley road work and Mishmi survey escorts, 1912 and 1913—Minor expeditions into the Abor and Mishmi Hills, 1914—The Great War and the Kuki rebellion—Riots in Behar—Daphla expedition, 1918—New lines completed at Sadiya, 1919—Elapoin punitive tour, 1920—Sedition and strikes, 1920 to 1922—Rampa State rebellion, 1924.

THIS brings us to the next occasion on which the Lakhimpur Battalion was employed in the field in conjunction with Regular troops, and which was brought about by the murders in March 1911 of Mr. Noel Williamson and Dr. Gregorson (missionary) at the hands of the Minyong Abors. The former, who had been Political Officer of the Sadiya tract from 1904, was a man of great tact and geniality with considerable knowledge of the characteristics of savage peoples, and had got on terms of friendliness with both Abors and Mishmis while maintaining a strong hand over them. In the winter of 1909 in company with Mr. Lumsden he had visited Kebang, the chief village of the Minyong Abors, where all was so friendly that another visit was decided on, with further exploration into the unknown up the Dihang valley to Thibetan borders. To this end Williamson, this time accompanied by Dr. Gregorson with some servants and orderlies, started off in March 1911, but at Komsing village, one march beyond Kebang, they were treacherously attacked and almost all cut up—Williamson shortly after arrival in the village, the Doctor about 3 miles back close to the river, where a cairn of stones marks the spot, as also another in the village where the Political Officer was killed. This outrage naturally caused a great stir, but the season being too late for military operations these were arranged to take place as soon as the rainy season was over.

Maxim gun Det. A.V.L.H.
32nd Sikh Pioneers
1 Coy. Sappers and Miners
1/2nd Goorkhas
1/8th Goorkhas Rifles
Lakhimpur M.P. Battalion
Detachment Lushai Hills M.P.
2 7-lbr. guns
Brigade Signalling Coy.
3000 Naga Carriers

To punish the tribe and also to explore and survey this country, for owing to China's moves in Thibet and along its south-eastern borders a real interest was at last being stirred in this long stretch of unknown border-lands, a large force under command of General Bowers was to be employed. It consisted of the troops marginally noted, and assembled in early October 1911 at Kobo, 43 miles up stream of Dibrugarh, where the main Base was established.

Before this the Lakhimpur Battalion had been busy, for directly news of the massacre was heard of in Sadiya, Captain Sir G. S. Dunbar, with Captain Hutchins and the Movable Column (150 men), made a forward move into the hills, managed to rescue the few survivors, and carried out some excellent reconnaissance work, when they were recalled from their headquarters, otherwise it is probable that they would have been able to inflict immediate and seasonable punishment on Kebang, which they were keen to carry out, both murdered Englishmen having been well known and most popular with all ranks. Dunbar was, however, allowed to move up more men (380 all told) and build stockade posts at Pasighat and Balek (Sketch Map 3) which they held throughout the rainy season, keeping the tribe in check. As a result of exposure and hard work Captain Hutchins, in charge of these posts, fell ill and died in December, to the great regret of all who knew him.

Being first at Kobo the Base, much work fell to the Battalion in forest clearing for camps and roads, and on the 20th October the first advance, delayed by the excessive rains, was made by 2 companies 1/2nd Goorkhas, 3 of the Lakhimpur Battalion, and a detachment of

Pioneers and signallers under command of Colonel J. Fisher, 1/2nd Goorkhas. This, called the "Ledum Column," was to guard the left flank of the main force in its advance up the Dihang valley, as the attitude of the neighbouring Galongs was uncertain.

Having no tracks to follow, this Column had to cut its way almost entirely through densest forests, the labour being very great. While a reconnoitring party of the 1/2nd Goorkhas and the M.P. was pushing up from Ledum to Mishing, the first contact with the enemy was made in surprising one of their picquets, several being killed. Mishing was reached on the 29th October, and a few days later a party of Goorkhas was able to punish a body of Abors crossing a "jhoom" (cultivation patch), evidently intent on attacking the Mishing post now in course of construction.

For some time during the halt here nothing but short outings were feasible owing to military orders *re* taking no risks and that nights were not to be spent away from Mishing, thus naturally obviating any chances of bringing the enemy to book or of active offence or wide reconnoitring. Rapid marches out and back in different directions only were possible in which on two or three occasions ambuscading parties were met and dispersed. On the 6th November a company of the 1/2nd Goorkhas and one of the Lakhimpur Battalion, under Captain Nicolay, made an attempt to reach Kaking village, some 6 miles across the hills to the south, but owing to limited radius of action did not get beyond Doshing, 4½ miles. After 6 hours' scrambling up and down ravines and hill-sides the scouts came on a strong stockade admirably sited at the top of a steep ascent and invisible through the jungle 10 yards off. The advance guard came under a heavy fire of arrows and a few musket shots, while some ten rock "shoots" were let down above the left flank, sweeping two British officers and several men down the hill-side. The position was rushed, many Abors being killed inside, and some wounded were found who were unable to escape with the rest of their fellows. These were pursued and Doshing village a mile beyond was burnt. Casualties in this little affair were 2 men wounded by arrows and 2 British officers and a number of men incapacitated by bad contusions from rock "shoots."

In mid November instructions were received relaxing the vexatious orders by which all had to be in Mishing post at night, consequently Colonel Fisher's sphere of activity widened, of which advantage was at once taken. Two mixed detachments of the 1/2nd Goorkhas and M.P. were dispatched by different routes to co-operate against Kharan, 10 miles south-east, a large village of the Galongs, whose men had fought at the Doshing stockade. Kharan was surrounded at night and destroyed, the Galongs receiving a severe lesson. The casualties here were slight, 1 man being killed and several hurt by "panji" stakes. This affair had the best results, for representatives of several Galong villages who had declined overtures came in at once professing friendship and promising not to take further part with the Abors. Detachments now moved north to the Sidè river and to Kalek village, which was destroyed after a short fight, but as now only 80 Naga coolies were available for hospital and other duties, the troops had to do their own porter work, to which they responded with fine spirit. The weather now had broken; it rained steadily for a fortnight, which with this severe extra work of carrying their own loads produced a considerable amount of sickness by the end of the month.

Meanwhile General Bower's main column, with which were 2 companies of the Lakhimpur Battalion, had left Kobo on the 22nd October and three days later reached Pasighat at the foot of the hills, a distance of only 23 miles, but rain had made the country-side anything but easy for marching. A halt was made here from the 26th to the 2nd November to build a stockade for L. of C. troops, and another at Janakmukh, 5 miles further.

Convoy crossing a Stream.

The Stockaded Post at Mishing—Abor Hills.

Supplies were also collected at Pasighat, which became the advanced Base, and reconnoitring parties entered the hills. The Sirpo river, 9 miles further, was reached on the 6th without opposition, the activities of the Ledum Column having inoculated the Abors with a disinclination to leave their big stockades at and beyond Rohtang. On November 7th and 8th contact was gained with the tribesmen, who attacked the advance guard in the forest on both days, in which our casualties were 2 men killed, Captain Hutchinson, A.V.L.H., severely wounded by a poisoned arrow, and several men hurt by "panjis." Incessant rain greatly hampered movements, and it was not till the 19th that the force approached Rohtang, 40 miles only from Kobo. Here it was found the large stockade believed to have been at the village was two miles south of it, defending the crossing of the Egar river from the top of a steep spur. As the advance guard neared it the Abors cut loose a number of rock "shoots," sending down an avalanche of boulders, narrowly missing the General, who was close up, and knocking one of his staff down the "khud." The Abors then opened fire with arrows and muskets, one of the former (fortunately not poisoned) hitting the G.O.C. slightly in the hand. Two companies climbing high up while the defences were held in front, outflanked the stockade, which was then rushed but found to have been evacuated. Casualties were slight, 2 wounded and several hurt by rock contusions and stakes.

The next ten days were spent at Rohtang concentrating the force, bringing up supplies, and improving the road. Two or three slight skirmishes took place, notably at Kalek, previously destroyed by the Ledum Column and where the Abors made a short stand. From Rohtang reconnoitring parties of Goorkhas and M.P. located a very large stockade some 3 miles up the Dihang valley at Kekyar Monying, the name for a precipitous rock face 500 yards long loping down to the river across which the track to Kebang ran. This rock face was very high, and above it towered the steep wooded hill dividing the Sirong from the Sidè rivers. Unlike other such defences, this one could be seen built down to the water's edge, while beyond it was a large Abor encampment, and here it was hoped to inflict a severe blow before the chief village was reached (Sketch Map 3).

The main force being now abreast of Mishing and the services of Colonel Fisher's Column no longer required on the left flank, it was broken up, orders being sent for 2 companies of the M.P. to hold Mishing, with 1 company at Balek, and for the remainder to push across the hills and join the main body at Rohtang. To capture the Kekyar Monying stockade a part of the force crossed the Dihang to enfilade the hostile left flank, and on the 3rd December, after much difficulty in getting a hawser across to which a raft was attached, they were on the other bank; not unobserved by the énemy, who attacked at night and killed 2 Goorkhas. Two companies 1/8th G.R. ascended the steep hill above and south of the position, and the remainder, with whom were 50 men of the M.P., formed the main attack. At midday on the 4th the frontal attack opened prematurely before the left flanking companies had gained the hill top, with the result that the Abors, being fired on in front and from across the river, bolted almost at once and the left flank companies were unable to cut off their line of retreat as intended. Only a few Abors were killed and the village of Babuk, 4 miles beyond, was destroyed. A further vexatious halt took place here in order to improve the road over the rock face, it being found somewhat difficult to get laden coolies over it in its then state, so that it was not till December 9th that Kebang village, a short march further, was reached, which reputed stronghold was found deserted and was burnt without opposition. However, Yemsing village, 6 miles beyond, was surprised by a detachment cutting its way through the forest instead of coming by the track, with the result that severe loss was inflicted on the tribesmen and the place was committed to the flames.

This brought actual military operations to an end. Komsing, where the massacre took place, was visited, but only fined, as it was found that though Williamson had been killed in this village the deed had been done by Kebang and Rohtang men, and not by any of Komsing. With villages destroyed, numbers killed and wounded, their food supplies destroyed or confiscated, by the end of December 1911 the Abors gave up the contest, and in early January they began sending in representatives from all tribal sections seeking peace.

The terms of Government having been explained to them were speedily complied with, the murderers of Williamson and Gregorson were given up to the Civil Authorities later, and political relations with other clans further afield were opened, with a view to the exploration and survey work which now followed. Into these it is unnecessary to enter as the Lakhimpur Battalion was not concerned in them, but the work was carried out very successfully with only one hostile incident, *viz.* at Shimong up the Dihang valley. This has been excluded from records and concerned a survey party with escort of troops under a Civil and a Military officer, and at one time it was touch and go whether another regrettable incident or even a massacre might not have taken place. The occasion arose through the Civil officer's mistaken energy and over-friendly attitude towards a people of obviously doubtful intentions, when with a young officer and a small advanced party he pushed on some distance ahead of the main escort, entered Shimong village without any precautions, and at once was surrounded by a mob of hostile armed Abors. The party were prisoners, and worse was on the point of following, for they had been disarmed, when the rest of the escort under a Goorkha officer arrived on the scene in the nick of time, on which the Abors released their prisoners, declaring their action to have been in jest, which it most certainly was not.

The total casualties in action to the force were small, *viz.* 5 killed and 7 wounded, while 2 B.O.'s and many men were severely hurt by contusions from rock "shoots" and "panji" stakes, but disease from the inclement season took a heavy toll of the force of 80 British officers and 2987 fighting men, to say nothing of the coolies, who suffered seriously.

In General Bower's despatches relating to the Lakhimpur Battalion the following were "mentioned" for excellent work, *viz.* Captain Sir G. S. Dunbar, Captain Masters, Mr. Dorward, Subadar Jangbir Lama, and Jemadar Sarabjit Thapa; while Subadar Jangbir Lama with No. 1120 Havildar Dalbahadur Thapa became recipients of the Indian Distinguished Service Medal.

Some notes by Major A. B. Lindsay, 1/2nd Goorkhas, in his official pamphlet relative to this expedition, and in happy reference to the work of the Lakhimpur Military Police Battalion, may be quoted. He wrote: "The account of this expedition's work would be incomplete without reference to the splendid pioneer work of the men of this Battalion under command of Captain Sir G. Sutherland Dunbar. On hearing of the massacre of Mr. Williamson's party in March 1911, a detachment of 150 men started practically at a moment's notice from Sadiya, and pushing up to Renging, 1 march south of Rohtang by forced marches (from which point they were recalled by Government), they were able to pick up and bring back the few survivors of the tragedy. A little later 90 men under Captain Hutchins (who died later from exposure) did a fine reconnaissance on the Mishing side, also building a stockade at Balek, which they held throughout the rainy season of 1911. The information on which the force was organised and operated was gathered mainly from the efforts of the Lakhimpur men during those long unhealthy months, and consequently it was a pleasure to the Regulars of the Field Force to find that a place had been kept in the scheme of operations for so fine a unit."

Shortly after the close of operations a trading post with a hospital was established at Rohtang, backed later on by 200 rifles of the Lakhimpur Battalion disposed as follows: at Pasighat 100, Rohtang 75, Yambung 25; but the Abors, finding themselves left more or less alone again after the expedition, adopted a sullen, truculent attitude and refused to trade, though they would come in occasionally for treatment in the hospital.

With a leniency which to the writer seemed somewhat misplaced the murderers of Mr. Williamson and Dr. Gregorson were sentenced to transportation for life in the Andamans, and from which about 1920 two were allowed to return to their villages.

The conduct in general of the Abor operations of 1911–12 compared with its results and the extremely high cost of the expedition formed the subject of much adverse criticism in the Press both in England and in India, but these are matters into which the historian of the Assam Rifles need not enter.

Having in 1910 ordered the reduction of the Battalion strength, this expedition and the new posts rendered necessary by it obliged the Government to raise its numbers again to 850, who were from now on arranged in 8 companies—5 of Goorkhas, 3 of Jaruas. While the expedition was in progress Subadar Ganbir Sing Gurung with 12 sepoys were sent to Delhi to take part in the ceremonies at the Royal Durbar in November 1911. Early in 1912 the post at Sonpura was given up, and that at Denning in the Mishmi hills up the Lohit valley was opened in its place, so as to facilitate the forwarding of supplies to the small column ordered to make a military promenade amongst that tribe prior to survey work being undertaken, as some slight signs of unrest, probably due to the Abors, had manifested themselves amongst these people.

The subject of trade communication with S.W. China *via* Rima having been under discussion for some time, it was now decided to try to open up and survey these

Mishmi hills, also making a trade route up the Lohit valley. The early winter of 1911–12 saw the 48th Pioneers and a company of Sappers and Miners with strong detachments of the Lakhimpur and the Naga Hills Military Police, under Captain C. Bliss (Commandant N.H.M.P.) and Captain A. Vickers (48th Pioneers), with several hundred coolies, start out on this work from Sadiya, Captains Nevill and Bailey and Mr. Dundas accompanying as Political Officers. Work was begun just beyond Sonpura, to which a road already ran, and a way cleared through the virgin forests in the flat country across the Digaru river to Tijoo and Tameighat, 37 miles, including 1850 feet of military bridges, whence the hills were entered up the Tamei valley by the end of November. Work went on steadily that winter and again in 1912–13, a good, wide, and well-graded bridle path being cut, often under infinite difficulties and in the vilest weather at considerable altitudes, as far as a point near Walong, when work was discontinued. But before this a better alignment had been found for the five earlier stages of the road, *viz.* from Sonpura to Payan (motor track), whence an easier ascent *via* Chorpani to Denning (Sketch Map 3), where a post had been stationed, and a little further on it joined the road cut from Tameighat.

At the same time as this work was in progress up the Lohit valley, exploration and survey under escorts from the Lakhimpur Battalion were being pushed up the Dibong and far into the Abor and Mishmi hills beyond points reached in the spring of 1912. These were under the control of Mr. Dundas, Political Officer at Sadiya, while Captains Trenchard and Oakes (Survey Department) conducted the various survey parties and Captain Sir G. S. Dunbar arranged the different escorts from his Battalion. In neither of these tours was there any active opposition by the tribes, the main difficulties concerning themselves with the high mountainous country and the excessive rainfall, the season proving an exceedingly wet one. During the whole of the open season of 1912–13,

THE LOHIT RIVER AT TAMEI GHAT.

DETACHMENT 2ND ASSAM RIFLES AT YAMBUNG POST—ABOR HILLS.

for instance, only eighteen days could be classed as good and clear for survey work. All were continually wet through, had the greatest trouble in keeping fires burning for cooking, and their only shelters were leaky waterproof sheets. Naturally there was much sickness, while in the higher ranges frost-bite had to be contended with. In spite of such adverse conditions an immense amount of country was surveyed and explored, and some 360 miles of fair bridle paths as far as the highest villages were made.

The experience of one of these survey parties may be mentioned as showing what patience, tact, and firmness are required in dealing with these wild folk. A party of 50 of the Lakhimpur Military Police and some surveyors under Captain Porter, when far into the Mishmi and Abor hills, reached a point where the tribesmen appeared ready to dispute any further advance. These had cut away the long swinging cane bridge just before our men arrived, in order to prevent a crossing being made. When Captain Porter's men began to build rafts the Abors started firing at them with bows and arrows from across the river and from the forest but doing no damage, and the sepoys took no notice of this hostility. At last, just before the rafts were ready, the Abors sent a man across inquiring why no notice was taken of their arrows and when were we going to fight? The interpreter was told to explain that fighting was not our intention, that we were quietly touring through their country surveying, and that early next morning we should cross to their village, whereupon the Abors withdrew. Next day the crossing was effected and the tribesmen came forward to make friends, confessing their foolishness in attempting hostility or to stop us, for which they now found themselves punished, in that all their "jhooms" (cultivation) lay on the far side of the river and our men had used all the canes and cut all trees suitable for anchoring the strands of a fresh bridge in order to make their rafts. Hence the people were confronted with the tedious and difficult task of making a fresh cane bridge elsewhere. This sort of bluff was often met with and, by being treated calmly as on this occasion, obviated loss of life, and showed a friendly spirit which was responded to when the wild people understood our reasons for being in their hills.

A change now took place in the headquarters of the Battalion, which in December 1913 was moved from Dibrugarh to Sadiya, the former place only having a detachment left in it. In the same month the new Darrang Military Police Battalion was raised at Dibrugarh, mainly by drafts from other Battalions, the Lakhimpur furnishing one of 10 N.C.O.'s and 90 men.

In January 1914, as the Padam Abors had not paid in their fines for assisting the Minyong clan against General Bower's advance it became necessary to send a Column to enforce payment, which Subadar Jangbir Lama and Jemadars Kali Prasad and Saji Ram with 120 men successfully collected. In March the same year Mr. Dundas with Captain Dunbar and 53 sepoys visited Elapoin village in the Mishmi hills to capture certain men concerned in a raid and murder. The outing, however, was not successful, for Elapoin was found deserted and its people had fled too far for pursuit.

The Great War now absorbed the attention of the Lakhimpur M.P. Battalion, which dispatched its first reinforcement to Goorkha Regiments in September 1914, consisting of 3 Indian officers, 4 N.C.O.'s and 200 men, all volunteers. The account of this period as it affected all Military Police Battalions is given separately in Chapter XVIII. The Kuki Rebellion which opened in December 1917 lasted 1½ years and caused all A.M.P. drafts to the Army to be discontinued, in order to supply a force to deal with this rising in the Manipur hills and to co-operate with the Burma Military Police in the suppression of the same. The account of this rising will be found in detail in Chapters XVI and XVII. In this latter period of active service the casualties sustained

SACRED POOL OF BRAHMA KHUND ON THE LOHIT RIVER A MILE ABOVE TAMEI GHAT.

-[From a sketch by L. W. S.

by this Battalion were 3 killed, 10 wounded, and 22 died of maladies due to exposure and strain of constant arduous marching. In the Appendix will be seen rewards gained by the Battalion both in the Great War and the Kuki operations.

Of other affairs during the period 1914–19 employing the services of the Battalion the following are mentioned in its records: In March this year (1917) the Battalion brought itself into line with Regular Regiments in common with the other units by reorganisation into 4 companies of 16 platoons, and in November the titles of all the Assam Military Police Battalions were changed to that of "Assam Rifles" by order of the Government of India, in recognition of the excellent services rendered by its men in various theatres of the Great War. In consequence of this the Lakhimpur Battalion from now on became officially known as the 2nd Battalion (Lakhimpur) Assam Rifles.

Serious rioting breaking out in the Behar and Orissa province, the Battalion was called on to send 2 British officers, 1 Indian officer, and 51 rifles to join a Contingent from other Military Police units, which proceeded to Patna and Arrah in early October 1917 under command of Major A. Vickers (3rd A.R.) to support the civil authorities in suppressing the state of disorder. But for the Great War this duty would have fallen to Regular units, the paucity of whom obliged assistance to be asked for from Assam, and the contingent returned after two months of arduous and unpleasant duties well carried out, which obtained for the Assam Rifles the thanks of the Behar and Orissa Government.

In April 1918 while the Kuki Rebellion was in progress and causing much anxiety, the Daphlas added to the general strain and stress by breaking out and raiding on to the Tezpur plains, capturing a number of people and destroying the village of Hellem. To put a stop to this a combined detachment of the A.R., to which the 2nd Battalion contributed Jemadar Jaman Sing Gurung and 50 rifles, was assembled at Tezpur under Captain Goodall with Captain Nevill, Political Officer of that Frontier, and entered the hills. Opposition was very slight, the villages concerned in the raid were burnt, the captives released, and the tribe paid up its fines.

In the winter of 1918–19 the question of linking the Burma railway system with that of Assam *via* the Hukong valley was again forced on the notice of Government owing to the exploits of the German cruiser "Emden" which seriously threatened the sea route to Rangoon. Survey parties under escorts of the 2nd and 3rd A.R. worked through the Patkoi range this and the succeeding winter, to discover a lower and more feasible pass than earlier surveys had found. This matter, however, was again shelved after the conclusion of the War.

The end of 1919 saw the practical completion of the new A.R. lines at Sadiya which had been commenced two years before. The cost of these was great, being of pucca brick and well built, but they were eminently needed for the benefit and health of all ranks, who up to date had been wretchedly housed in wattle, daub, and thatched huts, such as had been in vogue in early days in the province, and which were frequently blown flat by the hurricanes which often sweep down the Lohit valley. New and improved lines, but less expensive, were also built at Pasighat, Rohtang, and Yambung for the 200 rifles distributed in those posts in the Abor hills since 1914. Rearmament with the long M.L.E. 303 magazine rifle took place about August 1919, and at the same time riots in tea gardens near Dibrugarh claimed the services of small detachments from Sadiya to keep order.

In 1920 the Chulikatta Mishmis started trouble by raiding into the Sadiya area, which necessitated a punitive expedition of 125 rifles of the 2nd A.R. under Captain R. P. Abigail (lent from the 3rd A.R.) and Lieut. J. Murray Grant, with Mr. O'Callaghan as Political Officer, being dispatched against Elapoin (EL.4300 feet) and certain other villages (Sketch Map 3). They moved out from Nizamghat in October up the left bank of the Dibong river, the precipitous nature of the country making the progress of men and transport coolies most difficult. Before reaching Elapoin the Mishmis held a stockaded position well sited, which brought about a sharp little fight before it was taken. Here the clan lost a number of men, amongst them being "Pangoo," the leader of the trouble, who was shot dead. Elapoin was duly destroyed, and two posts were left for a few months in that part of the country till all fines were paid up. The following year it was deemed desirable to make a military promenade through these hills, which was conducted by Subadar Kan Sing Cachari and Jemadar Surbir Ale with 133 rifles, since when neither the Abor nor the Mishmi tribes have caused further trouble.

Owing to the activities of Bengal seditionists who fomented serious strikes on the Assam Bengal Railway and amongst tea gardens in other parts of the province during the hot weather and rains of 1921 and on into 1922 the Battalion, in common with its sister units, had to dispatch various detachments to suppress disorders and guard important points, also to take part in a military promenade under Major J. B. Gordon through the disaffected areas. These duties split up all A.R. Battalions considerably for the next year and a half, at the end of which time the 2nd Battalion was issued with the 303 M.L.E. short rifle, with which all units are at present armed.

The year 1924 saw the last bit of active service as far as this record is concerned, when in January the Assam province dispatched a Contingent consisting of detachments from all the A.R. Battalions to assist the Madras Government in suppressing a rising in the Rampa State Agency, details of which will be found in Chapter XVIII. The Sadiya detachment consisted of Captain Burke, Jemadars Bhailal, Surbir Ale, and Sibcharan with 103 rifles, who left Gauhati by steamer on the 13th January and returned to Sadiya at the end of June. In recognition of the excellent work rendered during this period by Jemadar Surbir Ale, 2nd A.R., this officer was rewarded by the presentation of the coveted King's Police Medal. In this year also Subadar Major Jangbir Lama's long and good service was recognised by the title of "Sirdar Bahadur" being bestowed on him.

The last item of interest in closing these chapters of the individual life of the old Lakhimpur M.P. Battalion is that of the affiliation of the Assam Rifles with groups of the Goorkha Regiments of the Indian Army and by which the 2nd A.R. became affiliated with the 5th Goorkha Group, *viz.* the 7th and 10th Goorka Rifles.

The actual orders on the subject will be found in the Appendix, as also a list of the Battalion's achievements at various Police and A.R. "Weeks," together with a list of Commandants from 1883 onward.

CHAPTER XI

1862 to 1881. The Naga Hills Frontier Police—Change in uniform—Survey work—Fight at Wokha, 1874—Butler killed, 1875—Wokha post established—New roads—Mozema expedition, 1877—Kohima sanctioned as headquarter station—Naga rising, 1879—Siege of Kohima and assault of Khonoma.

EARLIER chapters have shown the need for a special body of Frontier Police and the first embodiment of such, *viz.* the Cachar Levy and the Jorhat Militia, the amalgamation of both, the division of the Cachar Levy into two portions of which the major portion became the Nowgong Frontier Police, the lesser those of the North Cachar hills. These two units represented the only formed bodies of Frontier Police under the sole orders of the Civil Government until 1863, when other bodies were raised. With the formation of these, the Nowgong F.P. (the senior unit) found its duties more and more concerned entirely with its own border and the hill tribes beyond from 1863 onwards, to the extent that they became unofficially alluded to as the Naga Hills F.P., though under the Nowgong administration, this title eventually becoming official in 1872, when the unit severed its connection with that district. The whole of its men were now on the border with Samaguting as its headquarters, an increase to the strength was sanctioned, and it was under the command of Captain Butler, son of Major John Butler of earlier years, who was also Political Officer of this border, and was given the services of an Assistant Police Officer.

At this time we find the F.P. uniform changed to one of dark blue cloth with white piping round collars, cuffs, and down the seams of the trousers, white metal buttons, and stiff brown canvas gaiters, the equipment and weapons remaining the same except that in 1868 the more useful " kookerie " replaced the cumbersome sword. The author had personal knowledge of this from Subadar Belbong Ram Cachari, who enlisted in the early 'seventies and had carefully kept his old kit, which he showed him about 1898 when the former was Commandant of the Naga Hills F.P.

From about 1862 then we can follow the fortunes of this F.P. unit, now with a separate identity of its own. The next few years saw much escort work to survey and exploration parties in different parts of the Naga Hills, which, though interesting from the point of view of exploring new country and settling the sources and flow of many large rivers, were for some time productive of but little in the way of stirring work for the F.P. The work was mostly conducted by Major Godwin Austen with Captains Butler and Badgely, and only on three of these tours prior to 1872 is fighting recorded, which occurred at Themakodima and Tesephima in the Lhota Naga hills, and at Tetchumi, a village far to the east across the Tuzu river. To strengthen these escorts a party of the 43rd A.L.I. was attached to each, this Regiment for some time having a detachment at Samaguting.

Assam in 1874 was made into a separate province under a Chief Commissioner, and at the same time the Angami Naga country was definitely taken over for administration under Captain Butler, who, being much occupied with distant survey and boundary settlement work, applied for an officer to assist in matters at headquarters. Captain J. Johnstone (later Sir James, of Manipur fame) was thus sent to act for him at Samaguting, the growing importance of which had now necessitated two other English officials being sent there, *viz.* Dr. Coombes, in medical charge, and Mr. Needham, better known in later years as Political Officer at Sadiya. Johnstone, having visited Kohima several times, was

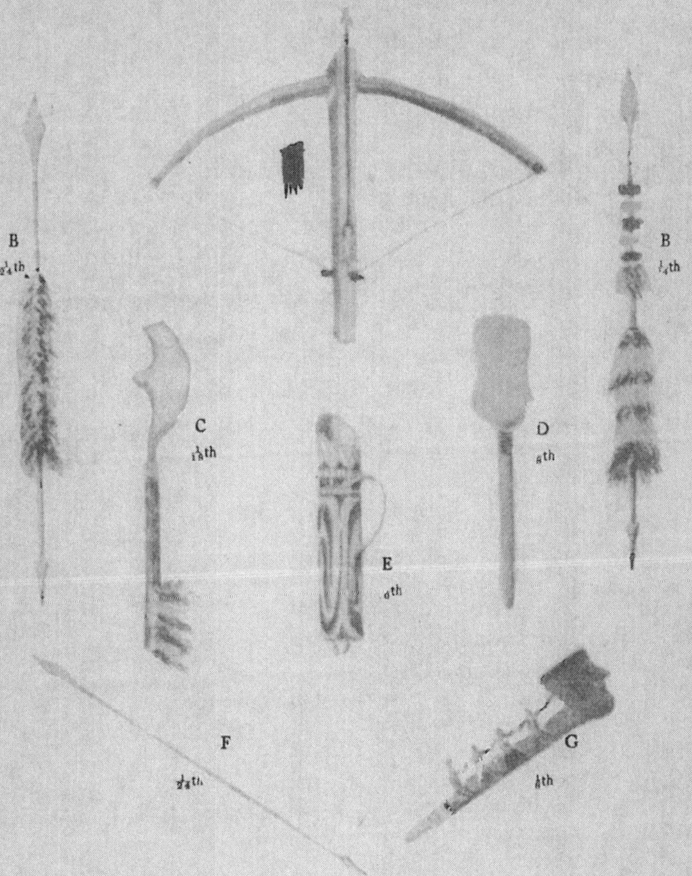

SOME TYPES OF TRIBAL WEAPONS

A. Cross bow used by Singphos Daphlas and Nagas on the Patkoi Range.

B. Spears used by the same with hair ornamentation. The circles denote owner's rank.

C. D. Different kinds of "daos" used by the Patkoi tribes. D is double edged.

E. A bamboo drinking cup adorned with real "poker work."

F. The plain shafted spear used for throwing.

G. Carved wooden pipe used on the Western Patkoi—the bowl represents a human head, and a row of monkeys stand along the stem.

From Sketches by L.W.S.

much in favour of abolishing Samaguting, which was none too healthy, and of occupying a site near the first-named village, a large and influential one of some 800 houses. This, he maintained, would form a more central position from which to control the Angamis. Government, however, did not see the necessity of carrying out this plan, which within three years was forced on it.

Captain Butler with Lieut. Woodthorpe and surveyors, 50 rifles of the 43rd A.L.I., and 80 of the F.P. left Samaguting on Christmas Day 1874 for the Lhota Naga hills, and on January 5th, when approaching the chief village Wokha experienced hostility, in some of his carriers who had straggled behind being cut up. That night they camped 2 miles from the village, almost on the site of the present Rest-house; shots suddenly rang out on all sides, and it was seen the camp was practically surrounded. A certain amount of confusion set in amongst the non-combatants, a number of whom were killed, but the attack was beaten off with considerable loss to the tribesmen. At dawn Butler, leaving a strong guard over the camp, attacked Wokha village with the remainder, the place was successfully rushed, 30 more Lhotas being killed, and the village was destroyed. This had an excellent effect, for no further hostility was shown during the tour, which was continued until events called for Butler's presence elsewhere, as narrated in Chapter IX, on the Lakhimpur F.P.

During the summer of 1875 Butler urged the establishment of a strong post with a Civil Officer at Wokha which would facilitate control of both the Lhota Nagas and the Sibsagor border, as well as the Angamis north-east of Kohima, but again this was objected to by Government until all surveys were completed.

This work was resumed in the cold weather by Butler and Woodthorpe, but was brought to a standstill in December 1875 by the death of the first-named officer. He, with a small portion of the escort, was approaching Pangti village (Lhota) across the Doyang river, and when close to the village entrance they were ambuscaded, Butler being mortally and one or two men slightly wounded by spears. Woodthorpe coming on behind with the rest of the escort at once attacked Pangti, killing several Lhotas and burning the place. Butler was carried down to Golaghat, where he died and was buried. This unfortunate affair lost us an officer who, like his father (Major John Butler), possessed first-rate qualities for dealing with wild tribes, and one who was not easy to replace.

Following on this episode came the sanction to establish a post at Wokha (Sketch Map 4), which was carried out by Messrs. Savi and Pugh (Civil Police) with Inspector Mema Ram, 150 F.P. constables, and 50 rifles 43rd B.I. before the year was out, Mr. Hinde being sent to join them a few months later. The first bridle path into the hills was at once taken in hand, the alignment running from Samaguting up the valley just south of the present Ghaspani Rest-house to Piphima village, where a small F.P. post was located, thence high above the present cart road to Keruphima, from which point it dipped down into and across the Rengmapani valley up to the saddle below Merema village, and from here on it is the same as in use nowadays. The first portion as far as Merema saddle was abandoned when the Manipur cart road was made in 1891. Mr. Broderick, who succeeded Savi and Pugh early in 1876, evidently took a lot of trouble during his sojourn at Wokha in laying out the little station, as shown by the remains of good paths cut round and about the place but now jungle-covered, and the old bathing lake a little beyond the present hospital. This he made by damming a ravine which filled out into a pleasant sheet of water. Even when the writer was in the Naga hills in 1897 it was still a pretty piece of water fringed by large trees, but it is now all silted up and covered with weeds, as no European has lived there since the Ao Naga country was taken over for administration in 1889. Broderick also made the road connecting Wokha with Golaghat *via* the Bagti valley (a great locality for shikar) and for some years had a post at Bandari to patrol it.

The following year the Nagas of Mozema broke the peace by a sudden raid on the small F.P. post at Gumaigajoo village in the north Cachar hills, killing a number of people and carrying off some guns and other loot. The offending village refusing all reparation, a punitive expedition proceeded into the hills commanded by Captain Brydon with Mr. Carnegy as Political Officer, and was composed of 200 rifles of the 42nd B.L.I. with 60 F.P. constables. On the 6th December, 1877, when the Column neared Mozema, a heavy fire was opened on them and the place was attacked and destroyed with a few casualties. The Nagas driven out dispersed, harrying the troops with night attacks, and interrupting communications with Samaguting and the plains to such an extent that a reinforcement of 100 rifles 43rd B.I. with 50 constables of the Garo Hills F.P. became necessary, these being brought up by Lieut. Macgregor (later G.O.C. Assam Brigade), with whom also came Captain Williamson, I.G.P. Desultory fighting continued for a month in which Mr. Carnegy was accidentally shot dead by one of our sentries. Mozema at last having experienced considerable loss submitted to the amazingly lenient terms given by the I.G.P., who had taken Carnegy's place, *viz.* a paltry fine of 50 rupees and the restoration of guns and loot. On this the force returned to the plains, but the detachment from the Garo Hills F.P. was transferred to the Naga Hills F.P., which was being increased in strength. About the same time there came a change in the arm of the F.P., the old muzzle-loading musket with its sword bayonet being replaced by the Enfield rifle with triangular bayonet.

Owing to Captain Johnstone's strong recommendations while he was at Samaguting to move the administrative centre from there up to Kohima, the Chief Commissioner paid a visit to the hills and the latter place in the winter of 1877, some months after which the move was definitely sanctioned. Mr. Damant, now Political Officer, moved his establishment up to Kohima in the autumn of 1878. The position selected for the new station lay on the undulating saddle and its spurs connecting Kohima hill, on which the village stands, with the slopes of "Poli Badze," an outlying portion of the great Barail range. This name means "Polly's seat" in the Naga language, and it was said to have been given by Nagas who accompanied her to commemorate the ascent of the hill by the first Englishwoman, *viz.* Mrs. Badgely (Polly), wife of Captain Badgely, on survey duty in the Naga hills in 1874. The elevation here is 4500 feet, and the site was not ideal from the point of view of modern weapons, but it was the best that could be found at the time. Rough wattle and daub houses and two stockades adjacent to each other for the garrison of a detachment 43rd B.I. and 150 F.P. were built on the site of the present-day fort, work on the new road up from Dimapur was put in hand, and for some months the tribal attitude appeared friendly. About this time it was intended to commence the reorganisation of the Frontier Police forces on the lines indicated in Chapter IV, but circumstances arose obliging a postponement of the plan until quieter times permitted it to be carried out.

It has already been shown how Bengalis as well as the Burmese traded old muskets to the hill tribes till most villages had acquired considerable numbers, and in April 1879 it came to our knowledge that the Khonoma clan were obtaining many more from the Cachar side which were being passed secretly through the hills. Thereafter followed a few isolated murders, and the attitude of the tribe generally became openly defiant, to the extent of refusing to supply carriers for the transport of supplies up or for work on the road, etc. An abortive attempt was also made to attack the post at Piphima, but these signs did not seem to impress themselves

Khonoma Village looking North.

Entrance to Henema Post- [illegible]rthwork.

seriously on Mr. Damant. However, as he was intending to make a tour through the Trans-Doyang country in the early winter, he decided to visit Jotsoma, Khonoma, and Mozema before going there, so as to see for himself what the disposition of the people really was.

On the 13th October, 1879, Mr. Damant set out with an escort of 65 constables of the F.P. and 21 rifles of the 43rd B.I., halting the first night at Jotsoma, and here he was warned by certain friendly villagers not to go on, as the Khonoma men meant mischief. Disbelieving in any danger, he continued his way down into the valley, and on arriving at the foot of the hill on which the large and well-defended village of Khonoma stands, he left his baggage with half the escort by the little bridge over a stream, and with the remainder climbed leisurely up the hill. Most of the way up the path a wall ran along the village side of it, at the end of which was the gateway. Arrived at this point and finding the heavy door closed, Damant called for it to be opened, and while standing there with his men rather clubbed together in the narrow pathway, the wall was suddenly lined with Nagas, who opened fire into the party, killing Damant and most of those with him. The tribesmen then swarming down the hill-side fell upon the baggage guard, cutting up many and dispersing the rest. Of the F.P., Jemadar Prem Sing with 25 constables were killed and 14 escaped with wounds, of the 43rd B.I. 10 were killed and 5 wounded, 3 servants also being killed.

The fugitives got back to Kohima that evening with the news, where at once preparations were made for resisting attack, which was not long delayed; in fact next day the Khonoma men, aided by some from Jotsoma, one "khel" (the Chutonuma) of Kohima, and several other villages, collected and began to besiege the roughly-stockaded post, into which all non-combatants had been drawn. The garrison here, excluding those with Damant, was down to 90 odd men of the F.P. under Subadar Mema Ram and Jemadar Kurun Sing, of whom 32 were recruits, and 80 rifles 43rd B.I. under Captain Reid, who was ill at the time; the only other Englishman was Mr. Cawley of the Civil Police, while Mrs. Damant and Mrs. Cawley with her two children as well as some 240 non-combatants swelled the numbers crowded into the stockades and added to the anxiety of the defenders. According to some accounts the enemy surrounding the place numbered quite 6000, but in all probability this was an excessive estimate.

At this time the post consisted of two large incomplete stockades, there were no doors to the entrances, no earthworks, and only a weak palisade. Damant had apparently been unduly confident as to the pacific attitude of the tribe, and there appears to have been friction between the civil and the military elements. He also had refused to allow surrounding jungle to be cleared, regarding the place as a civil station, whereas it actually was an advanced military post. Its generally unprepared condition excited much comment later, and was the occasion for a Court of Inquiry. Food supply was also very limited, the water supply coming down in an open channel from a distance was liable to be cut off, and the ladies and children had to be housed in the large oven shed, which formed the only shot-proof building.

Cawley at once dispatched messages by trusted friendly Nagas for help from Wokha, Manipur, and the plains, being at once responded to in the two former cases. Mr. Hinde, in charge of Wokha at the time, taking 40 rifles of the 43rd B.I. and 22 F.P. constables—all he could spare—covered the 50 odd miles rapidly. Marching at night and avoiding villages, he managed to reach Kohima without losing a man on the 19th October. Major Johnstone at Imphal, on receipt of Cawley's urgent message, collected his escort of the 34th N.I., a party of 50 of the Surma Valley F.P. on temporary duty there at the time, and 2000 Manipuri troops, which the Raja immediately offered, and set off for the scene 80 odd miles off over bad hill-paths. He also obtained the Raja's permission to send 200 more of his men up the Typhini (Zupvu) valley to Paplongmai, whence they might be able to cut off the retreat of the Khonoma men to the south and west.

On the 21st October the tribesmen attacked the Kohima post in strength and a sortie was made under two Native officers, but was driven back with several casualties. Each day the enemy crawling up fired arrows with burning tow into the stockades, which were close together, and succeeded in firing the lower one, which was destroyed. Between the hill crowned by the village and the stockade was a stretch of fairly open ground (now the 3rd A.R. parade ground and the lines), covered here and there with light scrub jungle which screened the enemy to a certain extent, enabling them to approach close to a point where, at night, they built a small stockade from which they could fire into the now crowded interior of Cawley's stockade. They also laboriously rolled large tree trunks along the more open patches of this stretch of ground, behind which they lay and fired. This went on for some ten days, Cawley's and Hinde's straits being rendered more desperate by the enemy diverting the main water supply, following this up by throwing a human head into the only other supply down the hill-side, which poisoned the water. In fact Cawley was about to negotiate for a surrender of the place if allowed a safe passage for all to Samaguting, which would have been fatal, for none would have escaped. Fortunately, a friendly Naga got in one night with the news that Johnstone was on his way up from Manipur with a force, which heartened all to hold out; and on the morning of the 27th October his bugles were heard in the distance and by noon the relieving force appeared, on which the enemy drew off.

Major Johnstone, now in command, sent off messages on the situation to Government, together with his proposals to attack Khonoma as soon as possible, and began clearing all jungle round the position and rebuilding and strengthening the stockades, the friendly "khels" of Kohima coming down to help. He also sent to Khonoma demanding Damant's head, which was brought back—his body had been destroyed—and buried in what is now the garden of the Deputy-Commissioner's house, with due ceremonial, where an inscribed stone marks the spot.

Communications with the plains and with Manipur were still difficult. In the former direction the bridle path which took off below Keruphima village and wound up the bottom of the valley below the present cart road ending in a steep ascent to Kohima was incomplete. Connection with Manipur was by a very rough path running below the cart road up and down deep valleys, through Mao Thana down to Meitheipham in the Barak valley 3 miles east of the Maram Rest house, rising again to a saddle near the old site of Kongnem village, whence it dipped to Kairong. From this point onward it was fairly easy going to Imphal.

The presence of Major Johnstone was a great factor towards improving the situation, for many of his old Naga friends came in, while Mozema, which had so far been neutral, now sent offers of assistance. As soon as possible arrangements were made to attack Khonoma, but before this could be done orders reached Johnstone directing him to await the arrival of General Nation's force, which was being dispatched to the scene of the trouble. This delay gave the Khonoma men time still further to perfect their defences, but Johnstone, knowing complete inaction to be the worst line to take with savages, and as his supply convoys coming up from Manipur were frequently attacked, proceeded to punish and destroy the hostile "khel" (the Chutonuma) of Kohima, who gave up a number of rifles captured and paid in a fine of 200 maunds of rice. Hearing that Phesama village had attacked one of his convoys, he dispatched a strong detachment of Manipuri and Kuki troops, who surprised and destroyed Phesama, killing over 200 Nagas.

On the 30th October Major Evans with 200 rifles of the 43rd B.I. arrived in the hills and strengthened the posts at Samaguting and Piphima on the way, not without a fight at the latter place and again at Sephama, a little to the north of Piphima, where Lieut. Maxwell (later Political Agent in Manipur) and 2 men were wounded, 2 being killed. Evans' arrival at Sachema was also opposed with three more casualties amongst his men. By 20th November General Nation's force of 1000 rifles made up of a Wing each from the 43rd B.I. and 44th B.L.I., 100 of the Naga Hills F.P., a detachment of the Surma Valley F.P., with 2 mountain guns and a rocket battery under Lieut. Mansel, R.A., were assembled at Sachema above the lower end of the Khonoma valley to the east of Mozema, and where the advanced Base was formed. Two days later the forward move against Khonoma was made. The men of Mozema, who this time held aloof from the struggle, warned Johnstone that the enemy intended particularly to fire at the English officers, and suggested they should cover their helmets to render them less conspicuous. This, however, was not done.

Khonoma, as described in Vincent's attack (1850), stands on a high conical hill jutting out into the valley and joined to the main range by a low saddle. To the south and overlooking it rise the great masses of "Japvo" and "Kahoo," both densely forested, the former being nearly 10,000 feet above sea level. Some 2000 feet higher up into these hills the enemy had built further defences called the "Chakka" forts, while still higher up they had sheltered their women and children in almost inaccessible caves. The village was, as formerly, defended very strongly and similarly to when it had resisted Vincent and Foquette, *viz.* with "panjied" ditches and "sangars" up the front spur, which was the best to approach by, while the upper portion was surrounded by ditches and tiers of loopholed walls with thorn entanglement in front of them (Sketch Map 5).

The whole formed a series of terraces, their scarps revetted with stone topped by walls or palisading, well loopholed and bullet proof. Each terrace formed a sort of separate fortification with which the whole hill was covered, each more or less commanding those lower on the slopes. Large piles of rocks were also collected at different likely spots to be rolled down on the attackers.

At 6 a.m. on the 22nd November the force advanced down into and across the valley covered by skirmishers from the 43rd B.I. and the Frontier Police under Captain Williamson, I.G.P., who knew the country. Two companies with 30 of the F.P. under Major Evans made a detour, eventually getting in rear of the village and occupying the saddle to cut off the enemy's retreat. The guns carried by Johnstone's Kukis at first took position on an opposite spur, but the distance being too great they were moved lower down. Two hundred of the Manipuri troops were also sent to a point where retreat to Jotsoma village could be prevented. Meanwhile Lieut. (later General) Ridgeway with Lieut. Henderson and the leading companies of the 44th B.L.I. had reached the foot of the northern spur and commenced the upward attack, a brisk fire being exchanged. The guns and rockets, moved still closer, began pounding the various "sangars" defending the way up. The troops fought their way slowly up over the steep ground covered with thorn and bamboo stakes, losing many men, till about 3 p.m., when all the lower defences were taken and a point had been reached a little below the main and most strongly fortified position crowning the top of the hill. The guns were now brought to within 100 yards of the walls and every effort was made to breach them, but the steepness of the ground on which the guns were in action, together with the heavy charges fired, caused them to upset and roll down at each discharge.

Two columns were now ordered to assault the upper defences, crowded with Naga warriors showering down spears and rocks and firing into the troops now close up. The assaults were led on the front face by the General himself with Major Cock, Captain Walker, Major Johnstone, and Lieut. Raban, while that on the right was led by Lieuts. Ridgeway and Forbes. Both assaults failed. Ridgeway reached a gateway and tried to force it with his men, the door was slowly yielding, when a Naga firing through a chink in it shattered Ridgeway's shoulder, who, however, gallantly managed to hold the door sufficiently open for single men to get through. Forbes with him was mortally wounded, and those who did get inside were overwhelmed and driven out or killed. For gallantry during this action Ridgeway was later rewarded with the Victoria Cross. The assault on the front face had to be made up an almost perpendicular hill-side under showers of spears, bullets, and rocks. Major Cock and Subadar Major Narbir Sahi were killed here, Captain Nuthall was badly wounded, numbers of men fell, and the assaulting parties had to retire. It being too late now in the gathering evening to attempt more, the force bivouacked lower down the spur, where they put up rough defences, and arrangements were made to assault again at dawn. The night was bitterly cold and it was impossible then to get the wounded back to the Base; in fact medical matters, none of the best, entirely broke down, and several wounded men died of gangrene through having to lie about on the insanitary village ground. Stretchers were also too few to carry all away, Ridgeway with his shattered shoulder having to walk back and climb the steep ascent to Sachema. At dawn it was found that the upper defences had been vacated by the enemy, who had retreated to their stronghold up in the hills, the misconception of an order early in the night having led to the withdrawal of the detachment on the saddle in the rear of the village, which opened the way for the enemy to escape by. So fell Khonoma, the chief centre of all trouble in these hills, at a cost to General Nation's force of 4 out of the 9 British officers and 25 per cent. killed or wounded of the troops actually employed that day. The actual casualty list of the Naga Hills F.P. detachment in the assault was 10 killed and wounded. It may be said here that but for the Afghan war absorbing all attention, public interest would have been drawn to these operations, which were eclipsed by the greater and more stirring doings on the N.W. Frontier, were hardly heard of, and were soon forgotten. Lieut. Forbes succumbed to his wound at Sachema, where a cairn of stones in a field close to and south of the village marks his grave. Major Cock and Subadar Major Narbir Sahi were buried where they fell, two stones, with their names roughly cut in, stand near an old tree just in front of the entrance to the present-day fort, held for some years by a detachment of Regulars, after which the Military Police took over the fort. In later years, about 1906 or 1907, a memorial to those who fell in this assault was set up on the highest point of the village by Sir William Reid, K.C.I.E., then Deputy-Commissioner at Kohima.

The whole attack of this Naga stronghold was a replica of that by Major Foquette and Captain Vincent thirty years earlier, except for the effort to cut off the line of retreat, which came to nothing. The Nagas also had many more guns at this time than in the past, which caused the troops heavier losses. For a few days after the assault detachments moved about the valley, one under Lieut. Macgregor meeting and dispersing a body of the enemy with considerable loss to them.

It was to be regretted that no attempt against the "Chakka" forts high up in the hills was made, which was certainly feasible though difficult; but General Nation was unwilling to risk further losses and now tried the effect of blockading the enemy. He did, however send Colonel Robertson, who had arrived with a reinforcement, on a tour to visit and punish certain eastern Angami villages who had sent men to help Khonoma, when the villages of Cheswejuma, Chadoma,

View in the Barail Range above Khonoma close to the Chakka Forts, El. 7600'.

The Zulhein Valley near Paplongmai, El. 7000'.

Kekrima, and Vishwema were burnt with only slight opposition. The troops now cleared up Khonoma, repaired the upper defences, and occupied the place during the winter. With the exception of sentries and water picquets being sniped at, often successfully, and some skirmishes, particularly a sharp one when the enemy attacked a convoy escort *en route* to the post at Paplongmai, nothing calling for special notice occurred for a time, though it is recorded that the Nagas caused the troops and the F.P. over 50 casualties in these desultory offensive acts.

In the end of January 1880 came news of a savage raid by a band of Khonoma men on the Baladhan tea garden in north Cachar, which, it transpired, had set out from their "Chakka" position, had evaded our blockading posts, and crossing the Barail range in its most difficult part had gone down the Barak valley to the Cachar borders 88 miles away. The raid was a rapid and daring one, the Baladhan garden was surprised at night, Mr. Blythe, the manager, with a large number of coolies was killed, the houses all plundered and burnt down, and the band returned with their loot as rapidly as they had moved out. It was not till they were back in their fastness that the troops in Khonoma heard of the occurrence. Naturally this created a panic amongst all the tea gardens in that part of Cachar, causing all those frontier posts to be strengthened.[1]

Reinforcements under Captain Abbott having reached Kohima, the blockading cordon was drawn tighter during February. Some skirmishes took place in the neighbourhood of Paplongmai culminating in a serious attack in the Zulhein valley 8 miles from Khonoma on a ration convoy and escort moving to the first-named post under command of Lieut. Barrett, 43rd B.I. The carriers, seized with panic, began to bolt, many being cut up;

[1] The Nichuguard stockade was also attacked, when 2 sepoys were killed and 6 wounded at the end of March, marking the Angami Nagas' last offensive action.

5 sepoys were killed and several wounded, obliging the escort to retire, having lost 20 loads of stores.

It was now decided to take vigorous action to end this unsatisfactory state of affairs by attacking the "Chakka" forts, and arrangements to this end were being made when, on the 27th March, the Khonoma clan sent down a deputation offering final and definite submission. At first, in further punishment added to their heavy losses in action, the whole of their fine terraced fields were confiscated, the community was dispersed among other villages, and punitive labour was enforced on them for new roads and the rebuilding of Kohima station and stone fort as it stands at present. The site and style for these were approved by the Chief Commissioner and General Sir C. Macgregor, Q.M.G. in India, who visited the place during the winter. As quietude settled down in the Angami Naga country after a few years, the people were allowed to return on to their old village site, and it was not long before Khonoma was once again a most prosperous place of some 700 houses, set in the midst of miles of the finest terraced cultivation to be seen in the hills, a veritable *vallèe d'or* in the autumn with the gold of the ripening crops. The upper portion of the village for some years held a detachment of 100 rifles furnished by the regiment at Kohima; in 1896 this duty was taken over by the Naga Hills Military Police, the strength being reduced to 50 rifles, dropping some years later to 25, and in 1923 the detachment was finally withdrawn. Many have doubted the wisdom of removing all show of force from Khonoma, whose people have the greatest name for turbulence in the hills, and who at once began intriguing against us when the rebellion of 1891 broke out in Manipur. It was believed, probably with some truth, that only the knowledge of the unexpected arrival of a Sikh regiment at Golaghat kept them from joining in the trouble of that year. Kohima was garrisoned from 1880 on by a Regular regiment and 4 companies of the Naga Hills

TERRACED CULTIVATION IN THE ANGAMI COUNTRY.

M.P., until in 1904 the former was removed, a Double Company from the regiment in Manipur being substituted, and in 1915 this detachment of Regulars vanished, leaving the watch and ward of these hills and borderlands entirely to the Naga Hills Battalion.

Following the close of these operations, Mr. Savi (Police) was ordered to make a tour through the Kaccha Naga and Kuki country south-west of the Barail range to ascertain the temper of the tribes. With an escort of 60 F.P. and a party of the 34th N.I., he visited most of the villages as far as Semkor (Sketch Map 4), and on his recommendation a post of 50 rifles was established at Henema early in 1881. Later reduced to 25 rifles of the N.H.M.P., it was finally abolished about 1916.

CHAPTER XII

1881 to 1889. The Naga Hills M.P., *continued*—Reorganisation—Change of uniform—Pipers and band—Rifle range—Escorts to tours—Political control areas—Trans-Dikkoo expedition, 1887—Mongsemdi massacre and expedition, 1888-89—Ao Naga country taken over.

WITH the settlement of these hills after the disturbances just narrated, the reorganisation scheme took place, all Frontier Police units becoming Military Police Battalions in the spring of 1882 and arranged territorially. Captain Plowden, 5th B.C., sent to form the new Naga Hills M.P. Battalion, started work as its first Commandant on a five years' tenure, with Sergeant Lyons to assist him with recruits and the Quartermaster's establishment. The old uniform now gave way to one of a rough sort of khaki drill which, as the fast-dyed material did not come into use till about 1888, had to have its colour renewed by being dipped in liquid abomination periodically by the Battalion "rangrez" or dyer, and which, when fresh, smelt to high Heaven. The Mackenzie equipment brown leather was issued, and bandoliers were for some years in use, but were discarded as being awkward wear for jungle work, and Snider rifles had in 1881 replaced the old Enfield. Plowden's first works concerned the housing of his men on the ground still occupied by their barracks in spite of their having been condemned frequently since 1898, the arrangement of a rifle range in the valley below and south of the present Dak bungalow, the establishment of a new post for 50 rifles under Mr. Walker (Police) at Lozema to control the western Sema Nagas, who were showing signs of likely trouble, which, later reduced to 25 rifles, was abolished in 1900, and various other affairs connected with the placing of the new unit well on its feet. He also started Pipers for the Battalion in 1884, the men being sent for instruction in the Pipes to the 78th Highlanders in Lucknow. About 1896, at the desire of the Battalion, the Pipes gave way to a Band, worked up by the help of the Bandmasters of the regiments which garrisoned Kohima, and this is still kept up but with a Bandmaster of its own. Samaguting, which since the occupation of Kohima had fallen to the status of a small post, was abolished in 1883, and a new post substituted in its place at Nichuguard at the foot of the hill, to control this end of the Golaghat cart road. At this time the posts held by the Naga Hills M.P. were as shown below:

Borpathar, 25 rifles in a masonry block house, abolished in 1887.

Dimapur, 25 rifles in a stockade, abolished in 1887.

Piphima, 25 rifles in a rough stone fort, abolished in 1887.

Nichuguard, 25 rifles in a stockade, abolished in 1896.

Wokha, 100 rifles in an earthwork fort, abolished in 1901.

Themakodima, 25 rifles in a stockade, abolished in 1895.

Lozema, 50 rifles in an earthwork fort, abolished in 1900.

Henema, 50 rifles in an earthwork fort, abolished about 1915.

The remainder of the Battalion was at Kohima, the total strength at first being 568 of all ranks which was raised to 700 a few years later. Two curious old wall pieces—long, heavy, muzzle-loading guns mounted on swivelled tripods—stand in front of the N.H.M.P. Orderly Room. These were got for the defence of Samaguting by Captain John Butler, junior, and were mounted later on the stockade at Nichuguard, being brought up to headquarters on that post being given up. The Nichuguard stockade overlooked the Nambhor forest stretching between the Mikir and the Naga Hills, the surprising deniseness of which has been alluded to in an earlier chapter, and an example of which may be given here in an incident which occurred not long before the post there was given up. The stockade stood on the end of a spur a little above the present Thana at no great height above the sea of foliage, and one afternoon a Havildar and 3 sepoys went out for a few hours shikar in the forest. Evening came on with no return of the party, and then those in the stockade heard shots followed by others. None, however, knew the direction the party had taken, and it was difficult to divine the situation of the shots muffled in the forest. Guns were fired periodically from the stockade to give the shikaris the right direction, and at dawn men went out searching, but with no result. The party did not return and a report was sent up to Kohima of their absence and of what it was believed had happened. The four had completely vanished and all were good men well versed in woodcraft. Nearly twelve days later at Dimapur, 9 miles from the stockade, a goatherd taking his animals to graze early one morning saw something being waved to him from the edge of the forest. On going up to see, he found a man in almost the last stage of exhaustion, hardly any clothes left on him, covered with leeches which had bled him almost white and reduced him to a skeleton. A native doctor was fetched and the unfortunate man was taken to the little dispensary and cleaned and tended. It was the Havildar, and how he lived through those days and nights was a marvel. His story, as he regained strength, was that they lost their bearings in the thick forest while following up a deer, and with hardly any sky to be seen through the canopy of green above there was nothing to guide them. They kept together for some days, their cartridges being soon expended in trying vainly to attract help. After three or four days, what with fatigue and trying different directions, no water or food except berries, leeches driving them mad, they

An Ao Naga Woman.

lost touch of each other and must have died under dreadful conditions. Of the Havildar's wanderings after the first four days or so and he was alone, he remembered nothing but that maddening green wall thick all round him, until he reached the open where he was found. He was in hospital a long time, but had to be invalided out of the service, and lived at Dimapur, where the author saw him frequently in 1898.

During the ten years following this reorganisation a large number of small punitive or exploring tours took place connected with the settlement of the country, minor raids, boundary matters, etc., many of which being devoid of any special interest, only the more important tours or expeditions need be mentioned. The boundaries of the Naga Hills District at this time were the Doyang river to north and north-east, the Kopamedza range to east, Mao Thana and the Barak river from below Bakema village to the south and south-west, and most trouble came from the tribes beyond these limits.

In July 1884, owing to the Ao Nagas of Manmatung having cut up and looted a party of Lhota traders within our border, a punitive outing of 50 Naga Hills M.P. and 40 of the 44th B.L.I. under Lieut. Tiernan took place. With them went Mr. McCabe, the Deputy-Commissioner. Manmatung was burnt without opposition though strongly defended, and the murderers were given up. Lieut. Tiernan and a few sepoys were injured by "panjis" while passing through the defences. The following January Mr. McCabe with an escort of the N.H.M.P. and Captain Plowden made a tour through the country lying between the Kopamedza range, the Lanier, and the Tizu rivers (Sketch Map 4), it having been under discussion to bring the eastern Angamis occupying that area under direct political control of the Naga Hills District. No revenue was to be taken from them as in the case of the other clans in the settled area. Their route lay *via* Mao Thana to Keza Kenoma, the chief village of the Kezami clan, thence across the Kopamedza range (7400 feet), our official boundary, to Razami, Tetcholumi, Lozephehomi, where friendly deputations from villages lying in independent territory beyond the Lanier and Tizu rivers were received. The party returned through Khromi and Purbami, and McCabe records the pleasantness of the tour, throughout which they were well received.

In the winter of 1884–85 it was found necessary to make a show of force in the Ao country to punish the Sema village of Nungtang for the murder of a British subject, to bring home to the Trans-Doyang people the fact that they were politically subordinate to our Government, and to determine the limits of the Naga Hills Control towards Sibsagor, the Deputy-Commissioner of which, Colonel Clarke, was to meet the party. Accordingly Mr. McCabe and Dr. Bora, C.S., escorted by Captain Plowden and 100 rifles from Kohima and Mr. Broderick from Wokha, crossed the Doyang river on the 15th January, 1885, reaching Nungtang next day. Some resistance was experienced, there was some firing, a few Semas were shot, and the place was destroyed. The Column then visited Nankam (Ao), Lopphemi (Sema), Ungma, and Longsa (Ao), the latter village together with Salachu having to be fined for various misdemeanours. At Bor Haimong, on one of the outer ranges, Colonel Clarke was met and the limits of the two spheres of influence and political control were discussed, as also was the desirability of locating a strong post in these hills to check raids and inter-village fighting. The tour was concluded in the end of February, and a year later the Government of India sanctioned the suggested limits of the Ao Naga Political Control area to include all the country west of the Dikkoo river to the Sibsagor border on the plains, this area coming under the jurisdiction of the Deputy-Commissioner at Kohmia.

A note by Captain W. M. Kennedy, later Deputy-Commissioner Naga Hills (years afterwards well known as the head of the Assam Labour Commission and who

AO NÁGA HOUSES.

[From a sketch by L. W. S.

THE GREAT MORANG OR GUARD HOUSE IN MASUNGJAMI.

was murdered in a train in September 1923), explains the condition and meaning of the term "Political Control Area." He writes:—

"The area of Political Control, and the policy to be adopted in the administration thereof, were decided by the Government of India in February 1886. The Political Control area at that time included the Ao Naga sub-division, which was not added to the Naga Hills District till 1890. The said area was constituted in order to stop raids and crimes of violence along the borders of the Naga Hills and Sibsagor districts, which, of course, had an unsettling effect on those tribes directly under our rule, as well as to interpose a barrier between our settled districts and the wild tribes beyond. Officers are not supposed to interfere much in the internal affairs of villages in a politically controlled area. It is only obligatory to punish murder cases, but officers may settle inter-village disputes if they can. Such villages pay no revenue, and are not even guaranteed protection against raids by independent tribes from beyond the boundary of our control. It is laid down that 'protection must depend on proximity and convenience.'"

Early in February 1886 it seemed as if trouble was likely to come from Khonoma again, and in this way. Hearing that three of their men trading just over the border in Manipur territory had been cut up at Shipvomi, Khonoma retaliated by sending a large body of warriors, who secretly crossed the Barail range by unusual passes. Collecting on their way more men from Kigwema and Vishwema, they descended upon Shipvomi, sacking and burning the village and killing numbers of people. Directly news of this raid was received in Kohima, Mr. Davis (then acting Deputy-Commissioner) with Captain Plowden and a strong force of the N.H.M.P. moved out rapidly and secured all the eastern exits of the passes through the Barail range, just in time to intercept the raiders returning laden with loot and heads, and arrested prominent leaders. Sixteen men of Khonoma were captured and sentenced to various long terms of imprisonment. The fact that several villages had assisted in this big raid gave it a serious aspect, but happily nothing further took place. Later Davis with an escort visited Shipvomi and from inquiries made it transpired that men of Tetcholumi in our control area had assisted Shipvomi in murdering the Khonoma traders. He then proceeded to Tetcholumi, which was found in a strong state of defence, with women and children sent away, showing they expected punishment. However, no resistance was met with, the place was burnt, and a punitive post of 30 rifles was quartered there for a year to ensure good behaviour. Other villages which had a hand in this affair were heavily fined.

The rifle range close to Kohima being only available up to 300 yards had been given up in 1885 and Plowden was given more extensive ground at Tesima, 7 miles out, where a good range was laid out up to 800 yards on an open broad ridge facing towards Nerhama village. A barrack was built here and a house for the officer, as detachments going through musketry had to stay out there several days.

Captain Plowden was succeeded in 1887 by Lieut. D. Macintyre, 2nd Goorkhas, during whose tenure of command the drab uniform was brightened by narrow scarlet piping round collars, cuffs, and down the trouser seams, and brown putties replaced the old black ones. About this time the custom came in of allowing definite transport to detachments moving about the hills, *viz.* coolies, at the rate of 1 coolie to every 3 men, and a certain number of pack ponies were allowed Battalion headquarters for the purpose of rationing posts. Previous to this and except when serving in expeditions alongside of Regular troops and sharing in their transport sometimes, the old Frontier Police fared badly, having to carry all their food and necessaries themselves when on trek. This, of course, made them most mobile and ready to move out at a moment's notice; they never bothered about coolies and were independent of the transport worries we of the present day know so well. As one old-time officer records in 1860: "It was the usual thing to see a N.C.O. with 10 or 20 constables move out on patrol, or larger bodies on escort duties, for ten days and longer without a single coolie. Each man fully equipped, carried his food in a 'chudder' (sheet), the two ends being tied either across the chest or supported from the forehead, the weight being on the back, while his 'ghi' chunga dangled from some convenient portion of his accoutrements. A most unsoldierly-looking lot imaginable, but hard as nails, very serviceable, very loyal and uncomplaining. They get free rations while on tour, which no doubt helps towards making them put up with the hardships of their job with smiling faces." This applies, not only to the Naga Hills, but also to all Frontier Police units of days prior to 1883.

In March 1887 the independent Sema Nagas of the Tizu valley began raiding certain Angami villages lying near the border, which occasioned a punitive outing with 80 rifles N.H.M.P. and 40 of the 42nd B.I. under Lieuts. Macintyre and Robins, Mr. Porteous, now Deputy-Commissioner, accompanying them. Sakai, the principal village for punishment, was reached on 1st April, and the fines levied on this and on Lhoshiapu's village near by were paid up without trouble.

The tour was then continued through the north of the Sema Political Control area (this region having been recently so constituted), where trouble occurred at Lukobomi and Sopphomi when the former village attacked the rear guard. A few volleys drove the assailants off and the place was burnt. Sopphomi was most aggressive, and a night was passed near there in readiness to repel a threatened attack. Next day the people came down and paid in their fine without further trouble. Kohima was returned to *via* Wokha by the end of April. During the rains this year another punitive tour had to be made against Ao and Sema villages just across the Doyang valley, and in view of much trouble with these, Mr. Porteous now strongly urged a post being placed at Nankam, which, however, was not sanctioned and the trouble continued.

Two years later it was necessary to make an extended tour through the north-east of the Ao country to visit and punish certain villages for raiding. Taking Lieut. Macintyre and 100 of his men, Mr. McCabe (now Deputy-Commissioner) accompanied by Mr. Muspratt from Wokha left on 13th March, 1888, reaching Waromong village ten days later, where investigation into murder and raiding cases was begun. Tamlu and Kanching were then visited and fined, and Kongan (Sketch Map 4), across the lower Dikkoo river, was proceeded against. On this march the baggage guard was attacked, 1 sepoy and several carriers being wounded. Camp was formed in Kongan village and, during the night, the tribesmen crept up and managed to fire the houses over the Column's head, the place being entirely destroyed. After visiting Jakhtung, one march further east, the Column returned to Tamlu and recrossing the Dikkoo paid the first visit among the independent Nagas (Changs), who were guilty of raids over the border.

Yasim, a large village, was found strongly defended by deep ditches bristling with bamboo stakes and stout stockades, and as it was seen to be crowded with armed Nagas who barred all approaches, Lieut. Macintyre attacked under showers of arrows and spears, and forced his way in. A number of dead were found inside, and on our side many sepoys were injured by bamboo stakes and 2 received spear wounds. It was seen that these tribesmen were using a large kind of cross-bow firing its arrow up to 150 yards or so, a weapon not met with as yet in these hills. Forming camp near Yasim, a portion of the force was sent to Chihu, not far away, which was taken and burnt, and while this was in progress a message came saying the camp and its guard were being attacked. Hurrying back, Macintyre was just in time to beat off

HEADMEN IN MASUNGJAMI.

VIEW IN A SEMA NAGA VILLAGE.

[From a sketch

the attack of some 1200 tribesmen who were all round McCabe and the camp. For two hours they persisted in attacks, and only drew off with heavy losses, while Macintyre's casualties were several with slight spear wounds. From Yasim the villages of Noksen and Litam were visited, opposition being met with only at the first-named place, where 6 Nagas were shot, and both villages were burnt for raids and murder. The Column thence made for Mokokchang and reached Kohima on 1st May.

Again it was strongly urged that the whole of the Ao Naga country should be permanently incorporated into the Naga Hills District, the people themselves being desirous of this and quite willing to pay revenue, and so have an end put to constant liability to raids with loss of life and property. The subject was still being discussed in the vacillating way common to all dealings with this frontier in those days, when Kohima was startled by news sent in by Dr. Clarke, a well-known missionary, of the destruction of the Ao villages of Mongsemdi and Lunkung and the massacre of 173 people in the former and 44 in the latter, by a combination of Trans-Dikkoo villages. This raid occurred in July 1888 and decided once for all that this distant part of the district should be taken over for administration and posts be established in it for protection and the preservation of order. To this end Mr. Porteous proceeded in August to the Ao country with 50 rifles of the N.H.M.P., whom he located at Mongsemdi. Here a stockade was built and godowns for stores required for the coming expedition, as soon as the rains were over.

In December a force of 200 men made up of 130 from the Naga hills under Lieut. Macintyre and 70 from the Lakhimpur M.P. Battalions under Lieut. Maxwell assembled at Mongsemdi, and Mr. Porteous having found out that several villages far to the eastward were also concerned in the massacre, decided to proceed against them as far as the large and hitherto unknown village of Masungjami at the head of the Yangnu valley (Sketch

Map 4). The force in two detachments crossed the Dikkoo to attack Noksen and Litam from different points, but the people fired both places on the approach of the sepoys, and vanished. Sontak, which stands very high, was then approached and found to be well defended with breastworks of timber and stone made across the path, and behind these crowds of the enemy were seen armed with cross-bows, spears, and daos. An attempt at parleying being only greeted with a stream of arrows, the force extended, opened fire, and attacked the position, on which the enemy fled. Some yards short of the breastworks the sepoys were pulled up by a deep broad ditch planted thick with sharp bamboo stakes and extending a long way down the hillside on either flank. Had the enemy held on to their position a little longer this ditch, a serious obstacle, would have caused the force a number of casualties, which as it happened were slight. A number of dead were found, and wounded were seen being carried away. Sontak with its granaries was then destroyed and the force descended into the Yangnu valley and occupied Masungjami on 12th January, 1889. On nearing this very large village it was seen to be full of armed men and a body of Nagas was noticed moving round the right flank, which Maxwell dispersed with 30 sepoys, who accounted for 4 of the enemy. Apparently thinking themselves secure, the inhabitants had made no attempt to remove any belongings, stores, or goods, and only had time to hurry their women and children away as the sepoys appeared in sight. On arrival at the village the tribesmen had all vanished and the men settled down in different houses. Although no enemy was seen it soon became evident they were lurking round, for the next evening 3 sepoys going for water were attacked, 2 being killed and their heads and feet carried off; the third escaped, though wounded. For this the upper "khel" was burnt. Other attempts on water parties were made and several of the enemy were shot. The rest of the village with all its contents and granaries was then destroyed in punishment for participating in the Mongsemdi massacre. By the end of January the Column was back across the Dikkoo, where Maxwell's detachment left on its return march to Dibrugarh. The results of this expedition were perhaps not as satisfactory as they might have been, for although considerable punishment was meted out in the loss of the villages, grain, and a large number of men, the ringleaders escaped capture. It had, however, good after effects, for that part of the country enjoyed an immunity from raids for many years.

CHAPTER XIII

1889 to 1892. The Naga Hills M.P., *continued*—Ao Naga country taken over—New roads—Battalions strength increased—Somra tour, 1890—Manipur rebellion, 1891.

In March 1889 formal sanction was obtained to establish posts in the Ao country (Sketch Map 4), *viz.* 100 rifles at Mokokchang, 50 at Mongsemdi, and 50 at Tamlu, which were to be relieved from Kohima every six months. The following year this area was incorporated in the Naga Hills District, a Sub-Divisional officer was appointed to administer it from Mokokchang, the first official being Mr. S. Walker (Civil Police). The only Trans-Dikkoo village to be taken into the new sub-division was Longsa, eleven miles from Mokokchang. It so happened the previous year had seen a reduction in the strength of the N.H.M.P. owing to more Civil Police having been sent to Kohima, and these new posts now obliged it to be again increased. The sanctioned strengths of all M.P. Battalions, it was now arranged, should stand at 671 for the Naga Hills, 819 for Lakhimpur, 797 for the Surma Valley, and 243 for the Garo Hills. With the establishment of the new posts in the Ao country came the need for proper communications, and good bridle-paths were at once put in hand from Mokokchang to Nakachari in the plains, to Wokha, Longsa, and Tamlu, and from the latter post to Geleki at the foot of the hills, whence supplies were drawn. About 1892–93 another road was commenced through the recently made Sema Political Control area *via* Emilomi along the northern slopes of the Kopamedza range to Cheswejuma, whence it descended into the Sijoo and Zulloo valleys and ascended to Kohima. All stages were provided with rough Rest-houses which in later years were improved.

A rifle range was laid out this year at Wokha, and as Kohima was somewhat crowded out, until more accommodation was given for the increased strength, all recruits with their drill instructors were sent out to this post for their training and musketry. The only changes in uniform in all M.P. Battalions at this time lay in the badges of rank for Native officers, the shoulder cords being replaced by cloth straps with two crossed kookeries for Subadars, a single one for Jemadars. The M.P. drill ground at Kohima, hitherto very roughly made, was during the next few years widened and properly levelled, the work being carried out from time to time by punitive labour from offending villages, until by 1896 sufficient space was available for the Regiment in garrison and the N.H.M.P. headquarter companies to drill together as a Brigade on it. About 1887, with a view to increase the efficiency of the M.P. units, the Chief Commissioner asked the G.O.C. Assam Brigade, when he found himself in the vicinity of M.P. headquarters or posts, kindly to inspect if possible and report on them. These inspections became a regular annual occurrence from 1890 on, but did not benefit the Lushai Hills Battalion, there being no Regulars in that area for him to visit. The Lakhimpur and Naga Hills units having Regiments at the headquarters stations, these underwent annual inspections, taking part also in field days, and were reported on to the Chief Commissioner, which kept all up to the mark.

In connection with these annual General's inspections, one, *viz.* that of General Fancourt Mitchell to Kohima in 1898, was of a most unpleasant nature. M.P. Commandants in those days were ordered to call upon the General on his arrival, hand him the Battalion "Present State," ask if he would inspect the Battalion, and generally to place it at his disposal. Previous to this and in subsequent years G.O.C.'s had always treated the Military Police units happily and as soldiers, but when

General Mitchell arrived at Kohima, and the Commandant called upon him, he flatly declined to look at the document or to inspect the Naga Hills M.P. Battalion, or to have anything to do with it. In abusing the Assam M.P. in general he stated the M.P. force had got too big for its boots as it were, had been drilled and trained beyond original intentions for such a force, that they now looked on themselves wrongly as if they were part of the Regular Army, and treated the Commandant with studied rudeness. In his indefensible attitude towards the Military Police he even went so far as to tell Colonel Molesworth, then O.C. 44th G.R., to order his Regiment not to return compliments paid them by the Naga Hills M.P. Battalion. At the same time he did not scruple to direct the M.P. Commandant to turn out his men for fatigue work connected with the Field Firing of the 44th, such as carrying and shifting targets, keeping the firing area clear of villagers, etc., and which was, of course, duly carried out.

Directly General Mitchell left the station a full report of what had happened was sent by the Commandant to the Inspector-General of Police for information of the Chief Commissioner of Assam, who in his turn made due representation to Army Headquarters and which resulted in General Mitchell apologising to the Military Police through the Chief Commissioner and giving a futile explanation of his reasons for such unwarrantable action. Naturally it was not easy for the Commandant to explain the General's attitude towards his Battalion and its Native officers, who were quick to resent the discourtesy and unfriendliness of the 44th arising from the General's order *re* no compliments, and an unfortunate state of social friction between all ranks of both units arose which took some time to dispel.

This system was not followed by the sister force in Burma, which came into existence after the annexation of Upper Burma in 1885–86, and which, priding itself on being an Irregular force and out of fear lest too great a display of efficiency might lead to their units being incorporated into the Indian Army, never joined with the troops their Battalions might be in touch with, as at Mandalay, Shwebo, and other places, and were never inspected by Brigadiers. About 1912, however, this was altered and annual inspections of all Burma M.P. by Brigadiers became the rule.

In the end of 1889 it became necessary to visit the Somra hills between the Lanier and Chindwyn rivers in order to settle the rights of the Manipur Raja over Arui Somra and its adjoining villages. Of this part of the hills nothing whatever was known. Unvisited and unsurveyed, it was hitherto impossible to say how far either Burmese or Manipuri spheres of influence extended. To define these Mr. Porteous (Deputy-Commissioner) made his last important tour in the Naga hills, leaving Kohima in mid December 1889 with Mr. Muspratt and 100 rifles N.H.M.P. Crossing the Kopamedza range through Kalajuma and Phulami, Melomi at the junction of the Tuzu and Lanier rivers, was reached in five marches. This village having been visited before and, being friendly, seemed a good starting point, as information regarding Somra was obtainable here and to which place Melomi had for years paid tribute. Learning of the smallness of the villages ahead and consequent difficulty in obtaining supplies, Porteous left half the escort at Melomi to support him if necessary and with the other half the tour was continued. Somra was reached after most trying marches at great elevations in early January 1890, where the people, by no means cordial though not actually hostile, were found to belong mostly to the Tankhul Naga tribe, with a good many Kukis amongst them. Having investigated the claims of Manipur over the Somra villages, it was ascertained they were so far under Manipur control as to have paid tribute to that State for some years past. Its power over this part of the hills, however, was not sufficiently strong to prevent the Somra people raiding and levying tribute where they chose, and this area was therefore deemed to come under the Naga Hills Control. Burma, it was found, had practically as yet nothing to do with these hills and its inhabitants. Primi, the furthest village eastward visited, marked the nearest approach to the great Saramethi mountain, dominating the country from a height of 13,400 feet, ever reached by Europeans until the Makware Expedition of 1911. Even then the chance of exploring this "Mecca" of so many officials in the district was not taken advantage of. Porteous returned *via* Kotisimi and recorded the pleasantness of the tour and friendly reception everywhere.

By now the communications between Kohima and Manipur on one side and Golaghat on the other had been improved, and a new cart road opened through the Nambhor forest to Nichuguard. Communication with the south-west and the north Cachar hills was by a good bridle path through Khonoma to the Henema post, whence on across the Chuleni river to Semkhor and Gunjong; the latter part was abandoned in 1896, to be reopened again from Haflong at the time of the Kuki Rebellion in 1918. Another road had been made in Butler's day to connect Samaguting with Paplongmai and Mozema, which ran *via* Raziphima up the west of the Chatthe valley to Chama cutting into the Henema road on to the Paona ridge. This stretch has, however, long since been given up, it being so rarely used after Kohima was occupied.

The next event to stir this side of the Assam province concerned itself with the Native State of Manipur, 88 miles south of Kohima (Sketch Map 6), where in the spring of 1891 serious rebellion broke out against the Raja, who was deposed, and a state of confusion ensued. This was due in great part to the supineness of the Political Officer there at the time, which cost him his own and other valuable lives.

It broke out suddenly, as so many of these troubles in the East do, and had a strong Political Officer worthy of the post been there, in all probability it would never have come about. Anyhow, as Sir James Johnstone, who was there in that position from 1878 to 1886, puts it in his book on Manipur, "The policy in which this incident originated did not reflect credit on the Government of India, while the actual explosion itself was precipitated by a series of blunders which have never been explained, as so many actors in that fatal business perished."

Of the forces belonging to this Native State their history is as follows. In 1824, when the first Burmese war was in sight, a trained body of 500 Manipuris was raised among settlers in Cachar, armed and paid by the British Government. This a little later was increased to 2000 men with three or four light guns under Captain Grant and Lieut. Pemberton to drill and discipline it. This force proved very useful, it was mobile, lightly equipped, and, like our Frontier Police, could move anywhere without the paraphernalia needed by Regular troops. It did good service in assisting to expel the Burmese from Cachar and Manipur in 1825–26, and remained in British pay till 1835, when a Political Officer (Major Gordon) was appointed at Imphal; and this Manipur Levy was then made over to its own Raja. In Colonel McCullough's time, who was the Political Officer from 1844 to 1867, the Raja's army was of the nature of a militia 3000 strong, of whom 400 men at a time were embodied for a year's service, after which they were changed for others, so that in course of time all in the militia received military training. This body, at first cantoned at Langthobal, 4 miles south of Imphal, where the Raja used to have a summer palace, now in ruins, was later moved into the fort, and Langthobal was occupied by the Political Officer's escort. It was after the annexation of Burma in 1885 that an Indian Regiment was sent to Manipur (Langthobal), which was gradually reduced to a Wing, and by 1891 to 2 companies from the Regiment at Silchar. The militia was also supplemented by a badly-trained body of Kukis, and both under Sir James Johnstone assisted us well in the Naga rising of 1879–80, as well as under the same officer in the relief of Kendat (Burma) and the suppression of revolt in the Kale Kabaw valley in 1885.

It is hardly necessary here to describe in detail the events and tragedy of March 1891, which has been written about by Mrs. Grimwood, wife of the Political Officer, who was present at the time, and by other writers, but a few incidents may be touched on which are probably not known so well.

Mr. Quinton, at that time Chief Commissioner of Assam, left Shillong for Manipur to inquire into the causes of the trouble, the deposition of the Raja, and the existing state of confusion which had arisen. At Golaghat he met his escort of 400 men from the 44th and the 42nd G.R. under Colonel Skene, who, having been told there was no likelihood of offensive trouble in Manipur, had allowed a fair number of very young soldiers to take part in the outing, and all were armed with Snider rifles, 40 rounds per man, but took no reserve ammunition. The 43rd G.R., who had Martinis, furnished the Resident's escort of 2 companies cantoned at Langtobal four miles off, with a detachment in Imphal. So little was trouble believed in that the two mountain guns in possession of each of the Assam Goorkha Regiments were not taken. This although it was affirmed that a private telegram had already been received, said to have been sent by a loyal Manipuri clerk in the Imphal office, to the effect that "a big tiger was to be killed in Manipur."

The warning was laughed at and the Column moved out. At Mao Thana on the border, 22 miles from Kohima and where a Manipuri detachment was on duty, it was noticed that these men kept inquiring: "Have you brought your guns? Aren't they coming too?" The information that these were not being brought was undoubtedly passed on down to Imphal. The capital was reached without incident and the Column bivouacked in the Residency compound, at that time a large thatched timber structure raised on piles and occupying the site of the present Residency. It faced the large earthwork ramparts of the fort about 200 yards off, with broad wet ditch nowhere more than 3 feet deep, which encircled the vast enclosure containing the Raja's palace, Durbar hall, temples, housing for troops, etc. On the north and south faces of this fort stood two large timber gateways, over each being an upper story arranged for defence.[1] The British officers with the Column were the Chief Commissioner, Colonel Skene, Major T. Boileau, Captains Butcher, Chatterton, Gurdon (in Civil employ), Lieuts. Brackenbury and Simpson, Mr. Cossins, and Captain Woods, an officer in civil employ going on leave from Kohima and who in order to see the country got permission to accompany the Column, intending to continue on to India *via* Silchar. He did so, not in the happy way imagined, but as a fugitive with all his baggage lost. There is no need to detail the series of blunders following the arrival at Imphal—how invitations on three successive days were sent to the Senapatti and other originators of the trouble to attend a Durbar at the Residency, at which it was intended they should be arrested, an action probably anticipated by them, who excused themselves on various pretexts; the doubts on our side as to the course then to be pursued; the dispatch of Lieut. Brackenbury and sepoys to arrest the Senapatti, and who, walking into a *cul-de-sac*, were shot down, Brackenbury mortally wounded but gallantly brought away by a bugler, who later received the Order of Merit for his act; the seizure of the south gate after considerable fighting by Captain Chatterton and a detachment, whence he commanded the line of ramparts facing the Residency and the mistaken order later for him to withdraw; the invitation of the Senapatti in the evening to a Durbar in the palace, responded to in good faith by the Chief

[1] The Manipuris had four 7-pounder mountain guns in the fort.

Commissioner and Colonel Skene accompanied by Messrs. Grimwood, Cossins, and Lieut. Simpson, none of whom came out again; the heavy attack with their guns on the Residency at 10.30 p.m. following on a call in Manipuri from the ramparts that "the Chief Commissioner will not return"; the burning of the Residency and general *débâcle*; the break up of the force of mostly immature soldiers who had fired away almost all their ammunition—all making the sorriest reading of all regrettable incidents in Indian Frontier history.[1]

Why a resolute attack of a place whose ditch and ramparts formed no insuperable obstacle was not made instead of frittering away the force in small isolated efforts will never be understood; or why the Chief Commissioner and party walked blindly into the trap, although it was stipulated they should come unarmed, and even at the gate the young orderly bugler with Colonel Skene was turned back by the Manipuri officer with the words, "We don't want children here," which all might have given a fair hint as to likely treachery. The two companies of the Political Officer's escort at Langthobal appear to have been unable to take part in events at Imphal as they were cut off and surrounded, until some days later Jemadar Birbal Thapa managed to cut his way out with his men and joined up with Lieut. Grant's small force from Tammoo which was in action at Thobal.

Some time afterwards Manipuri officers told ours that there had been no intention to put up a big fight, and that if a resolute attack by us had been made they were all prepared to evacuate the place by the north gate; but our evident indecision and half-hearted efforts stimulated them to greater resistance. The force broke up in parties and retreated, some reaching Kohima by long detours in which many were cut up, as also two officials of the Telegraph Department who were murdered at

[1] The strength of the Manipuri force at Imphal was estimated at 5000 men variously armed with Snider, Enfield, and Martini rifles.

Mayankhong, their graves lying close to the present cart road. The largest party, with which Major Boileau, Captain Butcher, Captain Woods, the Subadar Major, and Mrs. Grimwood went, effected their escape before midnight from the blazing Residency and retreated towards the western hills and the Silchar road, up which they knew two companies of the 43rd G.L.I. under a British officer were marching to relieve those at Langthobal.

This British officer with his detachment left Silchar for Manipur in the ordinary course of relief of the escort there, and in complete ignorance of what was happening at Imphal. After a few marches he noticed incivility from Manipuri officials and disinclination to produce supplies. On reaching the Laimatol hill above Kaopum and descending into the valley, firing was heard on the far side and the refugees from Imphal were seen pursued by Manipuri troops which, on becoming aware of the new arrivals on the scene who opened fire, ceased their pursuit and drew off. On the two parties meeting at the Laimatak river below, the newly-arrived officer learnt what had happened and here made his mistake. Instead of taking his companies on according to his orders in Silchar, and attacking the Manipuris on his own, letting the fugitives find their way to Silchar along a road devoid of danger, as most energetic enterprising officers would have done, he allowed himself to be persuaded by demoralised men to turn back and escort them to Silchar. On arrival there news had been received of the massacre of the Chief Commissioner and party. Had this officer gone on, as he quite well could have done, he would undoubtedly have been able to co-operate with Grant's little force and those at Langthobal, sharing in the honour that fell to Grant, who, on his own initiative on hearing of the rising, had marched at once from Tammoo (Sketch Map 6) with 50 of the 12th Madras Infantry and 30 of the 42nd G.R. to assist if possible in relieving the situation. He was held up at Thobal, 14 miles from Imphal, and surrounded for ten days with continuous fighting, where he was joined by Jemadar Birbal Thapa and the Langthobal detachment. After a most gallant defence at this point which gained the young fellow and his men honour and glory, orders reached him to withdraw and await the arrival of the Burma Column. The return of the two companies on the Silchar road formed the subject of a Court of Inquiry on the conduct of the British officer in command which was classed as neglect of duty. The remark by Lord Roberts endorsing the proceedings was to the effect that it was sufficient punishment for this officer to realise he had wilfully missed the golden opportunity which comes to every officer, though perhaps only once in his service, and that such would never come to him again. And it didn't. Concerning Major Boileau and Captain Butcher, the seniors left in the Residency that night, both were court-martialed and cashiered for gross neglect of duty in the face of the enemy, but there were other and more private reasons for this sentence which were not made public.

Three Columns were formed and advanced into Manipur from Kohima, Silchar, and Tammoo (Burma) to exact retribution for the rebellion and outrage, the latter Column only experiencing some sharp fighting at Palel and again near Thobal, and the disturbed condition of the little State ended with the public hanging of the Senapatti and the Tangal General, the two most deeply implicated in the trouble. The troops remained in the State during the rest of the year, after which a Regiment from India formed the garrison of Imphal until the Great War, when this duty was made over to the 4th Assam Rifles.

Turning now to the N.H.M.P. in March 1891, directly news of the fighting in Imphal reached Kohima Captain Macintyre, the Commandant, with 200 of his men, accompanied by Mr. Davis, the Deputy-Commissioner, left with the intention of reaching Imphal. It was found that the Mao Thana detachment on the border had been reinforced, also that Manipur was intriguing with Khonoma to ferment trouble in these hills. Fortunately, the Khonoma clan, learning of the moves of troops up the road and of a Regiment being stationed in reserve at Golaghat, wisely decided not to embroil themselves with the "Sirkar." Mao Thana was attacked by Macintyre's detachment, rockets being fired into the place from the end of the last spur on the cart road and covering the skirmishing line, which moved round the upper end of the last re-entrant and drove out the defenders with some loss. Macintyre and Davis then pursued them to near Maram, and would have gone on had not orders reached them, to their great disappointment, to return at once and await General Collett and the 42nd G.R., who were on their way up. Macintyre's action, however, had cleared the road of the enemy, and picking up three companies of the N.H.M.P. General Collett's column arrived in Imphal unopposed. Here they remained a few months, being employed in guard and escort duties, and losing a number of men in a bad outbreak of cholera.

This rebellion, in a locality not easy to get at, led to the making of the present cart road through the hills from Nichuguard to Imphal through Kohima (122 miles). It was commenced in the winter of 1891–92 by detachments of the Bengal and the Madras Sappers and Miners, whose inscribed stones at different points of their tasks can still be seen. It was finished, rivers were bridged, and permanent Rest-houses built at the various stages by 1896, and a few years later was metalled and made passable for motor cars.

The settled condition of the Naga hills by 1892 and with crime and inter-tribal troubles diminishing, the reduction was ordered of certain posts, *viz.* Wokha, to 45 rifles, Mongsemdi to 25, Themakodima was abolished, and Khonoma, hitherto held by 50 rifles from the Regiment in Kohima, was now handed over to the Naga Hills M.P.

CHAPTER XIV

1894 to 1924. The Naga Hills M.P., *continued*—Abor expedition, 1894—Patkoi railway survey, 1896—Band replaces pipes—Trouble on the A and B railway construction, 1898—Trans-Dikkoo tour and Yachumi affair, 1900—Camp of exercise, 1901—Murder of Sergt. Tolley—New class composition—Duty in aid of Civil power, 1907—Makware expedition, 1911—Tour in Tantok area, 1911—Abor expedition, 1911—Mishmi and Lohit Valley escorts, 1911/12 and 1912/13—Chinlong expedition, 1912—Aka expedition, 1913—The Great War—The Kuki rebellion, 1917/19—Aid to civil power, 1920/22—Rampa State Column, 1924.

THE Abor Expedition of 1894 claimed the assistance of the Naga Hills Battalion, which was ordered to send 100 rifles under Captain Little, who had succeeded Captain Macintyre as Commandant, to Sadiya in January. An account of this expedition appears in Chapter IX, on the Lakhimpur M.P., so it will suffice here to say the detachment took part in practically all the actions, losing Subadar Inayat Ali and 3 sepoys killed and several wounded. In a stiff fight at the Silli stockade Havildar Major Bakshi Ram Dogra earned and later was decorated with the Order of Merit for his gallantry. Mr. Driberg, then Inspector-General of Police, in recording this expedition especially notices the services of "Captain Little and his company of the N.H.M.P., who performed many acts of bravery," while Captain Maxwell, who commanded the operations, stated in his official report: "I would particularly mention the name of Captain Little, whose company of the N.H.M.P. was *par excellence* the best in the force, clean, obedient, and ever ready for hard work."

By 1895 the road through the ·ma Political Control area *via* Emilomi begun in 1891 was completed, many

N.C.O.'s and men having been employed superintending the work at various points, and in this year also rifle ranges were opened at Mokokchang and Tamlu, which had been entirely constructed by the sepoys.

During the winter of 1895–96 the first survey of a railway route over the Patkoi range and *via* the Hukong valley to link with the Burma railway system near Mogoung was carried out with escorts of 50 rifles each from the Naga Hills and the Lakhimpur M.P. under Captain Row of the latter unit. The route taken lay from Margherita over the Patkoi to Hasham and on to Nyngbin at the southern end of the Hukong valley, where a similar survey party from Burma was met. The tribes were not hostile and after five months the detachments returned.

It has been shown that in Captain Plowden's time Pipers were started in the Battalion, but towards the end of 1896 at the desire of all ranks these were discontinued, their place being taken by a Band of 25 instruments, the services of the Bandmaster of the Regiment in garrison being kindly lent to train the musicians. In later years this Band was increased in numbers and with 100/- per month from Government instead of the previous 50/- plus the monthly subscriptions from all ranks, it became able to support a Bandmaster on its own. The tenure of Captain Little's command was marked by thorough organisation of the interior economy, as during this period there were fewer tribal and trans-border troubles, thus giving the one British officer with the Battalion more leisure to attend to such matters. The methods of duties, relief of posts, clothing and equipment matters, discipline, etc., were now carried out precisely on the lines of a Regular unit, to the great benefit of military efficiency.

Various small punitive tours across the eastern borders chequered the next few years, and in April 1898 the Commandant, Captain L. W. Shakespear, was ordered to take 2 companies down to Lumding to keep order amongst the thousands of coolies of all tribes and classes, even from far distant Mekran, who were employed on the construction of the new Assam and Bengal railway. This line was being built in sections, those through the North Cachar hills and the Nambhor forest (130 miles) entailing an enormous amount of work in tunnelling, earthwork, and forest clearing; and in these two sections were congregated the greater number of workers, amongst whom there was much prevalence of crime, culminating in the murder of Mr. R. Wylde, one of the principal engineer officials. The companies marched down to Lumding—then a mere jungle clearing, and now an important junction—whence the sepoys were distributed in posts from Maibong to Rangapahar near Dimapur, patrolling being constantly carried out between them to keep order amongst the heterogeneous mass of labouring humanity. After six months of the hottest and most unhealthy in this low country, their presence was no longer necessary, and they returned to Kohima.

Sibsagor district, having no Military Police of its own, and suffering from many minor raids by Nagas in the hills east of the Dikkoo river, called on Government in the winter of 1899–1900 for action to put a stop to this trouble; and in early January 1900 Captain Woods, Deputy-Commissioner Naga Hills, was directed to take a small Column and punish the offending clans. With Captain L. W. Shakespear the Commandant, Subadar Arjun Rai, Jemadar Belbong Ram, and 100 rifles he left Kohima, and as no route had been prescribed and both officers were keen to explore new country a route was taken over the north end of the Kopamedza range and up the Tita valley, hoping so to reach Masungjami and one or two other villages in that neighbourhood which it was desirable to visit on the way as their fines for various offences had not been fully paid up. Coolies were taken from village to village and all went well till Khukemi, at the head of the Tita valley, was reached on the 6th February, and the following day a move to Yachumi

The First House (Thornhill's) built in the Jungle where the Important Junction of Lumding now stands, 1898.

village was made, this part of the hills never having been visited by Europeans (Sketch Map 4), and here trouble was met with. From a spur lookihg down a broad open valley Yachumi was sighted 1½ miles off, and a halt was made while "dobashas" (interpreters) went forward to the place to let the people know we should be friendly if they were. After an hour's absence the village war drums were heard, men were seen running up from their cultivation, and the "dobashas" came hurrying back saying the people would not listen and had thrown spears at them. At the same time a mob of armed men was observed collecting in increasing numbers on open ground near the village. The Column moved on, the "dobashas" waving green boughs as a token of peace, and the mob began a war dance, throwing up their spears and chanting. It was hardly thought likely they would attack and that this was merely show and bravado, till the chanting ceased and the mob began racing along the hill-side towards the Column, which with some 150 carriers was strung out in single file along the narrow path, the hill rising above them crowned with thick forest. The small advance guard halted and extended, and as it was evident now that hostility was intended a few rounds were fired over their heads in warning. As they still rushed on a volley was fired into the mass which brought down three or four warriors, and the mob stopped for a brief space to look at the fallen men and see what was being thrown at them with so much noise, evidently in ignorance of fire-arms.

The rush was resumed, this time under flights of arrows, as they were only 150 yards off and it was seen men were using a heavy sort of cross-bow. Firing now being in earnest, 19 warriors were soon lying within 80 yards and less of the sepoys. This checked them and they began moving back, but flanking sepoys on the hill above called down that there was a gathering in the forest evidently intending to cut into the long line of carriers and sepoys. Leaving Captain Woods with the advance guard, the Commandant climbed the hill with a section, and after a skirmish in the jungle in which the enemy got sufficiently close to wound 3 sepoys, 1 with a dao cut, 2 with spears, the hostile mobs retreated into the village. This was found to be defended by a thick stockade and barricaded gateway, the long grass in front of which was so densely sown with "panji" stakes that sepoys had to cut poles and sweep the ground clear before it could be crossed. Here the tribesmen attempted to prevent an entrance, more firing was necessary, and Kupu, the head interpreter, and a sepoy were severely wounded by "panjis" and a Naga carrier by a spear. The village was a large one of over 500 houses, well built of stout timbers with thatched and in some cases shingled roofs, and for its hostility was destroyed. In all 45 dead warriors were counted and many must have been carried away wounded. As several more large villages could be seen in the distance which might be equally hostile and the Column might find itself in greater difficulties, it was decided to return to the Tita valley and take another line of country. At Longsa Mr. Noel Williamson from Mokokchang, with more ammunition and supplies, joined the Column, and Masungjami *via* Sontak and Nokching was reached, after some very stiff marches and climbing. The people were found most unfriendly, declining to give carriers or pay up their fine in full. Two days were spent here trying to induce the headmen to comply, which they flatly refused to do, until, finding parties of sepoys posted about the village with orders to fire it by a certain hour if the carriers and fine were not produced, they climbed down and complied, enabling the Column to continue *via* Yasim and Yantalang to Tamlu. Here the Dikkoo was crossed to Kongan at a point where the valley was filled with the smell of kerosene, and iridescent bubbles of the oil were seen coming up from the bed of the river. By the end of February the area in which lay villages to be punished for raids into Sibsagor was entered, but here the country was found in the throes of a severe famine, the crops having failed. This, together with very faulty information from Sibsagor officials and the stupidity of their "Kotokies" (interpreters), made it impossible to affix blame on or to punish any particular village. The headmen, however, took oaths not to molest the plains any more and the Column returned to Kohima in late March, after 2½ months of strenuous marches in difficult country, often in bad weather and considerable cold, in which all ranks did well. The local Government later took exception to the border having been crossed up the Tita valley, thus inviting hostility, and strict orders were issued against such action occurring again.

During the winter of 1901–02 a Camp of Exercise was held in the Mayankhong valley attended by the 43rd and 44th Goorkha Rifles and the 3rd Bengal Infantry, the whole being under command of Colonel Lumsden, 3rd B.I. The Commandant N.H.M.P. obtained sanction to join this camp with 250 of his men, where a most useful fortnight of work was carried out to the benefit of all ranks in the Battalion through experiences under service conditions alongside Regulars. Shortly after this the N.H.M.P., in common with other M.P. units, received Martinis in place of the Snider rifles, and Wokha and Mongsemdi were now abolished as M.P. posts.

The following year a tragedy occurred at Kohima which cost the life of Sergeant W. Tolley, who had succeeded Sergeant O'Callaghan in the Battalion. He was shot dead while sitting at dinner with his wife and a friend by a Bandsman with a small grievance, who then turned the weapon on himself. After this incident it was decided to appoint an Assistant Commandant to each unit and have no more British N.C.O.'s. This was a great improvement, as what with greater efficiency being expected and musketry training, long absences inspecting posts, all falling on one British officer, it was by no means easy to maintain the degree of excellence demanded by military work under the stimulus of the recent South African war.

Early in October 1904, disturbances being feared in the Manipur State, the Battalion received orders to dispatch 200 rifles at once to reinforce the garrison at Imphal. The order was received late at night, and the Deputy-Commissioner, then Mr. W. Reid, being a most energetic organiser, at once got Kohima village to provide the requisite number of porters, although not the turn of that community to supply such labour. They were all mobilised and ready at dawn and left under the Commandant, Captain Thompson, on the 6th October, each man carrying 100 rounds in addition to his usual pack, and reached Imphal the third day, the marches having been 26, 30, 28 miles—a good performance which merited the thanks of the Chief Commissioner.

The next two years were quiet for the Battalion, save for tours to Masungjami and Yachumi to exact fines for various misdemeanours on the border. In both cases there was slight opposition necessitating a little firing, when a few Nagas were killed. Kehomi was found to be the guilty village, not Yachumi, which still remembered its rough lesson of five years earlier and was on good behaviour. Kehomi, proving continuously troublesome, had to have another drastic visitation the following year before its people learnt wisdom.

Since 1892 the class composition of the N.H.M.P. had been 3 companies of Goorkhas, 2 of Jaruas, and 1 company of Dogras and Garhwalis, and for various reasons it was decided in 1906 gradually to eliminate the two latter elements until the Battalion should be constituted in 4 companies of Goorkhas and 3 of Jaruas. This was eventually carried out and has remained so.

The Assam Military Police were now to have their first experiences of the extremely uncongenial duties of suppressing disorders in Eastern Bengal which were the outcome of Swadeshi and anti-partition agitations. Of the N.H.M.P., Lieut. Bailey with Subadar Singbir

Rana and a strong detachment left Kohima for Dacca in April 1907, where one half was detached to Mymensing. For some months they were moved about to different scenes of rioting and disorder, and carried out their arduous duties in aid of the civil power, as an official report states, "with exemplary patience and good conduct under trying conditions."

For three years no further trans-border troubles worthy of note occurred, and then early in 1910 the Aishan Kukis towards Somra began a series of murders of Nagas visiting Melomi in our sphere of control, as well as worrying the Chindwyn valley side. This resulted in orders to the Deputy-Commissioner to visit Aishan and exact fines in punishment. A Column of 150 rifles under Captain Bliss, Commandant, with the Deputy-Commissioner, proceeded to Meloni at the end of January, whence Subadar Singbir Rana was sent to place protective posts in certain villages living in fear of Kuki depredations, while the remainder moved on Kangjang and Aishan, further south-east.

It was hoped to be able to co-operate with a detachment of Burma M.P. from Homalin, but this was found impracticable. However, a number of Kukis prominent in raids and murders were rounded up and captured and numbers of guns were confiscated without fighting, the force being strong enough to overawe the tribe, and for some time a post of 50 rifles was stationed at Melomi for the protection of this part of the border. The following year (1911) much raiding on our side as well as on that of the Chindwyn river by the people of Makware, a large and unvisited village in independent territory on the northern slope of Saramethi mountain (Sketch Map 4), necessitated the co-operation of two Columns from Homalin on the Chindwyn and from Kohima, the latter comprising 5 British officers and 100 rifles under Captain Bliss, while Burma sent 75 rifles of the Chindwyn M.P. under Captain Simpson and Mr. Street. A supply Base was formed at Melomi in early January 1911 and the Kohima force moved towards the north end of Saramethi *via* Tetchumi and Primi, the actual position of Makware being somewhat obscure. On the 16th helio communication was established with the Burma force, which had reached Niemi *via* the Nantaleik river (the Tuzu) and on the 23rd both Columns joined at Tetchunasami. Very bad weather now hampered movements at considerable altitudes, a most difficult range of 8000 feet having to be crossed before Chimi was reached on the 27th. Here a stockaded post had to be arranged for in which to leave a number of sick men under a guard, and Makware standing very high and overlooked by Saramethi, 13,400 feet on one side, and by another peak of 11,000 feet to the north, was approached on the 31st. Here opposition was expected and to a certain extent was offered till the attack opened, and after about ten minutes' firing, in which several warriors were killed, the defenders fled, and the village, a large and well-stockaded one, was entered, with two sepoys wounded by arrows, of whom one died. Next day the place with its granaries and belongings was destroyed. Both forces then returned to their respective stations by mid February; the Burma detachment, taking a new line of country out of these hills, reached the Chindwyn at Heinsun. It seemed a pity the opportunity was not seized of exploring Saramethi while the Column was in its vicinity, but the vileness of the weather militated against pushing further afield, also Captain Bliss was due for leave home and had to catch a certain steamer, so the idea was given up.

While this outing was in progress another of 80 rifles from Mokokchang and Tamlu under Captain Hamilton was taking place across the Dikkoo river to the east, into territory which had been officially brought under political control the previous year. A certain amount of unrest manifesting itself amongst these people (Tantok clan), who had also made one or two small raids, a show of force was deemed desirable. The village of Chinlong, where some opposition was encountered calling for a little firing

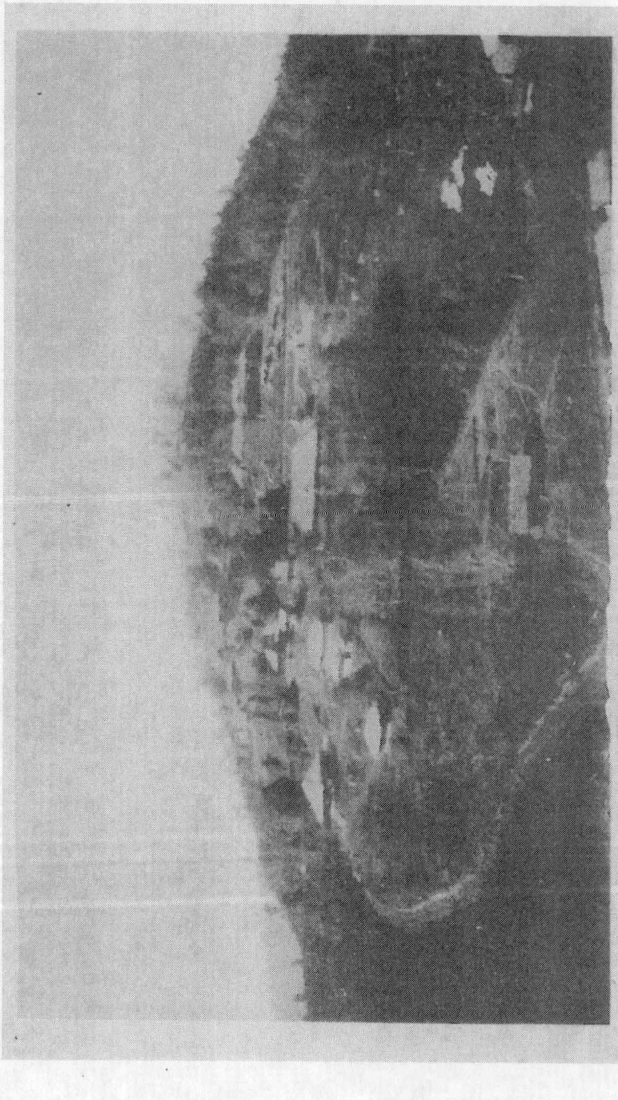

VIEW OF MOKOKCHANG IN THE AO NAGA HILLS.

which disposed of four or five Nagas, had to be burnt, Longkai paid up its fine, and the little force returned to Tamlu, having made, it was thought, a proper impression on this somewhat truculent group of Tantok villages.

The following winter the Royal Durbar at Delhi was attended by Subadar Major Arjun Rai, 1 Havildar, and 10 sepoys of the Battalion, when the Subadar Major received at His Imperial Majesty's hand the Order of British India, 2nd Class, and the coveted King's Police Medal, in recognition of long and excellent service.

The N.H.M.P. did not take active part in General Bower's Abor Expedition of 1911–12, but they dispatched 100 rifles under Captain Hardcastle and Lieut. Dallas Smith in early September to relieve the Lakhimpur detachment at Balek which had been holding that post just on the border from early April after Williamson's murder. They were on duty there till mid October, when they were sent to join the Mishmi Mission and Lohit valley trade route escorts. For this the N.H.M.P. furnished 200 rifles under Major C. Bliss, the Commandant, Captain Hardcastle, and Lieut. Dallas Smith, the rest of the force comprising the 48th Pioneers under Major Vickers, the 5th Company 1st Sappers and Miners under Captain Le Breton, R.E., 150 rifles of the Lakhimpur M.P. under Captains Bally and Bethell, a survey party under Captain Gunter, R.E., Mr. Dundas and Captain Bailey being the Political Officers. All were assembled at Sadiya by 6th November, 1911, and the road work from Sonpura up the Lohit valley began, which has been described in Chapter X. The Mishmi Mission, moving up the Dibong river to open up those hills, was at work at the same time. There was no hostility, but as both the country and people were unknown the Columns conducted their work as under active service conditions, which was carried on again in the winter of 1912–13.

The next occasion on which this Battalion was employed across the border occurred in June 1912, when

Chinlong, a Tantok village of the Konyak Naga tribe east of the Dikkoo river (Sketch Map 3), cut up some men of the British Naga village of Wanching in retaliation for the latter having led Captain Hamilton's Column into those hills the previous year when Chinlong was punished. Other murders occurring, a small force of 75 rifles N.H.M.P. was dispatched to this area which established posts at Wanching and Chingphoi, which were to remain until completion of the Lohit valley escort work, when 200 rifles would be sent to exact punishment. However, earlier action being thought desirable, orders were issued for the dispatch of 150 rifles of the Dacca M.P. Battalion in addition to those of the N.H.M.P. already in those hills, to proceed against the Tantok group of villages under command of Colonel Loch, C.I.E. from Aijal, with whom were also Captain Bally and Hardcastle, Lieut. Dallas Smith, Major Gidney, I.M.S., and Mr. Webster, Deputy-Commissioner. This force left Tamlu, and reached Chingphoi on the 5th February, 1913, from whence the village of Chinlong was proceeded against. The hills in this locality were not so thickly forested as in most parts but had a lot of tall grass jungle covering slopes not cultivated. After crossing the Aoyeng river opposition was met with which continued until Chinlong was in sight. The place was then attacked and occupied, 1 sepoy of the N.H.M.P. being killed, but before the attack was completed the transport carriers, parked some little distance off under a guard, were rushed by a large body of the enemy, causing a loss of 4 sepoys and 9 carriers killed, 3 sepoys and 28 carriers severely wounded. The carriers stampeded and for some hours could not be induced to go back for their loads. Eventually the enemy was beaten off and the force concentrated in Chinlong village, the outer circle of houses being pulled down to give a field of fire. Desultory efforts at attack were made by the Konyaks during the night, and next day the village with its granaries was destroyed. Jemadar Pokul Thapa now

Konyak (Tantok) Nagas from across the Dikku River.

came up with 25 more men of the N.H.M.P., but Colonel Loch decided, in face of this opposition and hostility and as fresh transport coolies were needed, to retire and call for reinforcements. This part of the expedition being of the nature of a reverse which might serve to stimulate other Trans-Dikkoo clans to join in against us caused anxiety. General Sir James Wilcocks with Major Stockley of the Headquarters Staff came to Nazira to inquire into matters, with the result that 200 rifles of the 1/8th G.R. with 3 British officers were ordered from Shillong and added to the force already at Tamlu and Wanching. The command of this phase of the operations was given to Major A. Wilson, 1/8th G.R., and it assembled on the 9th March at the Shimiang river Base camp, which had been built by the N.H.M.P. On the 11th the force advanced and Totakchingko with two other villages were burnt with slight opposition. The force was then divided into five small columns, which operated in different directions through the Tantok hills, destroying Changwi and other principal offending villages and hunting down and dispersing with heavy loss numbers of hostile gangs. This drastic punishment was concluded by the end of March 1913 and the force broke up, leaving 25 rifles N.H.M.P. at Wakching one march east of Tamlu, where a stockaded post was built, the post at Tamlu being given up. In this expedition Jemadar Harka Sing Rai was rewarded with the Indian Distinguished Service Medal for gallant conduct.

The winter of 1912–13 had seen the Battalion supplying 200 rifles under Major Bliss and Lieut. Dallas Smith as escort to the second phase of the Mishmi Mission of the Dibong Survey, as it was now styled. They were out seven months and as a result 5000 square miles of country were added to the map and some 300 miles of very fair 4 feet wide paths were made, over amazingly difficult country at great altitudes and in severe cold, which caused many bad cases of frost-bite. Friendly relations were also established with people as far as the borders of Thibet.

Major Bliss returned to his regiment in August 1913 after having had a distinctly strenuous time in command, being succeeded by Captain Graham, 5th G.R., and in January 1914 both officers became recipients of the King's Police Medal, Major Bliss being further decorated with the C.I.E. in recognition of his good services on this frontier. Unfortunately, neither lived long to wear these honours, as they lost their lives early in the Great War. At the same time the decoration of the Order of British India, 2nd Class, was conferred on Subadar Sanjai Suba of the N.H.M.P. for long and meritorious service.

A small expedition to Tetchumi with 50 rifles and a long tour with the Deputy-Commissioner with an escort of 50 through the Konyak hills east of the Dikkoo valley occupied Captains Graham and Hensley during the early winter 1913–14, where all was found in a tractable quiet state, and at the end of the year a political and survey mission into the Aka country claimed the services of the N.H.M.P. as escort. This consisted of 200 rifles under Captain Graham, with whom went Captains Molesworth 8th G.R., Mathew 2nd G.R., Dunlop S. and T. Corps, Lieuts. Kennedy I.M.S., and Huddlestone, and 3 S. and T. Sergeants in charge of 800 transport coolies. A Base supply Depot was established at Balukpung on the border, and the forward move towards Jamiri village on the Tenga river was made on the last day of 1913. Jamiri was reached on the 5th January and a halt was made for survey purposes, while Captain Nevill, the Political Officer, with an escort visited and established friendly relations with Rapa and other villages. From here on the 18th an advance was made to Medhi, the chief village of the Akas, where an advanced supply Depot was arranged for. From Medhi the force split for a time into two Columns—the Bechom river one with 70 rifles and surveyors proceeding north up that river, with whom Graham, Nevill, and Huddlestone went —the other, called the N.E. Column, with Captains Molesworth and Mathew, 50 rifles, and surveyors, making for the head waters of the Bhareli river. All went well, some 4000 square miles being mapped, and both parties met to replenish stores at Medhi.

A further survey eastwards was now started with Graham, Nevill, Molesworth, Mathew, and Kennedy, 60 rifles, surveyors, and 135 coolies. The objectives were Yefan and Riang villages right on the Daphla border and inhabited by both Akas and Daphlas. Both were reached and found none too friendly, but they allowed the party through, surveys in the neighbourhood and along the border being carried out. This being the limit of operations and as supplies were low, the return march commenced. It was noticed how the Column's movements were continually watched by small parties of armed Daphlas, who on the 6th March opposed the return passage through Riang. The Daphlas were beaten off, losing many men and the place was burnt, but the tribesmen in increasing numbers hung on the flanks and rear of the Column all the way down to the Puchung river, causing a few slight casualties. A thick mist descended suddenly, greatly adding to the difficulties of the situation, which were further increased by the smoke from the men's rifles (Martinis) hanging in dense clouds in the narrow valley, so much so that after a little firing nothing could be seen. The cane tubular bridge over the Puchung river was found destroyed by the Daphlas, and the detachment had to retrace its steps some distance, and then cut a new track down to another point where it was possible to construct hastily another bridge, which was ready by 2 p.m., and half an hour later all were safely across. The enemy made persistent attacks with spears and arrows while the work was in progress, getting in so close that Molesworth was able to shoot three with his revolver. But for Captain Mathew and Jemadar Harka Sing Rai with a few men seizing a small ridge above and covering to a certain extent the work on the crossing and who were able to repel a flank attack, matters would have gone very seriously for the party. The enemy lost a number of men, and Yefan village was then destroyed for its participation in the attack, and Medhi was reached with fortunately only a few casualties. To anyone with experience of jungle fighting this affair must appear most creditable to all concerned, for the almost invisible enemy did not cease his attacks till the last man was across the Puchung river, and it certainly raised the prestige of both officers and sepoys amongst the Akas and Daphlas (Sketch Map 3).

The Great War now occupied the interest and activities of the Assam Military Police, whose Battalions were called on for drafts to Goorkha Regiments in various theatres of operations. Before the first draft went off the N.H.M.P. were inspected by General May, G.O.C., 8th Lucknow Division, whose report stated that he considered "this M.P. Battalion to be as good as most Indian Regiments for frontier defence, and being more self-reliant and thoroughly accustomed to roughing it, its men are in many ways far more efficient. I was greatly pleased with all the work I saw carried out." All who went with the War drafts were volunteers, and the drafts in order of their dispatch were as follows:

1st Draft, 18th Oct., 1914—3 Havildars, 100 sepoys—to the 3rd and 8th G.R.

2nd Draft, 4th April, 1915—2 N.C.O.'s, 50 sepoys—to the 3rd G.R.

3rd Draft, 11th Aug., 1915—2 N.C.O.'s, 50 sepoys—to the 1/6th G.R.

4th Draft, 12 Oct., 1915—Subadar Hari Ram, 50 sepoys—to the 8th and 2nd G.R.

5th Draft, 22nd Jan., 1916, 65 sepoys.

6th Draft, 23rd March, 1916, 35 sepoys.

7th Draft, 23rd May, 1916, 50 sepoys.

8th Draft, 23rd July, 1916, 50 sepoys.

9th Draft, 23rd Sept., 1916, 50 sepoys.

10th Draft, 23rd Jan., 1917, 50 sepoys.

All for active service with Goorkha Regiments in France, Egypt, Gallipoli, and Mesopotamia.

That their services were appreciated thoroughly will be seen from the letters of different Commanding Officers in the Appendices. In order to provide and train these drafts, two additional Assistant Commandants were sent to each Battalion and their strengths were raised to 1000 rifles.

Serious riots breaking out in the province of Behar and Orissa, the Assam Military Police were called on to send a force there in aid of the civil power, and a strong Column under Major A. Vickers formed by 300 men of the Naga Hills, 100 of the Lushai Hills and 100 of the Lakhimpur Battalion with Captains Ostrehan, Davis, and Copeland were dispatched in October 1917. Their duties lay mostly in the districts of Patna and Arrah, in which during their six weeks' presence in the disturbed areas they succeeded in arresting some 1400 prominent rioters, who were imprisoned.

It was at this time that in order to mark its recognition of the excellent services rendered in the Great War by men of the Assam Military Police Battalions, the Government of India sanctioned the old title of the force being changed to that of "The Assam Rifles" of which the N.H.M.P. now became the 3rd Battalion.

In the end of 1917 troubles nearer home, *viz.* the rebellion in the Chin hills and amongst the Kuki tribes of Manipur, obliged the cessation of the war drafts to the Army, as it was not long before every available man of the Assam Rifles was required to suppress the rising in co-operation with the Burma M.P. force. It took a year and a half of continuous active service in mountainous country on the part of 2400 of the Assam Rifles and 3000 of the Burma M.P. before order was finally restored, which was achieved by means of a scheme by Major A. Vickers, Commandant 3rd A.R., and officially approved.

An account of these operations forms the subject of a separate chapter. The casualty list of this Battalion was small, *viz.* 7 killed, 8 wounded, and a number succumbed to exposure and disease. Four Goorkha officers of the

Battalion specially distinguished themselves in these arduous operations and were rewarded as under :—

Subadar Hari Ram Mech Subadar Nain Sing Mal Jemadar Hanspal Limbu	With the Indian Distinguished Service Medal.
Subadar Pokul Thapa	With the King's Police Medal.

During the Kuki operations the platoon system had superseded that of the company, a platoon of 50 men or so being found the best unit for service in the hills. The strength of the Battalion, fixed at 840 rifles on conclusion of these operations, was arranged into 14 platoons of 60 rifles each, two of these being headquarter platoons in which were placed all who on mobilisation for service would remain at Battalion headquarters, such as Pay Havildars, office clerks, Band, Drill Staff, etc. During the hot weather, this unit, in common with the others, was re-armed with the ·303 rifle, long, non-charger loading, and this year also saw 8 Pipers added to the Band, who received instruction in the instrument at the hands of a Piper of the 48th Pioneers.

The years 1920 to 1922 were a period of much anxiety for the local Government, confronted one after another with tea-garden strikes and strikes on the Assam Bengal Railway fomented by non-co-operators and seditionists, in the suppression of which and restoration of order the 3rd A.R. sent out 9 platoons at different times to aid the Civil power, also sending all available signallers to assist in keeping open the railway telegraph line, and signals, unpleasant and arduous duties which were well carried out by all ranks. Owing to the political situation in early 1922 it was found advisable to show force in disaffected districts by marching a strong Column of 450 rifles drawn from all units through them, under Major Gordon and Captain Abigail, the 3rd A.R. furnishing 3 platoons. Assembling at Moriani on the 10th February the Column marched through the disturbed tea areas in Upper Assam *via* Nakachari, Jorhat, Sibsagor, Charali, and Bhojo. At

KOHIMA PARADE GROUND.

CAPT. W. B. SHAKESPEAR, CAPT. ABIGAIL (ARM IN A SLING), SUBADAR-MAJOR JAMALUDDIN AND INDIAN OFFICERS, 3RD ASSAM RIFLES, 1921.

this point they railed back to Moriani and traversed the area Titabar, Mohima, Nigriting, and Golaghat. Here the Column was railed to Sylhet and marched through Kalaura to Karimganj, getting back to their respective headquarters by early April. The year 1920 also saw the raising of a new 5th Battalion to the Assam Rifles, to which 4 Goorkha officers and 82 rifles were transferred as a nucleus from this Battalion.

While the demonstration march was in progress the independent village of Tetchumi beyond Melomi began giving trouble, necessitating 2 platoons under Major Vickers with the Deputy-Commissioner being dispatched in February to inflict punishment. Slight opposition only was met with and the place was destroyed. In April this year the post at Khonoma, held since 1880, was abolished, and that at Wakching beyond the Dikkoo was moved to near Kongan village, one march northwards and in the vicinity of the Borjan collieries, which employed a large and very mixed crowd of workers, who in these days of seditious troubles were likely to cause anxiety.

The following year, 1923, found the Government for economic reasons constrained to effect temporary reductions in the units of the Assam Rifles, the strength of each being reduced by 1 British officer, 2 Goorkha officers, and 2 platoons. The permanent posts held in the Naga hills by the Battalion were now only two, *viz.* Mokokchang and Kongan, such being the quiet, contented condition existing in this area, the last punitive outings of mention being those to Yungya and Yasim, across the Dikkoo valley. This was under Captain W. B. Shakespear and 2 platoons with whom went the Deputy-Commissioner in November 1921 and March 1923. After some stiff and rapid marches both places were reached and attacked, as the inhabitants opposed the little Column. The villages were soon taken, 3 of the wanted murderers being captured, the fourth having been killed in the short action. The year 1924 saw the official affiliation of the Assam Rifles with the Goorkha Regimental Groups of the

Indian Army, by which the 3rd A.R. became affiliated with the group of the 1st and the 4th Goorkha Rifles, a measure appreciated by all A.R. ranks, and which should make for the easier working of mobilisation and for dispatch of reinforcements when need for such arises.

The last of this Battalion's activities with which this history concerns itself took a detachment down to the Madras side, where a state of rebellion had broken out in the Rampa State Agency near the east coast, the assistance of Assam being asked to suppress it. This was sanctioned in January 1924, and a force of 400 rifles, reinforced later by 200 more, was furnished by detachments from all A.R. Battalions, this Battalion sending 3 platoons under Subadar Kainbir Limbu and Jemadar Bagirathi Thapa. The account of these operations, which did not close till June, is given in Chapter XVIII, and Subadar Kainbir Limbu was presented by H.E. the Governor with the King's Police Medal for his excellent services during this period.

Before closing this account of the life and services of the 3rd A.R., mention must be made of Subadar Major Jamaluddin, who retired on a well-earned pension on the 1st January, 1924, after nearly thirty-eight years' excellent service, with the title of " Khan Bahadar " and the Order of British India. He was born in the Battalion and following the example of his father and grandfather, who had both served for years in the armed Civil and then in the old Frontier Police, he entered the ranks of the N.H.M.P. in 1882 and rose through all grades to his last high rank, having also taken part in numerous border expeditions. A first-rate example of a Mahommedan gentleman, he enlisted when our M.P. ranks were still of very mixed classes, and was retained by reason of his fine and loyal qualities long after the ranks received only Hindoo elements—Goorkhas and Jaruas—by whom he was greatly liked, looked up to, and respected as the father of the Battalion, and whose final departure was the subject of great and general regret.

CHAPTER XV

1913 to 1924. **Further increases to the Assam Military Police—Raising of two new battalions, the Darrang Battalion (4th A.R.) and the 5th A.R., in 1913 and 1920, respectively.**

About 1910 the withdrawal of the Indian Regiments from Dibrugarh, Kohima, and Silchar having caused heavier duties to fall on the Military Police Force, Battalions were allowed to enlist up to 10 per cent. over strength. Although this helped matters in a measure it did not lessen the difficulty always experienced by the Lakhimpur and sometimes by the Naga Hills Battalions, in furnishing, rationing, and relieving the posts along the distant Darrang and Kamrup borders. Wherefore it became necessary to raise another unit to take over these remote duties, and this was sanctioned in early 1913. This unit, at first called the "New Battalion" but afterwards officially styled the "Darrang Battalion," was raised at Dibrugarh by Major C. Bliss (8th G.R. and at the time Commandant of the N.H.M.P.), with Captains Ostrehan (later Goodall) and Montifiore and Lieut. Coote as Assistant Commandants. Its nucleus was formed by parties of 95 N.C.O.'s and men from the Lakhimpur, 31 from the Lushai Hills, and 60 from the Naga Hills Battalions, while a little later the independent detachments at Silchar and Tura (the last remnants of the old Surma Valley and Garo Hills units), *viz.* 4 Indian officers and 73 men from the latter, 4 Indian officers and 130 from the former, were added to it. The sanctioned strength was 800, increased as with all other Battalions to 1000 for the duration of the war, and recruiting in the usual way brought in the remaining number required, so that by the time the permanent Commandant, Captain Croslegh, was able to join (31.7.14) and Major Bliss to return to his own command, the new unit was practically at full strength and was armed and equipped as the rest of the force.

Before it was ready to move to its rightful district from Dibrugarh the irony of circumstances stepped in, the Great War causing the 123rd Outrams Rifles to be withdrawn from Manipur, which had since 1891 been garrisoned by a full Regiment, and the new "Darrang" Battalion had to be sent in March 1915 to take its place there. A year or two later, it having been decided that no Regulars would garrison Manipur again, Imphal became the permanent location of the new Battalion, the title "Darrang" was given up, and it became the 4th Assam Rifles in September 1917, in which month it suffered a serious loss in the murder of the Subadar Major Dhanbir Lama by a Havildar, and Subadar Hetman Rai succeeded the deceased in the position of senior Indian officer in the Battalion. The following year the two 7-pounder R.M.L. mountain guns belonging to the Lakhimpur Battalion were made over to the 4th A.R. and 87 short Lee-Enfield Rifles were received for the training of war drafts, as all units were still armed with old Martinis.

In common with its sister units, this Battalion turned vigorously to the dispatch of drafts as reinforcements to Goorkha Regiments in various theatres of the Great War. Those sent between October 1914 and April 1917 totalled 5 Indian officers and 649 of all ranks, who served some with the 2nd Goorkhas, others with the 3rd, 6th, 7th, 8th, and 10th G.R. Of this total 7 signallers joined a signal corps at Poona and 1 Subadar, 2 Jemadars, and 20 sepoys went to the 22nd Labour Corps. All were on active service in France, Egypt, Gallipoli, Mesopotamia, and were dispatched as under :—

From Dibrugarh—

1st	Draft left 18.10.14,	strength	50	Goorkhas.	Joined 2/10th G.R.
2nd	" " 2.11.14,	"	50	"	" 7th G.R.

From Imphal.

3rd Draft	left 31.10.15,	strength	25 Goorkhas.	Joined 2nd G.R.
			25 „	„ 7th G.R.
4th „	„ 15. 1.16,	„	25 „	„ 2/10th G.R.
			35 Jaruas.	„ 1/7th G.R.
5th „	„ 15. 3.16,	„	50 Goorkhas.	„ 1/6th G.R.
6th „	„ 15. 5.16,	„	50 „	„ 2/7th G.R.
7th „	„ 15. 7.16,	„	50 „	„ 1/7th G.R.
			10 Jaruas.	„ 1/6th G.R.
8th „	„ 15. 9.16,	„	51 „	„ 1/8th G.R.
9th „	„ 15.11.16,	„	40 Goorkhas.	„ 1/7th G.R.
			10 Jaruas.	„ 1/8th G.R.
10th „	„ 13. 1.17,	„	40 Goorkhas.	„ 2/3rd G.R.
			10 Jaruas.	„ 2/8th G.R.

All acquitted themselves thoroughly well, which is vouched for by the letters written by O.C.'s of the Goorkha Regiments to which they were attached, and which will be seen in the Appendices.

In May 1917 Major Croslegh rejoined his own Regiment and was succeeded by Colonel G. Row, a former M.P. Commandant who retired in 1913, rejoined the Army in 1914, and had been serving at Suez as Base Commandant. Under him the formation of a Mounted Infantry platoon was sanctioned, but which, for various reasons, chiefly that of expense, was not kept up, and in September 1917, owing to the title of Military Police being changed to that of Assam Rifles, this unit became the 4th Battalion A.R.

In mid December 1917 the outbreak of the Kuki Rebellion obliged a stop being put on the dispatch of drafts to the Army, as it soon became apparent that all available men in the Force would be needed to deal with this trouble and to co-operate with Military Police Columns from Burma, that province also suffering from the rising. The detailed account of these operations in the hills surrounding the Manipur valley which did not close until May 1919 is given in Chapter XVI, and on their cessation it was necessary for the 4th A.R. to hold the hill areas concerned in the rebellion by a series of

posts, until each area was completely quiet once more. These posts held until late 1922 were:—

Ukrul (Tankhul)	1 Indian officer	40 rifles		
Kamjong (Chassadh)	1 " "	20 "		
Mombi	1 " "	20 "	Southern Hills	
Chura Chandpur	1 " "	40 "		
Hengtham	nil	20 "		
Tamenglao	1 Indian officer	40 "	Western Hills	
Nantiram	nil	20 "		

For their good work during the Kuki operations Subadar Birman Thapa and Jemadar Satal Sing Cachari were rewarded with the Indian Distinguished Service Medal, and all ranks who took part in it received the British Service Medal or a clasp to it. It was also ordered that the detachment of 1 Indian officer and 100 rifles on duty in the Garo hills (Tura) should be furnished from now on by the 4th A.R. Early November 1919 saw the Battalion's strength reduced from 1000 to 840 of all ranks, and in June of the following year an experiment was made in enlisting our late rebels the Kukis, of whom it was intended to have two platoons. At first they deserted fairly frequently, disliking our discipline. Then finding that service in the A.R. exempted them from doing coolie work, which they greatly dislike, they came in more readily and have been shaping fairly well as soldiers, and the future may see them taking more kindly to military life and duties.

On 1st March, 1920, Colonel Row retired on pension and for nearly a year Captain Hebbert and Major Gordon acted as Commandants till Major Dallas Smith, 2nd Goorkhas, then on field service in Persia, could arrive to take command, and in August the Battalion was re-organised into 14 instead of 16 platoons, *i.e.* 2 Staff platoons and 12 service ones, each 60 strong. A draft of 1 Indian officer and 40 rifles was also transferred to form the nucleus of the new 5th A.R., and at the same time Subadar Major Hetman Rai was created a "Rai Bahadur" on the occasion of the King Emperor's birthday and in

Group of Indian Officers, 4th Assam Rifles, 1922.

The Tamenglao Stockaded Post, Manipur Hills.

recognition of his long and good service. The presentation of the title was made at a public Durbar held at Shillong by the Lieut.-Governor.

The years 1921 and 1922 were full of trouble for the province by reason of seditious propaganda resulting in serious disturbances amongst the coolies on many tea gardens, and a prolonged strike on the Assam Bengal Railway. The 4th A.R., like other Battalions, was called on to assist in the suppression of disorder and sent two platoons under Lieuts. Williams and Askwith to the Sylhet district, also 12 signallers to assist in keeping railway communications open. With them went a detachment of the Maharaja of Manipur's police, who did duty in guarding the junction of Badarpur, all being absent for many months. During this year Pipes were instituted in the Battalion, the Pipers being trained by those of the 3rd Goorkha Rifles.

On the occasion of the Prince of Wales' visit to Calcutta, the Assam Rifles were given the honour of being allowed to send a detachment there from each Battalion under Major Gordon to form a guard of honour, the 4th A.R. sending Jemadar Satal Sing Cachari and 6 riflemen.

In January 1922 two platoons under Subadars Babu Lal and Ganga Lal were dispatched to the plains in aid of the Civil authorities, and at the end of that month three more platoons under Lieut. Williams rendezvoused with those from Kohima at Dimapur, whence they took part in a military promenade under Major Gordon through the disaffected areas in the province. This tour ended in April, when the platoons returned to Imphal except the two under the Subadars above-mentioned, which were kept at Haflong for the hot weather months, that place being on the railway whence they could more readily be used if further trouble arose.

During this year the Battalion, in common with other units of the A.R., suffered a reduction in strength as alluded to previously, and the last bit of active service for the 4th A.R. to be recorded is the request of the Madras Government for assistance in quelling a serious rising in the Rampa State Agency, when 600 of the Assam Rifles drawn from all Battalions were sent under Major Goodall. The 4th A.R. sent two platoons under Subadar Birman Thapa and Jemadar Jagatsher Limbu to this disturbed area, whence after nearly six months of continuous pursuit and hunting down of rebel gangs whose leaders were either shot or captured, they returned to Imphal in June. Subsequently Jemadar Jagatsher Limbu received the King's Police Medal in recognition of good work performed in the operations. In this year an annual training camp was started for instruction in jungle warfare, each platoon going to Sengmai, where the camp was held, for ten days during the winter.

In January 1925 this Battalion was inspected by Sir John Kerr, Governor of Assam, accompanied by the I.G.P., and although all previous reports had been creditable to the 4th A.R. the Governor's closing remark on this occasion may well be quoted in concluding this account of its thirteen years' existence. He records how very favourably he was impressed by the smart soldierly appearance of all ranks and their movements on parade, while the I.G.P. remarked the " turn out was a model of smartness and cleanliness."

Of the history of the youngest unit of the Assam Rifles there is naturally as yet but little to set down here. The 5th A.R. was raised on the 10th June, 1920, to control the Kamrup and Darrang borders owing to recent raids by Akas and Daphlas tribes, and which border was too remote to be easily guarded from either Sadiya or Kohima. That spring the D.I.G. Assam Rifles, with Captain Nevill, the Political Officer for this frontier, had prospected for a suitable site and had decided on Lokra, 3 miles from Balipara, at the end of the light railway from Tezpur. Here certain buildings belonging to the Political Officer were taken over for the new Battalion, he and his officials moving to Charduar, 3 miles west. Captain Hooper,

I.A.R.O., was transferred from the 4th A.R. and was first on the scene at Lokra to receive the various drafts sent by all Battalions, until Captain Ogilvy, 1st Goorkhas, appointed Commandant, could arrive to take up his duties. By the end of June these drafts, totalling 12 Indian officers and 498 riflemen, had arrived, full strength being reached by recruiting during the early part of 1921. For some time the men had to occupy tents and thatched huts while the barracks were being built, which were completed during 1922. The new Battalion was armed with the ·303 Lee Enfield rifle, long, magazine, and soon had to furnish posts at North Lakhimpur, Harmati, Dikulmakh, Hathipaithi, Udalguri, and Darranga. All these being low down on the plains and consequently more liable to unhealthiness than other units, the desirability of a hill post was discussed. It happened that 2½ miles out of Shillong was a disused camp called the Happy Valley, which had belonged to the 123rd Outrams Rifles when quartered in Shillong. A certain number of barracks and quarters for officers were standing but in considerable neglect. These in 1921 were auctioned and eventually bought by Government at a pleasingly low figure, and made over to the 5th A.R., which sent up two platoons under Captain Hooper to occupy the place and start putting all into proper repair. This has been one of the Battalion's posts ever since. The first duties outside its own area on which the 5th A.R. were engaged were the unpleasant and onerous ones of aiding Civil authority in suppressing rioting and disorders connected with the Non-Co-operation movement in 1921–22, several detachments being dispatched to the disturbed districts of Bishnath, Nowgong, Kamrup, Goalpara, Mangaldai, and Tezpur, where they acquitted themselves well. In January 1924 the Battalion was called on to form a portion of Major Goodall's Column sent to suppress revolt in the Rampa State of Madras. Two platoons were sent from Lokra under Captain Keene, with Subadar Ropotram and

Jemadar Sunman Thapa, and later a third platoon was dispatched under Subadar Jitman Gurung. All took active part in the operations which ended in early June with the capture or death of the leaders and the complete dispersal of their gangs, after which they returned to Lokra.

A DAPHLA WARRIOR.

STOCKADED POST ON THE DAPHLA BORDER (5TH ASSAM RIFLES).

CHAPTER XVI

The Kuki and the South Chin Hills rebellions, 1917 to 1919.

In early October 1917 in order to assist the Inspector-General of Police with the Military Police Battalions of Assam who were training and dispatching large drafts to Goorkha Regiments during the Great War, a Deputy Inspector General was appointed to Assam to deal with all matters concerning this force. Colonel L. W. Shakespear, a former Commandant of M.P. whose period of service on the Staff in Mesopotamia had recently expired, was posted to the new billet, and took charge in mid November 1917. The Military Police Battalions had a few months before this been given the new title of the "Assam Rifles," each unit being numbered, in recognition by Government of their services in the world struggle to which they had dispatched 23 Indian officers and 3174 riflemen, all of whom had volunteered and were seeing active service in France, Egypt, Mesopotamia, Gallipoli, and on the N.W. Frontier of India. This, of course, had considerably reduced the effective strength of the Battalions in Assam, whose best men had all gone, leaving those somewhat too old or too young and still being trained. An unfortunate time for trouble to break out in the province, but so it happened and thus.

Labour Corps had been raised for France in 1916 amongst various clans of Nagas, Lushais, and others, who willingly came in, having in many cases done this sort of work for Government before in border expeditions, and knew the work and good pay. Such had done extremely well wherever they were sent, but in 1917 more were needed, to supply which it was necessary to tap other sources, *viz.* the various Kuki clans inhabiting the hill regions of the native State of Manipur, a people who had never left their hills and knew but little of us and our ways. Optimism too strong with the higher authorities soon showed the fallacy of trying to induce these people to leave their country for the unknown, and the Chiefs, with whom the first attempt was made, declined to send men. A further effort on the part of the Political Agent only produced angry refusals. This Political Agent was then sent to France with Labour Corps and another officer took his place, who was directed to explain to the Chiefs the reasons why their men were wanted, the nature of the work required of them, pay to be received, etc., to which end he arranged for a Durbar and invited the Kuki Chiefs to attend. To this the principal recalcitrant Chiefs, Ngulkhup of Mombi and Ngulbul of Longya, in the southern hills (Sketch Map 6), returned insolent replies, refusing to attend and stating that if we used force to compel them to do what they had no intention of doing, they would also use force against us. It was also believed, though not actually proved, that Bengal seditionists in Sylhet and Cachar, quick to divine where discontent could be fanned, sent emissaries amongst the southern Kukis urging them to rebel and thus to cause more trouble to the British Raj. To add to the discomfort, a Manipuri set himself up as a pretender to the Manipur "gaddi" (throne) and commenced collecting a following. This effort of his, however, did not last long, as the man was captured in a few months and his small band dispersed. The insolent messages from Mombi and Longya requiring active notice being taken, the officiating Political Agent, with Captain Coote and 100 rifles, marched in September to visit Mombi, six days out from Imphal, where open hostility greeted them. A skirmish followed and the place was destroyed, after which they were *en route* for Longya, when orders were received to return and to take no further action with the Kukis. Had they been

Cane Bridge in the Kuki Hills.

The Residency at Imphal, Manipur.

allowed to punish Longya as well, it is probable the clans would have thought better than to rebel; as it was, the speedy retirement of the detachment heartened both Chiefs, who sent in messages to the effect that they closed their country to us. And so matters remained until December 1917, neither side doing anything, when the men of Mombi started a series of petty raids into the southern end of the Manipur valley. At this time a notably plucky effort at maintaining if possible a state of peace with the Kukies, was made by Mrs. Cole, residing in Imphal, whose husband, Colonel H. W. G. Cole, C.S.I., formerly Political Agent in Manipur, had gone to France with a Labour Corps. Both she and her husband had known Ngulkhup of Mombi personally, and relying on friendship with him she had a message sent out to Mombi to meet her at the foot of his hills beyond Shuganu by a certain date. Ngulkhup agreed, and Mrs. Cole set out alone, except for an interpreter, and reached Shuganu, four long marches from Imphal. Ngulkhup, with two or three of his leading men, was duly at the appointed place, met Mrs. Cole quietly and courteously, and a talk on the situation took place, in which the lady's high hopes were frustrated by the chief, who declined to listen to reason. So a most plucky effort—for the temper of that tribal section was already up, as she well knew, ended in failure, and Mrs. Cole had to return to Imphal, matters thereafter taking their own course. It may here be stated that during the Great War with its attendant crop of difficulties, felt in Assam as well as in other provinces in India, it was found necessary, owing largely to all M.P. units having sent their best men to Regular Goorkha Regiments, for the authorities to overlook tribal impertinences which ordinarily would have been dealt with promptly on lines advocated by Major John Butler (the elder) in the early 'fifties. He then wrote in his book that "greater boldness and presumption are always sure to be manifested by savages when their aggressions pass with impunity or their acts of violence are not instantly chastised. On such occasions procrastination or forbearance on our part is construed by them into fear." The start of this rebellion was largely due to our procrastination in not dealing at once and fully with it when the trouble first showed itself.

Here digression must be made to explain events which occurred in the far south of the Chin hills (Burma) and which first called for the services of the Assam Rifles. It happened that in those hills the Burma authorities in the early winter of 1917 were confronted with a somewhat similar trouble in an effort to raise a Labour Corps in that area, and this trouble, aggravated by tribal discontent due to certain action taken by the authorities to check slavery which still existed in that region, caused a serious outbreak of rebellion. The ignorance as to any cause for anxiety in which the authorities dwelt, and the suddenness with which the southern Chins rose, were remarkable. In early December 1917 the D.I.G. Assam Rifles received a wire from the Superintendent Chin Hills inquiring if he had any knowledge of likely trouble on the Chin Lushai border. The reply stated he had no such knowledge, the only minor trouble known of concerned Zongling in the Unadministered Area towards Arrakan. Twelve hours later came an urgent wire to Shillong from Falam, the headquarters station in the Chin hills, saying the southern Chins had risen, Haka station was surrounded, and begging for urgent assistance. Permission to act having been obtained, the D.I.G. sent orders to Captain Falkland, Commandant 1st A.R. at Aijal, to march at once with 150 rifles for Haka, and in a few hours they were *en route* to cover the 16 marches as rapidly as possible. A few days later another urgent wire from Falam called for more help, and as active trouble had not as yet started in Manipur, Captain Montifiore with 150 rifles of the 3rd A.R. at Kohima was ordered to the Chin hills, travelling as expeditiously as possible—by rail to Chittagong, river steamer to Rangamatti, country boats to Demagiri, whence onwards a fortnight's hard marching to Haka. As neither Falkland nor Montifiore could reach the disturbed area till well after Christmas, and details of their moves and actions in the Chin hills did not reach Shillong for some weeks, we can turn to the Kuki troubles fermenting in the Manipur State.

As previously mentioned, the Mombi and Longya Chiefs started petty raiding in December, and were soon joined by those of Hinglep and Ukah in the south and western hills (Sketch Map 6). A serious raid on the Itoll police Thana near Shuganoo and another into the valley near Moirang obliged active measures to be taken, and two detachments of the 4th A.R. at Imphal were dispatched, each 80 strong—one under Lieut. Halliday to Mombi, with whom went the Political Agent, the other under Captain Coote and Lieut. Hooper to Hinglep. The former was unsuccessful. Halliday found the Chokpi river crossing beyond Shuganoo strongly stockaded and held, in attacking which he had 3 killed and several wounded, and finding the rebels in too great strength he withdrew to Imphal. Coote had a little more success. He had scarcely entered the hills below Moirang when he was attacked, and after two actions, in which he punished the Ukah men well, he returned with slight casualties. The first somewhat unfortunate occurrence and the first reverse (there were only two in the whole operations) sustained, served to put the Kuki rebels' tails well up; the whole southern and south-western hills were now in active rebellion, serious raids following, in which they closed the road to Burma, destroying the Rest-houses, killing the chokidars, and damaging the telegraph line.

The D.I.G. went down to Imphal and began a systematic organisation for effective operations, and Burma was wired to for men to assist, which was responded to as rapidly as possible, for the Kukis were now worrying the Chindwyn valley and the north Chin hills areas as well. Transport entirely lacking had to be arranged for, and a corps of Naga carriers 800 strong was collected at

Kohima and sent down together with a platoon 3rd A.R. Further, as the 4th A.R. at this time mostly consisted of old men or half-trained young soldiers, these were made to undergo intensive training in jungle warfare for three weeks until all was ready. A reinforcement from the 2nd A.R. at Sadiya of 100 rifles was also called for which left Silchar under Major Cloete. Medical arrangements were attended to, rations collected and disposed at Palel and Shuganoo, from which bases two Columns were to advance when all was ready, and the porters had been trained to carry the two 7-pounder mountain guns which were to be taken.

By the 22nd January, 1918, both Columns were ready, each of 120 rifles and a gun—one under Captain Coote, and Mr. Higgins, I.C.S., was to move through the Mombi and Longya area, and with this went the D.I.G., as it was intended to join hands with a Burma Column from Tiddim in the northern Chin hills under Captain Steadman, with whom further arrangements for co-operation could be personally made. Steadman was to make for and deal with Longya; the junction of both Columns, it was expected, might be about Khailet. The second Column from Imphal under Captain Hebbert, with whom was the Political Agent, was to proceed towards Tammoo, reopen the Burma road, and punish rebel villages in that neighbourhood.

The terrain of operations for suppressing this rebellion eventually included the entire hill country surrounding the Manipur valley and covering an area of 7000 square miles. The valley of Manipur, 1000 square miles in extent and exceedingly fertile, alone is level, an ancient silted-up lake, of which the Logtak and Waithok lakes with certain swamp localities are the last dwindling remains.

It is an intensely mountainous country encircling this valley, beautiful in its forested rugged ranges, cut into everywhere by deep narrow valleys and ravines, the higher portions covered with pines and rhododendrons, the latter making a glorious display of blossom in the spring, while thick "ooyang" (Manipur oak) and the flowering Bauhinia woods cover the lower slopes. The highest ranges overlook the north end of the valley on the north-west and north-east, Kaupru and Sirohi rising to 9100 and 8400 feet, respectively, while many others are well over 6500 feet, the south end of the valley being closed by the fine solitary peak of Haobi, about 6000 feet, with the "massif" of Khatong, 7906 feet further to the south-east.

The Kukis, being a people of nomadic habits, constantly change their village sites, consequently their homes, unlike those of the Angami Nagas, are lightly built and as a rule not stockaded. Their defences, in the shape of stout timber stockades with thorn or "panji" abattis in front, or skilfully-concealed log breastworks loopholed, are placed at some little distance from the village to block or cover likely approaches. These people used to be expert bowmen and as such were much feared by other tribes, as well as by reason of the autocratic rule under which they live, and which gave their Chiefs a greater power for combining effectively against any foes. The gradual acquisition of numbers of old fire-arms had led to the disuse of the bow and arrow, their other weapons being the spear and dao. They also use a curious sort of leather cannon made from a buffalo's hide rolled into a compact tube and tightly bound with strips of leather. A vent is bored in the proper place, their own rough powder poured in, and a quantity of slugs or stones is then inserted. The weapon is usually fastened to a tree so as to command a turn in the track up which the enemy is approaching, and is either fired by hand at the head of the party as it appears in sight, or is arranged to be fired by a trip cord which our flankers may touch, and which drops a stone on to a percussion cap on the vent which fires the charge hoped to hit our men coming up the path. Such weapons sometimes can be used twice, but usually burst with the first discharge. The Civil authorities were inclined to treat the idea of the Kukis having many fire-arms as absurd, giving as their view that perhaps 100 or so were at most scattered about the hills. It was soon shown that the number had been greatly underestimated; in many actions in different parts of the hills the rebels had 70 or more in use at a time, and the total number of fire-arms confiscated by the end came to nearly 1000 weapons, which, though old flint-lock or percussion muzzle-loaders, were good enough for their jungle fighting and guerilla tactics at fairly close range. Only in a few cases did they make any prolonged stand behind their defences, but their firing into detachments on the march and into camps at night was frequent, as also were their sudden raids on open villages in the valley, which they burnt, killing numbers of people and driving off cattle, after which the gangs would retire rapidly into the hills, making pursuit most difficult and laborious.

As the labours and experiences of the numerous punitive Columns acting in the rebel areas were more or less of a similar nature, the account of one Column will suffice to show the kind of active service conditions in which the A.R. now found themselves engaged, for strong detachments of all Battalions were sent to take part in it, making a total of 2400 rifles eventually. The Column chosen as an example will be Captain Coote's into the Mombi area (Sketch Map 6).

This Column, with which Mr. Higgins, Assistant Political Officer and the Deputy-Inspector-General, went, left Imphal on the 23rd January, 1918, and three marches along the level valley with a divergence to punish Aihang village, brought it to Shuganoo, its supply Base.

From here the village of Longyin was destroyed for its share in the attack on Itoll Thana, and the low hills were entered with the going still good. On the 28th Coote prepared to attack the stockade at the Chokpi river crossing, where Halliday's party had had a reverse before Christmas, but scouts found it was not occupied. The

Coote's and Hibbert's Columns at Imphal, ready to move out.

Attack and Burning of Longyin Village.

Coote and Higgins inside the Mombi Stockade.

bodies of the men killed with Halliday were found flung into a small ravine after their heads, hands, and feet had been cut off. As it was known the direct route to Mombi up the Tuyang valley was strongly stockaded at three points, Coote decided to turn these by moving straight up into the hills east of the Tuyang, and proceeding *via* Nampho Kuno, a rebel village. The Column began its climb in single file, the only way to advance, up a steep spur covered with small trees and scrub jungle, when after going for about an hour several shots rang out in front, to which the advance guard replied. Not a single Kuki was seen, but they had wounded 3 riflemen and had vanished. Later on, crossing the top of the ridge, the same thing occurred again but without effect, and as it was dusk the Column camped in a small but friendly hamlet and was subjected to sniping during the night, in which one man was mortally wounded, dying next morning. The next march was along a ridge covered with the long grass of disused cultivation, at the far end of which Nampho Kuno was in sight, glasses showing the presence of many armed Kukis in it. At this point firing was suddenly opened on the Column from both flanks accounting for 3 more wounded, *viz.* 1 rifleman and 2 carriers. No enemy was seen in the long grass, which was thoroughly searched, while the mountain gun opened on the village at 900 yards. The first round plumped into the place, dispersing all in it, and it was then destroyed. While this was going on a great column of smoke was noticed far to the south-west, which was taken to be Longya being punished, though it was doubted if Steadman from the north Chin hills could have reached it so soon. A steep descent and most fatiguing climb brought Coote on to Mombi hill the following afternoon, a few ineffective shots being fired from the forest *en route*, but the stockaded defence was empty, as was also the site of the village burnt the previous September, and here the Column bivouacked. Mombi stands about 5000 feet up and commands a most extensive view to south and west, the eye ranging over a sea of tangled hills and valleys from the Manipur valley to the far distant Chin hills, the great mass of Khatong, 7900 feet, closing the view to the south-east. Helios at once tried all hill points around in the hope of getting in touch with Steadman, but without success. Here a halt had to be made to escort the wounded to the Shuganoo Base and to bring up a further supply of rations. This was done by Coote with 70 rifles, and on the way down the Tuyang valley he ran into a Kuki war party, who in the ensuing scrap lost 4 killed and from blood trails apparently carried off some wounded in their flight. One body, evidently from its ornaments and weapons showing a certain importance, was sent back to Mombi, where it was identified by a Manipuri official with Mr. Higgins as one of those prominent in stirring up the trouble. The first night at Mombi the camp was fired into but no damage was done, and the next day those left on the hill heard faint sounds of distant firing, but as a high wind was blowing the actual direction of the sound was not easy to locate, but it was thought to be Steadman in action somewhere. A reconnoitring party discovered the new village of Mombi, some 4 miles along the ridge to the east, which was destroyed unopposed, and the camp had a few more shots fired into it at night.

On Coote's return with fresh supplies the Column moved towards Longya, being fired at on two successive days at Letkulon and Khailet, both places being destroyed. At the latter place the first view was obtained across the Manipur river of Longya, which was seen to be in ashes, and the signallers, climbing the hill near by, flashed their helios all round trying every likely hill-top for the Burma Column. After a couple of hours of this a faint answering flicker of a helio was seen far to the south, and a message was received from the Subadar at the Lenakot post (north Chin hills) from which Coote learnt that Captain Steadman's Column had got to Longya quicker than expected on the 27th January and burnt it without opposition. He then descended, crossed the Manipur river and climbed to Haika *en route* to Khailet, where the two Columns were to have met. A very long stockade barred his path, against which Steadman made a frontal attack and failed to take it, losing 11 killed and many wounded. Steadman, the only British officer with them, was badly wounded in three places, the carriers began to bolt, and the Column was obliged to retreat to Lenakot—a most unfortunate incident, due to inexperience of the British officer in command.

As any meeting or co-operation was out of the question now and there were no signs of the Kukis who had opposed Steadman, Coote proceeded to carry out the rest of his programme in punishing the Mombi Chiefs' eastern villages. Five strenuous marches, incessantly climbing up or down, bivouacking in forests which had first to be cleared for camp spaces and strands of barbed wire fixed round the perimeter to prevent it being rushed, and Coote reached Nungoinu. Its strong stockade was evacuated on his approach, which with the village and a similar neighbouring one were destroyed; and on the 7th February, as his Column was threading its way along the top of a densely-wooded ridge, shots rang out, killing the leader of the left flankers, the advance guard extended and was soon busy. No enemy or position could at first be discerned, and pushing through the tangled jungle it was found that a high ridge of rocks crossed the ridge at right angles, a dip in the centre through which the narrow track led was heavily stockaded, and the space in front of the rocks for some 40 or 50 yards was littered with a mass of trees felled by the rebels and forming a serious obstacle to negotiate. Two of the advance guard were killed and several wounded at the near edge of this obstacle. Mr. Higgins and the D.I.G. with parties tried to turn each flank, but the ground being very precipitous and covered with dense thorn jungle, no way could be found. For three-quarters of an hour heavy firing went on, the gun was brought up to break down the stockade, but at the third round the gun Havildar and the gun layer were badly hit, also two others of the gun's team, putting it out of action, while Higgins received a somewhat severe contusion on his shoulder from a spent bullet. All that could be seen of the enemy were the muzzles of muskets thrust through interstices in the rocks, fired, and rapidly withdrawn again. The Kukis must have had some 70 or 80 muskets here, and the whole time the most astonishing din of men shouting and drums beating arose from their position, adding to the noise of the action. As no way round either flank was possible, Coote decided to rush the position, Jemadar Kharga Sing's platoon on the left to advance, covered by the fire of another holding the front. With the Jemadar went the D.I.G., and the platoon advanced; to rush was impossible, as each man had to climb over or under the innumerable tree trunks thickly littering the ground. One outburst of fire came from the rocks as the platoon broke cover, but no one was hurt, then a sudden silence in the position, and as the first lot of men began climbing the rocks, Coote's firing ceased. The enemy had all bolted, carrying off their wounded, for many blood patches were found, also some weapons and drums left behind in their hurry. The position, by nature strong, had been rendered still more so by the piling up of more rocks and timber breastworks at weak spots, while the passage through was stockaded with a double row of heavy timber posts loopholed. From the large number of sitting places for firing from, the trampled state of the ground, food left, etc., there were probably some 300 Kukis holding the position and of whom there was now not a sign. A mile beyond this the large village of Khengoi was reached, well situated on an open spur overlooking the Kale Kabaw valley (Burma), with glimpses of the broad Chindwyn river further eastward winding its way through forests. Khengoi was empty, a huge tiger skin stuffed and set up on trestles greeted Coote at the village entrance, and accommodation for all was soon arranged in the houses.

From here the signallers got in touch with Tammoo, 40 miles off to the north-east, and rations now needed were asked for to meet the Column at Withok in the Kale Kabaw valley, for which place Coote now headed. Khengoi village was burnt next morning, and as the rear guard moved off it was fired on from the jungle, but no damage was done. The Column was now in the low hills covered with magnificent teak forests, from which it emerged into the cultivated rice lands of Withok, a pretty Burmese village surrounded by a loopholed palisading of thick teak timbers. The Myouk (Civil official) met Coote and led him and his men to a large field in which rows of shelters for them had been run up, with supplies stacked near by, also a clean house had been allotted to the three British officers, and here two days were spent. Captain Grantham (Burma Police) and Lieut. Kay Mouatt (Burma Bombay Trading Co.), both in the I.A.R., rode out from Tammoo, 22 miles off, bringing carts to take Coote's wounded and sick back to their hospital, and with news of the spread of the rebellion up the Chindwyn valley. It was learnt a Burma Column was being formed at Tammoo which would shortly be joined by another coming up from Tinzin under Captain Patrick, both intended for operations against the Chassadh Kukis, who had begun serious raids near Kangal Thana and Homalin. A letter from Imphal showed the rebellion to have spread north from Hinglep, the Silchar road had been closed and Rest-houses destroyed by the Kukis, who had also cut up a number of people. Major Cloete, 2nd A.R., with 100 rifles from Sadiya, had reached Silchar and was now on his way to clear this main road to Imphal. Altogether the rebellion was spreading rapidly.

On the 11th February Coote left Withok, and after a few miles across the open the forest swallowed the Column again. Beyond the destruction of Changbol,

Gnarjal, and Pantha, all rebel villages, but which had been deserted, a little firing into camp at night, and a last short scrap near the top of Rekchu hill (7000 feet) nothing of very particular interest occurred. It was all hard marching and climbing, but the men were all in good training by now. The skirmish on Rekchu hill evidently was intended to be a big affair, the enemy having prepared a line of breastworks and shelter pits commanding the track up which the Column was toiling. But they opened fire too soon, and did not notice the flankers, also in ignorance of the presence of an enemy until the shots rang out, and each little party found itself on the right and left of the Kukis. These on seeing their flanks turned bolted down the far side after a brief interchange of shots. From Pantha, the last rebel village punished in this area, the Column left the hills, descending into the Manipur valley at Palel, whence two marches brought it —now a ragged and in many cases a bootless crowd— to Imphal after an extremely hard five weeks' tour, the experiences of which had vastly improved all ranks.

Captain Hebbert's Column, which had left when Captain Coote did, had returned a few days earlier, having punished several villages with one skirmish near Suampo, but these places being at no great distance from the Imphal–Tammoo road had not entailed quite so much hard marching as fell to Coote's Column. A detachment of 200 rifles, 2nd Goorkhas, under Major Cruickshank, Captain Duff, and Lieut. Buss, had been sent to Imphal and Kohima (100 at each) for garrison duty and to release more of the A.R. for active operations. Major Cloete with his detachment of the 2nd A.R. was now at Kaopum on the Silchar road, where he had experienced some fighting, particularly at Laibol north of the road, and had punished several villages. The Hinglep and Ukah men being particularly active in raiding near Moirang, Captain Goodall and Lieut. Carter with 120 rifles had moved out in late February and destroyed both places with some sharp fighting at each, in which they sustained some casualties. March saw the trouble spreading into the Jampi area north-west of Imphal between the Barak river and the north end of the Manipur valley, and Dulin, the chief village, being too far for Major Cloete to reach, Major Vickers with Lieut. Sanderson and 150 rifles 3rd A.R. were directed to proceed to Henema, whence, crossing the Barak, they reached and destroyed Dulin after some fighting at Chanjung and Kumpung, in which 1 rifleman was killed and 2 or 3 were wounded. The rebels bolted, some south, others north-east, where they induced the villagers of Laikot a little west of Maram to rise and raid near the cart road, endangering traffic. In early April detachments of the 4th and 3rd A.R. were sent out, who dealt thoroughly with Laikot and one or two other villages, and established posts at Kairong and Kanpopki for the protection of the cart road.

CHAPTER XVII

The Kuki and South Chin Hills rebellion—*continued.*

THE rapidly spreading rising amongst the Kuki clans was disconcerting and most difficult to deal with, all villages in the valley nearest the hills were in a panic, many suffered from sudden savage raids, and the number of rifles at Imphal was insufficient to maintain constant pursuit of raiding gangs in every direction. More men were wired for from Sadiya and Kohima, as a strong Column would shortly be needed to co-operate with the Burma Military Police in the Chassadh hills, where a most active Chief, Pachei, had destroyed many villages in both the Chindwyn and the Manipur valleys. As soon as Major Cloete's detachment from the Silchar road had reached Imphal it had to be dispatched at once to move through the Maphitel range against certain rebel villages in that direction. Supplies of clothing and boots which wore out rapidly under the wear and tear of this sort of life proved a source of great difficulty in replacement, the authorities not at first understanding the urgency of conditions expensive and new to them.

In early March the D.I.G. was ordered to Tammoo to meet the D.I.G. Burma (Colonel ffrench Mullen) and arrange a system of co-operation between his force and that of Assam. With an escort of 50 rifles under Jemadar Babu Lal, 4th A.R., Tammoo was reached without incident and arrangements were made for 4 Columns—2 from the Chindwyn side, that from Homalin under Major Hackett and from Kangal Thana under Captain Patrick—2 Columns from the Assam side, that from Imphal under Captain Coote, another of 200 rifles from

COOTE'S COLUMN HALTED AT THE TUYANG RIVER.

THE D.I.G.'s OF BURMA AND ASSAM WITH COLUMN COMMANDERS AT TAMMOO, MARCH 1918.

Kohima under Lieuts. Prior and Sanderson into the Somra area, while the other three operated on the Chassadh side. Orders were also issued to the 1st A.R. at Aijal to dispatch 100 rifles under an Indian officer to Bangmual on the south-west border of Manipur to guard that locality and co-operate if possible with either an A.R. Column operating in the Hinglep–Manhlung region, or with a Burma one due to operate up the Nankathe valley. Sketch Maps 2 and 6 show these localities. When all details had been settled and orders issued, the D.I.G. returned to Imphal, experiencing a little opposition above Tengnopal, where breastworks commanding the road had been put up and a little desultory firing took place. Here one of the curious leather cannons previously described which had failed to explode was taken, and Chenam village, partly rebuilt after punishment by Hebbert's Column, was burnt again.

In mid March a combined Column of 150 rifles (platoons from the 2nd, 3rd, and 4th A.R.) under Captain Coote with Lieut. Parry and Mr. Higgins left for the Chassadh hills, not without trouble at the start, when the Naga carriers suddenly struck and refused to carry loads. The wholesome spectacle of the 11 ringleaders being publicly flogged soon induced all to think differently, and they quietly resumed work. The route taken lay through the Aya Parel villages, certain of which had to be punished while others submitted, and on the Mangha river near Kangal Thana Coote joined hands with Patrick; both Columns then moved on north and attacked Kamjong, Pachei's principal village, in which action several casualties occurred and Lieut. Molesworth (Burma M.P.) was killed. The two Columns then proceeded by different routes against Chattik and Maokot, and in the fighting at the latter village Coote had 1 man killed and 6 wounded, Lieut. Kay Mouatt (Burma) being amongst the latter. Pachei, evading capture, fled into the Somra hills, an almost unknown tract. Lieuts. Prior and Sanderson with Mr. Hutton meanwhile had entered north Somra from Melomi with 200 rifles 3rd A.R. and advanced down the Nantaleik (Tuzu) river to block rebels from escaping into the Saramethi range and unadministered territory. They were opposed at Yungnoi and another place in which slight casualties occurred and one rifleman was killed.

At Sayapo, where there was some opposition, Coote linked up with Major Hackett's Column from Homalin, who had had a considerable action at Dansagu. It being now mid April and the heat being great, when little more could be done here, it was decided Coote's Column should move to Homalin, go by river steamer to Kendat and return *via* the Kale Kabaw valley, visiting and punishing Tuithang and Samdal villages in the hills south-west of Tammoo, this being an easier route than that of recrossing the difficult Chassadh country. This was done, and it was not till the middle of May that they reached Imphal.

During the last half of April further raiding by the men of Hinglep, Ukah, and Manhlung obliged another Column of 150 rifles under Captain Goodall with Lieut. Carter and the Political Agent to be sent out on that side, while the 1st A.R. was directed to order Subadar Bhowani Sing at Bangmual to co-operate in that region. Several small actions took place, causing Goodall a few casualties, particularly at the well-arranged night surprise of Bamkushan village, where he had 2 men killed and several wounded, but accounted for a number of rebels. Subadar Bhowani Sing was also successful in a fight and the burning of Gnarljang village, where he had two or three casualties. From Hinglep Goodall moved across the southern end of the Manipur valley to assist Lieut. Tuker, who, with a detachment, was near the Burma road, where the Kukis were still active in spite of previous punishment, and who had cut all the telegraph line down again. Aihang and Aimol were again destroyed when a little opposition was met with, and both detachments returned to Imphal, it being too late in the hot weather for operating. Just before this there was

GATEWAY OF SWINGING TIMBERS AT THE KAMJONG STOCKADE.

CAPTURE OF A KUKI BREASTWORK IN THE CHASSADH HILLS.

nearly a serious affair between Bishenpur and Kaopum on the Silchar road, to which latter place Lieut. Hooper was escorting a ration convoy, for the post recently established there. At Terelpopki a large gathering of Kukis from Laibol and Manhlung attacked him, his coolies bolted, many being cut up, and Lieut. Walker with 50 rifles had to be rapidly sent out to extricate him. After further skirmishing on the Laimatol hill, Kaopum, which had also suffered from attacks, was reached and rationed, the rebels retiring and leaving that post in peace for a time. In fact, the great heat being now well advanced made activity on either side impracticable, the Kukis appearing to feel it equally with us. Strong posts were put out at prominent points round the edge of the valley for protection at Moirang, Bishenpur, Shuganoo, Palel, and below Kanjupkhul, while in the hills those at Ukrul and Kaopum east and west of the valley were strengthened. Posts from the 3rd A.R. at Kohima were also put out at Kerami on the Somra side, and at Thalong and Chanachin on the Jampi side.

The D.I.G. was returning from Imphal to Shillong in early May 1918 when a wire was received at Kohima informing him that Kuki raiding parties were out in the north Cachar hills, the little civil station at Haflong and the tea gardens were in a state of panic, and measures for protecting that area were to be taken. The 2nd A.R. were ordered to dispatch 100 rifles at once under Captain Copeland to Haflong, where the D.I.G. met them. Here it was found that a raiding party of 70 to 80 Kukis had come to within 14 miles of the station but had retired again. The state of panic was such that a detachment of the Railway Volunteers with a maxim gun had been railed to Haflong, but returned on the arrival of Copeland. Posts were then established at Laitek, Hangrung, and Baladhan on the Manipur border, which were kept out till November, but nothing further transpired on this side.

We can now turn to the doings of Captains Falkland, 1st A.R., and Montifiore, 3rd A.R., who had been the first to be employed in suppressing the revolt in the Chin hills and of whose operations for a long time nothing was heard. Neither of them arrived at Haka in time to relieve it, having such long distances to traverse before reaching the scene. Haka, besieged for a fortnight, was relieved by a Burma M.P. Column under Captain Burne after two considerable actions between Falam and Haka and just before Falkland arrived. Being then sent southwards, his Column co-operated with two Burma ones under Colonel Abbay, Major Burne, and Mr. Wright, the Superintendent Chin Hills. They were engaged frequently, the principal actions being against the Yokwa Chins at Kapi, Aiton, Shurkwa, Naring, Sakta, and many other places where severe opposition was met with, for the Chins are stout fighters (Sketch Map 2). Falkland sustained many casualties and Mr. Wright and Mr. Alexander were badly wounded. Captain Montifiore, on reaching Haka, was sent first against revolting villages north-east of the Tao range, where at Bawkwa and Bwenlon much opposition had to be overcome. In late February 1918 he was sent with a mixed force of his own and Burma M.P. to Lenakot in the north Chin hills, whence he entered southern Manipur to retrieve the disaster to Captain Steadman's Column. He successfully attacked and destroyed the big stockades near Haika, incurring a few casualties and causing much loss to the Kukis, amongst whom was the redoubtable Gnulbul Chief of Longya, shot while trying to escape from the stockade with his little son in his arms. Later he punished the village of Tolbung on the Khatong range, which offered but slight resistance. In April Montifiore's Column found itself operating on the upper Boinu river (Koladyne), with fighting at Wantu and still further south at Laitet and Ngapai, where he linked with Colonel Abbay and Captain Broome's Columns. By June Falkland was allowed to march back to Aijal, and in July Montifiore and his men left for Rangoon, Calcutta, and Kohima. Both Columns received much kindly assistance in clothes, etc., supplied by the Ladies' War Society in Rangoon, which was greatly appreciated, and both had an extremely strenuous seven months' active service, Montifiore receiving the O.B.E.

The southern Lushai country was also not without its stir, for Chin raiding parties in May 1918 crossed the upper Koladyne, necessitating Mr. Bartley (Civil Police), in charge of Lung Leh, moving out with a detachment of the 1st A.R. to drive them back. Ambuscaded half-way down the Narchong ravine near South Vonlaiphai (which post had been given up a couple of years earlier), he had 2 men killed and 2 or 3 wounded, but eventually drove the raiders through Sangao back into the Chin hills with some loss.

Returning to Manipur, the hot weather precluding further operations, the detachment of the 2/2nd Goorkhas was sent to Peshawur, there being sufficient numbers of the A.R. to carry on through the rains. Petty raiding still continued but on a much smaller scale, and it was evident further extensive operations would be required in the coming cold weather. In Shillong many conferences were held at which the needs of the A.R. were set forth: more British officers, clothes, boots, etc., new rifles to replace the old worn-out Martinis (old when issued in 1900!), rifle grenades, mountain guns, transport animals, besides many other items, against the obtaining of which came naturally the argument of expense. Simla was appealed to for urgent assistance and promised to do what was possible, and in June the Chief Commissioner went up there, taking the D.I.G. with him, to interview the C. in C. and other officials relative to such aid, as well as personally to explain the situation. But before going there trouble suddenly arose on the Darrang border across the Brahmaputra, where in late May the Daphlas started raiding on the plains, burning Hellem and one or two other villages and carrying off captives. Captain Goodall with 100 rifles from the 3rd and 4th A.R. was dispatched to Tezpur, whence they proceeded to the border and entered the hills.

Two Daphla villages were punished without opposition worth mentioning, all captives were restored, and the force returned.

The visit to Simla resulted in orders being issued to re-arm at once the A.R. Battalions with new rifles, 4 more mountain guns and a supply of rifle grenades were sent, also more I.A.R. officers, while fresh kits were to be issued free to all ranks. Troops at this time could not be sent owing to the exigencies of the Great War, but the C. in C., who approved the fresh plans for the coming winter's operations, said he would place these under General Sir H. Keary, shortly to take over the command in Burma, with Colonel Macquoid to command at Imphal under his orders. On return to Shillong plans were perfected, all Commandants being ordered to reduce their local posts to a minimum so as to release every available man for active service when the rains were over. New rifles, ·303 long Lee-Enfield magazine, began arriving at the different Battalion headquarters, and training in these weapons, as well as of teams for the new mountain guns, was at once commenced. The new scheme for this second phase of the operations, originated by Major A. Vickers, 3rd A.R., and carried through with but slight alterations, was to divide the rebel hills into areas, appointing detachments for each, in which lines of posts were to be established sufficiently strong to enable them to combine in a number of small handy Columns with which to harry the rebels till they gave in; movable Columns also in each area were to drive the Kukis on to the line of posts. A difficulty existed in the numbers of friendly villages in amongst the rebel localities, and it was often not easy to distinguish these people from those to be dealt with. This was to a certain extent overcome during the hot weather by the Political Agent arranging for concentration camps in the Manipur valley to which all these friendlies were advised to repair in order to avoid the wrath to come. Large numbers responded, but many refused to leave the hills and so in some measure unavoidably suffered later with the guilty. But as undoubtedly these so-called " friendlies " gave succour and information to the rebels, much attention was not paid to any suffering those who remained behind may have experienced. In all some 54 posts came into the scheme, but the number was afterwards reduced.

The various areas into which the rebel hills were divided for this scheme were :—

Jampi area—between the Barak river and the cart road —its Supply Bases being at Bishenpur, Henema, Tapoo.

Hinglep–Manhlung area, south-west of the Logtak lake. Supply Base at Moirang.

Mombi area, south of the Manipur valley. Supply Base at Shuganoo.

Burma road area. Supply Base at Palel.

Chassadh area, east of the valley. Supply Base at Yangaipopki.

North Tankhul area, north-east of the valley. Supply Base at Tadapa.

North Somra and Tuzu river area, south-east of Kohima. Supply Base at Melomi.

Burma M.P. supply Bases for the areas on the Chindwyn side are shown in Sketch Map 6. A bullock transport train of 400 animals was organised in Imphal for supplying these Bases, and transport mules were purchased in Burma, but unfortunately proved useless, as " surra " disease broke out so badly amongst them.

In August General Keary, with Colonel Macquoid, arrived in Shillong and examined the scheme of operations, generally approving and only altering certain minor details. He then left for Burma, accompanied by the D.I.G., to meet and explain all to the Burma authorities and to fit in our plans with theirs.

Lieut. Sanderson's tour down the Nantaleik (Tuzu) river in April had resulted in the establishment of posts at Kerami and at Niemi and Matong north of that river which commanded the principal crossings, so as to prevent Pachei's gangs from escaping into unadministered territory, and desultory scrapping occurred near Kerami during June. In August Subadar Hangspal Limbu, commanding the post at Niemi, on receiving information from "friendlies" that a large body of Chassadh Kukis was approaching to cross the river, met them and in a sharp fight killed 30 of them and drove the rest back into Somra.

On the west the Jampi Chief had been captured, but the rebels on that side were now headed by two ruffians, Tinthong and Enjakoop, the last named having been some years previously in the 3rd A.R., and they kept the trouble going. In September Pachei, apparently tired of rebellion, had the impudence to send in to Burma his terms of surrender, which were referred to Assam and naturally not accepted. His people were now raiding in the Tankhul Naga country and about Ukrul, so Lieut. Parry was out in that part with a detachment for a long period during the rains, endeavouring to round up Pachei or any of his following. He was successful in a night surprise of Hoondong village, where a number of rebels were captured after a sharp fight. At Shipvomi also the Havildar Major 3rd A.R. with some of Parry's men had a short affair in which several people were killed and the place was destroyed.

Major H. D. Marshall
Captain H. B. Fox
Captain W. P. Reid
Lieut. R. G. Black
Lieut. G. D. Walker
Lieut. Scott
Lieut. E. J. Askwith
Lieut. C. F. Jefferys
Lieut. P. A. Armstrong
Lieut. G. Congden
Lieut. Needham
Lieut. Mawson
Lieut. Rees
Lieut. Goldsmith
Lieut. Mack (Transport)
Lieut. Willis
Dr. Crozier

By mid October the marginally noted additional British officers had arrived at Imphal and were distributed to various areas and duties; practically all belonging to the Indian Army Reserve and many had served in different theatres of the Great War.

They made, together with the permanent British officers of the A.R., a total of 30 officers for service during the second phase of operations. For the different areas and their various posts the following officers were detailed:—

Jampi area—Major Marshall, Lieut. Walker, Captain Montifiore, Lieut. Needham.

Hinglep area—Captains Goodall and Fox, Lieut. Carter.

Mombi area—Captain Coote, Lieut. Askwith.

Chassadh area—Captains Parry and Black.

Tankhul area—Lieut. Mawson.

Somra area—Captain Prior, Lieut. Rees.

Remaining officers were for movable Columns, Transport, and headquarters duties, Colonel Row being O.C. at Imphal, Major Vickers at Kohima. The Columns operating from Burma were:—

Major Broome's, from Kangal Thana.

Major Hackett's, from Homalin and Maungkan.

Captain Patrick's, from Tammoo.

Captain Rundall's, from Lenakot, and this Column was assisted by the friendly Kamhow Chief Howchingkoop and his men.

By the latter half of October the different detachments from Sadiya and Aijal began to reach Kohima and Imphal, but not without worry and delay, for a bad epidemic of "'flu" broke out, a detachment of 240 men 1st A.R. getting it badly, which caused them to be halted at Kairong, where they lost 11 men and 31 coolies, while numbers had to continue the march in carts, being too weak to go afoot. With this also came an outbreak of cerebral meningitis amongst Mack's Naga Labour Corps, which for a time had to be segregated. The posts in the North Cachar hills were now withdrawn, the men being sent round to Imphal.

However, all was ready in early November, and the force (2400 rifles) was handed over to the Brig.-Gen. Macquoid, who with his staff (Captains Coningham, Henderson, Lowry Corrie and Major O'Malley, P.M.O.) reached Imphal on the 7th, and a day or two later all Columns were in movement into their respective rebel areas. Gen. Sir H. Keary, G.O.C. of the whole operations, made his headquarters at Mawleik near Kendat. The total number of Indian officers and men from each Battalion were :—

1st A.R.	10 I. officers, 595 rifles
2nd A.R.	9 I. officers, 479 „
3rd A.R.	22 I. officers, 779 „
4th A.R.	16 I. officers, 709 „

In late November 1918 Marshall and Walker, moving from Kaopum against Tinthong's and Enjakoop's gangs, had an action at Laibol incurring slight casualties and burning the place which had been rebuilt. They then pursued the rebels westwards, having actions at Kebuching and Layang, where they were able to inflict considerable punishment. At the same time Montifiore and Needham from Tapao were moving on Nantiram and Dulin to co-operate with Marshall and establish posts at Chanakin, Lamlaba, and Layang. During December and January 1919 Goodall's Column was doing good work in the Hinglep–Manhlung area, experiencing much opposition from the offending villages of Ukah, Hinglep, Manhlung, Hengtham, and Chungyan, establishing posts and linking up with the Bangmual Column from the Lushai hills. Coote co-operating with Rundall from Lenakot succeeded after an extremely hard pursuit of Ngulkhub, the Mombi Chief, in driving him towards Tammoo, where he surrendered with his following. At one part of this pursuit Rundall's men covered 97 miles of stiff mountainous country in five days, several times coming on the rebel fires and nearly rounding the gang up, which to their great disappointment always just managed to evade capture. Several men fell ill and died of fever and exhaustion as a result of their strenuous time.

In the Chassadh area Parry and Black established their posts at Poshing, Langli, Chattik, and Maokot, linking up with the Burma Column, which had been delayed by " 'flu," and pursuing Pachei and his following into the Somra area, where Hackett and Parry after

CAPTAINS PARRY AND BLACK BUILDING THE STOCKADE AT POSHING IN THE CHASSADH HILLS.

TANKHUL NAGAS.

TANKHUL WAR DRUM.

some little skirmishing near Kalinoi dispersed the gangs by early March. Mawson at Chullao in the north Tankhul hills experienced but little excitement, but Prior in north Somra had some fighting near Lapvomi and south of Kerami and joined with part of Hackett's force at Mawvailoop.

By the spring it was evident the Kukis had had enough; they began slowly to surrender on all sides, and in April Pachei himself, having been driven all over the hills but never caught, came suddenly into Imphal and gave himself up. This, together with the capture of Tinthong and Enjakoop in Jampi area, marked the end of active rebellion, and in May operations were brought to a close, Columns were called in and dispatched to their different headquarters, leaving certain strong posts out in the various areas until the people settled down. These posts furnished by the 4th A.R. were Ukrul, Kamjong, Nantiram, Tamenglao, Chura Chandpur, Mombi, Poshing, Chanakin, and Kerami, the last two named being from the 3rd A.R.

Very little was known to the public of these operations; one or two Calcutta papers only published short and erroneous accounts of what they wrote of as "outings of Political Officers and their escorts," and generally belittling a long, hard "show" carried through eventually to a successful issue by the combined Military Police forces of Assam and Burma.

Had the Great War not been in progress it is more than likely a large force of Regulars would have been employed in suppressing the rising. The silence observed *re* these operations and their cause can be traced to the fact that the trouble arose through Governmental mistakes, and that when the trouble first showed itself it was not firmly dealt with. It grew therefore into the largest series of military operations conducted on this side of India since the old expeditionary days of Generals Penn Symonds and Tregear in the late 'eighties, or the futile Abor Expedition of 1911–12, eclipsing them all in casualties and arduousness of active service. During these operations all the advantage lay with the active scantily-clad Kukis, armed certainly only with the old "Brown Bess," but who know their hills and forests, carry no packs, do not bother themselves over supplies, who are rarely seen in their forests, and who are adepts at guerilla and jungle warfare.

Allusion has been made earlier to the belief that the rebellion had been still further fomented by emissaries from Bengal seditionists, but any idea that the hand of the Hun could possibly have been in it occurred to none. However, at Tammoo in May 1918, where a Column was assembling prior to breaking up after the first phase of operations, the Medical Officer going through the sepoys' huts found some Sikhs tearing up papers which they told the officer they would not want any more. He looked at the papers torn and whole, and found photos of one or two white men, obviously Germans, one being in uniform, and on them was written in Hindustani: "If you fall into the rebels' hands show these and they will not harm you." The sepoys could only state that when they were leaving Bhamo for the scene of disturbances a sahib had given them these papers. Who the sahib was, or if any strange sahib had been on the Chindwyn side, never transpired.

It is of interest to enumerate the results of the operations from December 1917 to 20th May, 1919.

86 rebel villages were destroyed.
112 ,, ,, submitted.
15 ,, ,, were deserted by the people.

970 muskets were confiscated in Manipur rebel areas and 600 odd in the south Chin hills, in spite of civilian disbelief in numbers in use amongst the Kukis, or that more than one or two hundred could possibly be found in the hills. The rebels also lost heavily, not only in killed and wounded, but also in grain and cattle confiscated.

Captain Montifiore's Column crossing the Upper Boinu River in the Southern Chin Hills.

The First Batch of Kuki Rebels taken Prisoners in Action in the Jampi Area.

Of the Assam Rifles the casualties were:—

Killed in action, 1 Indian officer, 34 riflemen.
Wounded in action, 1 Indian officer, 47 riflemen.
Died of disease contracted on service, 84 riflemen.

Of the Transport followers, 7 were killed and 393 died of disease.

On the Burma side the casualties were:—

Killed, 1 British officer and 38 sepoys.
Wounded, 4 British officers and 99 sepoys.

A large number of followers also succumbed to disease.

In addition to rebel areas being fined for their share in the rising and the imprisonment or deportation of all the prominent leaders, the Kukis were now made to open up their country by constructing fair bridle paths through their hills connecting with points in the Manipur and the Chindwyn valleys, and also connecting the various posts with each other. Many of these were begun by both forces, N.C.O.'s supervising their completion, and during 1919 and 1920 nearly 740 miles of decent bridle paths were thus made. It was also urged that a cart road should be made from Palel at the end of the existing road in the Manipur valley to Tammoo, and so on down the Kale Kabaw valley to Mawleik on the Chindwyn. The project presented no great difficulties, but expense precluded its construction.

In comparing the operations just narrated with the earlier important expeditions we find that General Penn Symonds' Columns in the Chin hills during 1889–90 had 66 casualties all told, those of General Tregear's in the same period barely reached 30, while of General Bower's force in the Abor Expedition, 1911–12, which was greatly written up in the newspapers, 4 were killed, 7 wounded, and 54 died of disease. The operations in the Kuki and Chin hills were included in the grant of the British General Service and Victory Medals and clasp for the N.E. Frontier.

To commemorate their combined operations together, extending for a year and a half, in suppression of this rising, the Burma Military Police Battalions presented the Assam Rifles with a handsome shield to be competed for in rifle shooting annually by the different Battalions.

General Sir H. Keary, K.C.B., K.C.I.E., D.S.O., in his final despatch on the operations, records that "the small losses sustained during so many months of incessant field service should not by any means be taken as the measure of resistance offered by the rebels, but rather is it a tribute, and a high one, to the fighting efficiency of mostly young troops, in all relating to the tricks and tactics of hill and jungle warfare, and to the use made of this knowledge by young officers in many cases with no war experience of any sort who had led them."

The following rewards were obtained for their good service during the Kuki operations: 1 C.I.E., 1 O.B.E., 5 Indian officers and 9 riflemen the I.D.S.M., 1 Indian officer the King's Police Medal. There were numerous "Mentions in Despatches," several were promoted on the field, and a number of "Jangi Inams" were granted.

CHAPTER XVIII

General items of information—Interior economy of the Force, pay, rationing, recruiting, signalling, etc.—The province of Eastern Bengal and Assam—Increase in strength—The Great War—The strikes and riots from 1920 to 1922—Expedition to the Rampa State (Madras)—Conclusion.

This history would not be complete without reference to the various changes which took place from time to time in the Assam Military Police Force in general, relative to pay, recruiting, rationing, etc. At the first start of the "Cachar Levy" in 1834–35 we have seen how this was intended to be a cheap semi-military body, its men enlisted for two years, clothed as were the armed Civil Police, and drawing pay ranging from 100 rupees per mensem for inspectors to 8 rupees for constables, with a small annual grant of 4 rupees per man for upkeep of kit. This obtained up to 1878, when the grant for upkeep of kit was found too small, so greatcoats became a free issue, and a few years later the annual kit allowance was raised to 6 rupees per man.

In 1882 on the reorganisation of the old Frontier Police units into Military Police Battalions, enlistment for three instead of two years was introduced, as under the shorter period resignations were too frequent. The following year saw the allowance of Good Conduct Pay sanctioned, as in the Army. After the occupation of Upper Burma, 1886–87, and the raising of new Burma Military Police Battalions, those in Assam began to suffer from numerous desertions to Burma, owing to men in that province receiving better pay, as well as to the more attractive conditions of life and service there. To counteract this trouble a grant of free passages to men going home on leave was made to the A.M.P., followed in 1890 by the annual kit allowance being raised to 30 rupees per man, while a ration allowance of Rs. 1/8 per mensem was sanctioned in the case of the Naga Hills Battalion, which unit being then nearest to Burma for long proved more attractive, desertions at last only being checked by the passing in 1891 of the Assam Military Police Regulation, in which, for the first time, provision was made for the due punishment of this offence.

The next improvement to be noticed took place about 1895 in the matter of rations, the permanent occupation of the Lushai hills providing the incentive to the procedure. Up to this period men of the force had had to provide their own food as in the Civil Police except in the Naga Hills M.P., whose men, as shown, received Rs. 1/8 per mensem. The prevailing attitude was that men's rations were no concern of Government, and that if a grant for the same were given it might only be spent in drink and gambling. In the Lushai hills, however, it was found impossible to buy food locally, hence arrangements were forced on Government to supply rations for the Battalion at Aijal. This was done, a ration scale was laid down, the Lushai Hills M.P. receiving what were called "free rations," but a deduction of Rs. 3/8 per mensem (only a fraction of the whole cost) was made from each man's pay on this account. A little later a corresponding but by no means identical concession was made to the other Battalions, but the fiction that the men provided their own rations was still maintained, though a cash allowance equal to the amount by which the cost of a standard ration exceeded Rs. 3/8 was made to each man. The pecuniary effect so far as the individual was concerned was the same as in the Lushai Hills Battalions, but Government was under no obligation to supply rations—it provided the cost and the man was supposed to buy his own. In practice, of course, such a condition of affairs was absurd, and the procedure actually adopted was that the rations were supplied by a contractor under the Commandant's supervision, and payments were made by deductions from the men's pay. Nevertheless the fiction persisted until 1922, when the men's pay was raised from 9 to 11 rupees a month, the deduction on account of rations being reduced to Rs. 2/8.

But long before these concessions made for general contentment in the force there had been trouble, notably in 1902, when the old problem of the better conditions of service and pay in the Burma Military Police gave rise to open discontentment. This showed itself chiefly in the North Lushai Hills Battalion, the men of which frequently had to operate in conjunction with their *confrères* of the Chin Hills Battalion (Burma), and who naturally thus learnt of the better conditions existing in that province. This state of discontent continued for a couple of years and spread to the small Silchar Battalion, where the inexperience of a very young Commandant proved incapable of dealing adequately with the first and only instance of organised insubordination which has occurred in the whole history of the Assam Military Police Force. A detachment of the Lakhimpur Battalion under a British officer was sent immediately to Silchar (1904) and succeeded in quelling the incipient mutiny before it actually attained serious proportions. The causes of discontent were removed, and under a new Commandant and with the imprisonment of the ring-leaders, the Battalion was brought into order again.

The period of the Great War produced the next change in internal economy, when the universal necessity for raising emoluments owing to the general rise in prices led to the conditions of service being examined. As a result of this concessions were made in 1918 in the monthly deductions from a man's pay in respect of rations, by reducing this to Rs. 2/8 instead of Rs. 3/8, thus virtually adding R. 1/- to his pay, while in addition the annual kit allowance was increased by Rs. 15/-.

This latter still proving insufficient with prices steadily rising, two years later the system of making a man pay for his kit was given up and replaced by a standard kit being issued and maintained by Government, provided a man took care to make the items last the prescribed time.

Regarding changes in uniform and weapons at different periods since the earliest days of the Frontier Police, these have already been detailed in previous chapters, and the Force is now dressed and equipped as are its *confrères* of the Indian Army.

Throughout the early years of their existence the Frontier Police were recruited in a haphazard way, the first bodies to be raised, *viz.* the "Cachar Levy," being filled with plainsmen from Bengal, and the "Jorhat Militia" mostly with local Shans long settled in that district. In Butler's day, about 1850, those from Bengal began to be eliminated, their places being taken gradually by Nepalese, Shans, and Cacharis. Ten years later Jaruas were tried, and proving their worth all F.P. units enlisted them when possible. A Recruiting Depot was opened at Sylhet in 1865 which, as it became known, brought numbers of Nepalese and Cacharis into the ranks, and this continued for some ten or twelve years, when it was closed down, each unit thereafter having to get its recruits as best it could. At one time an attempt was made to enlist Sikhs, Punjabis, and Dogras; the last-named, however, only proved a success, being freely enlisted for many years. The Naga Hills M.P. had two companies of Dogras up to 1905, when they were reduced to one company, being finally given up when the Great War confined recruiting temporarily to within the province only.

About 1887 the Government of India prohibited the enlistment of Goorkhas (Magars and Gurungs) from Nepal, as it might interfere with their recruitment for Goorkha Regiments of the Indian Army, which in 1886 had had their numbers increased by the raising of second

Battalions. This occasioned some difficulty in filling the M.P. ranks and recourse was had in all units to trying for more Cacharis and Jaruas, and even to seeing if local hill tribesmen could not be developed into good soldiers, but in this latter case without much success. The situation was relieved in 1891 when a new recruiting Depot was opened at Purneah near the foot of the Darjiling hills for the recruitment of eastern Nepalese, *viz.* Limbus, Rais, and Moormis, to which M.P. units were allowed to send recruiting parties. A few years later this Depot was moved from Purneah up to Darjiling.

After the withdrawal of the Regulars from Dibrugarh, Kohima, and Silchar in 1910, heavier duties falling to the M.P., they were allowed to enlist to 10 per cent. over strength. In 1897 the sanctioned strength of each M.P. unit was: Naga Hills 672, Lushai Hills 970, Lakhimpur 848, Silchar (the remains of the Surma Valley M.P.) 372, Garo Hills 202, and in 1910 these strengths were changed to 704, 850, 673, and the Dacca Battalion to 784, this latter unit having come into the Force with the amalgamation of Eastern Bengal and Assam. After one more numerical change the strength was finally fixed for each Battalion at 800 rifles in 8 companies or 16 platoons, *viz.* 4 companies of Goorkhas, 3 of Jaruas, 1 company of Cacharis, and a few local tribesmen. As we have already seen, two new Battalions were raised, the 4th A.R. in 1913 and the 5th A.R. in 1920.

Regarding the British officers with the Force, prior to 1882 the Frontier Police were officered from the Civil Police, but on the reorganisation into Military Police Battalions each unit was given an Army officer as Commandant, with an English sergeant to assist in training recruits and in certain matters of internal economy. With only one British officer per Battalion work was continuous and heavy, or less so according to the energy and conscientiousness of officers; but it taught young men to rely on their own initiative, to accept their own responsibility and much else that would not have been acquired in their regiments till they were far more senior in rank. This was altered in 1904 when the sergeants vanished and an Assistant Commandant was given to each Battalion, these officers being lent by the Indian Army for periods—in the case of Commandants four years extendable to five as heretofore, in that of Assistant Commandants for two extendable to three years. In 1915 a further stimulus was given to the efficiency of the Force by increasing the sanctioned strength of British officers per Battalion to 4, *viz.* the Commandant and 3 Assistant Commandants, but for some years a third A.C. was not posted to Sadiya. Many of these additional officers were from the Indian Army Reserve, as most of the Army officers had to rejoin their Regiments during the Great War. Mounted Infantry detachments were also tried in the 1st, 3rd, and 4th A.R., but being expensive and difficult to keep up did not last long, the ponies being then given up to transport purposes.

The wastage of all ranks throughout the Army becoming great from early days in the Great War, found the Indian Army Reserve unable to cope with the numbers of reinforcements wanted, especially in Goorkha Regiments, and the Indian Army turned to the Assam Military Police for additional men for these particular units. The response was immediate, volunteers came forward in numbers, 500 being dispatched on active service in the early days of 1915. The energies of all were now turned to training with a view to the requirements of modern warfare, and to enable this to be carried out all posts were reduced to a minimum, and Battalions were allowed to recruit up to a strength of 1000 rifles each. A small number of ·303 rifles and a Lewis gun were sent to each headquarters station, so that drafts for the Army could be trained in these weapons which they would have to use when joining regiments, as the A.M.P. were still armed with old Martinis. A certain amount of barbed wire and entrenching tools were also supplied for instructional purposes, and the Musketry course was brought more into line with that in the Indian Army.

As a result of this organisation and labour on the part of all concerned the A.M.P. by 1916 were supplying drafts to Goorkha Regiments at an average rate of 200 men a month until the end of 1917, when the Kuki rebellion obliged these Army drafts to be discontinued, as every available man was needed to suppress this trouble nearer home. Thus all above the normal strength of Battalions who would have gone to the War were retained. In all, the Lushai Hills Battalion sent 8 Indian officers and 817 men, the Lakhimpur Battalion 7 and 988, the Naga Hills Battalion 3 and 720, the Darrang Battalion 5 and 649, making a total of 23 Indian officers and 3174 men furnished as reinforcements to Goorkha Regiments, or an equivalent of the whole sanctioned strength of the Force. These drafts served in every theatre of the War in which a Goorkha Regiment was employed, *viz.* in France, Egypt, Gallipoli, Mesopotamia, North Persia, and the N.W. Frontier of India. That they proved their worth is shown by letters from C.O.'s of Goorkha Regiments to the Inspector-General of Police which will be found in the Appendices, and by the fact that 11 Indian officers and 69 other ranks received various honours which include 3 Indian Orders of Merit, 5 Indian Distinguished Service Medals, and 12 Meritorious Service Medals. The total casualties incurred by the Assam Rifles during the Great War came to 5 Indian officers and 237 other ranks killed, 6 Indian officers and 247 other ranks wounded.

Indeed so much was their value appreciated that the scheme originally put forward by Colonel Villiers Stuart, O.C. 5th G.R., but lost sight of for some years, was revived in 1924, when the formal sanction of the Government of India was accorded to the permanent affiliation of the A.R. Battalions to Goorkha groups of the Indian

Army, based as far as possible on the connections formed during the War. Thus the

1st A.R. (Lushai Hills Battalion) is affiliated with the 2nd Group, 2nd and 9th G.R.
2nd A.R. (Lakhimpur Battalion) is affiliated with the 5th Group, 7th and 10th G.R.
3rd A.R. (Naga Hills Battalion) is affiliated with the 1st Group, 1st and 4th G.R.
4th A.R. (Manipur Battalion) is affiliated with the 4th Group, 5th and 6th G.R.
5th A.R. (Darrang Battalion) is affiliated with the 3rd Group, 3rd and 8th G.R.

and the scheme provides that each A.R. Battalion shall be officered as far as possible from its own Goorkha Group, thus making for continuity of tradition, for mutual interchange of *personnel*, and for the reservation of each Battalion in time of War as a reinforcement for its own group in the Indian Army. The sanction states that "This affiliation takes place without interference with the status of the Assam Rifles as a Military force under the Civil Government." And so it should ever remain, for to incorporate the A.R. into the Regular Army would not only obliterate its *raison d'être*, but would deprive the Civil Power of the province, surrounded as it practically is by wild tribes of varying degrees of turbulence, of its best protection—a trained and mobile force ready to move anywhere at the need and will of the Governor, unhampered by all the red tape and officialism unavoidable in a Regular Army. Meanwhile, as a measure of recognition of the War services of the Assam Military Police, sanction was accorded to the old title being changed to that of the "Assam Rifles," the units being henceforth numbered as in the Army, *viz.* the 1st A.R. (Lushai Hills Battalion), 2nd A.R. (Lakhimpur Battalion), 3rd A.R. (Naga Hills Battalion), 4th A.R., 5th A.R.

Unfortunately at the time this numbering took place,

in September 1917, little if anything was known by those on the spot as to the history and development of the force, and the only one who did know arrived too late to make any change. Otherwise the Naga Hills Battalion, the senior unit, dating from 1835, should undoubtedly have been the 1st A.R., while the Lushai Hills Battalion, developed out of the old North Cachar Hills F.P. (1850), would have been the 2nd A.R., the Lakhimpur Battalion (1862–3) the 3rd A.R., and so on, as shown by old records and the general history of the province. With the changes of title in 1917 the whole force adopted the black buttons and badges of Rifle Regiments in place of the silver ones of the Military Police.

It had been long ago thought advisable to have a Deputy-Inspector-General appointed to Assam to relieve the Inspector-General of Police of the increasing work entailed on him by the M.P. Force, and whose own duties were heavy enough. This, however, did not materialise till the strain of the Great War and all the training and dispatch of drafts to the Army brought the matter up again seriously, and the billet was created, but not till the latter part of 1917. Colonel L. W. Shakespear, a former Commandant of the Naga Hills M.P. whose time on the Staff of the 15th Division in Mesopotamia had come to an end, was appointed D.I.G. and held the post till October 1921, when it was abolished on his retirement from the Service. Local recruiting within the province enforced in 1915 not being very successful, a Recruiting Officer with his headquarters at Shillong and a Depot at Gauhati was sanctioned early in 1920, to explore all possible fields for recruits, including also certain hill tribes. This, however, did not last long, for the billet was abolished in 1922, shortly after that of the D.I.G., owing to the need for financial retrenchment. The same year also saw a temporary reduction in the strength of the Battalions by 1 Assistant Commandant, 2 Indian officers, and 2 platoons owing to need for economy.

Reference must here be made relative to signalling, in which all Battalions from 1892 onwards made excellent progress. From 1895 to 1901 the Lushai and the Naga Hills units stand out pre-eminently, reports by the Army Signalling Officer at his annual inspections showing in the latter year the N.H.M.P. to have been 54 points better than the regiments stationed in the province. Two years later the annual report showed the same Battalion signallers to have been equal with those regiments standing second in the Indian Army, while the Lakhimpur M.P. equalled those standing tenth. This efficiency has been well maintained ever since. Long-distance signalling was carried out at different times, Shillong being linked by helio with Sadiya and Manipur *via* Kohima, and from Aijal in the Lushai hills helio communication was kept up in the fair season with Tuipang by two intermediate stations. It was also possible to connect with Falam and Haka in the Chin hills (Burma). The forested condition of both plains and hills in the Sadiya area made signalling communication not so easy.

A detail of this long-distance signalling carried out may be useful to future Commandants, especially as these chains of communication had been lost sight of for some years prior to the Kuki rebellion, as no records appear to have been kept. Particularly was this the case in the Lushia hills, where on the outbreak of trouble in the south Chin hills in 1917 no one had an idea as to where signalling stations could be located. Fortunately, the D.I.G., with memories of his early expeditionary days, 1889–90, in that area, was able to supply information.

Taking the Battalions in their order, the following are known chains of communication :—

1st A.R.

Aijal to Tuipang in extreme south *via* Maiphang, Sarep, Tuipang, 110 miles.

Aijal to Champhai through Lumtui hill, 50 miles.

Aijal to Bangmual through Lumtui hill and Chellám, 56 miles.

Aijal to Falam through Maiphang and Aikon Klang, 70 miles.

The latter had not actually been tried but is feasible.

Aijal to Shillong through the Bolpui stage on Silchar road to Cherrapoonji, thence to the Shillong Peak, about 130 miles. This also has not actually been tried but is feasible, with possibly one intermediate station between Bolpui and Cherrapoonji.

Lung Leh to Haka (Chin hills) through Fort Tregear, Tao Peak, or Hriankan village visible through the low saddle south of Tao, and the top of the Boipa Klang above Tlan Tlang village, 60 miles.

Lung Leh to Tuipang *via* Sairep, 45 miles.

Lung Leh to Aijal *via* Maiphang, 60 miles.

Maiphang to North Vonlaiphai, 30 miles.

2nd A.R.

Sadiya to top of Dibrugarh church, 54 miles.

Sadiya to Denning post, 35 miles.

Sadiya to Tamlu through Dibrugarh (church tower) and so to Kohima, 200 miles.

3rd A.R.

Kohima to Tamlu and Dibrugarh through Kohima, Nankam, Tamlu, 100 miles.

Kohima to Imphal through Japvo to Nongmaiching hill and Imphal, 65 miles. This only in clearest weather, as the distance from Japvo to Nongmaiching is great.

Or through Telitzu Peak near the Mao Thana, a peak above Mayankhong village, Sengmai, and Langol ridge.

Or through Sirishi, a peak 20 miles east of Kairong visible from both Imphal and Kohima.

Kohima to Shillong through Japvo to a point on the Hendong range south-west of Henema, to Shillong Peak, 150 miles.

4th A.R.

Imphal to Kohima as in 3rd A.R.

Imphal to Lenakot in North Chin hills through a point near Mombi, or one on Haobi Peak, 65 miles.

Imphal to Tammoo through Yaripok, Aimol Kulyen, Kongan, 52 miles.

Imphal to near Homalin on the Chindwyn river through Sirohi Peak, 70 miles.

5th A.R.

With a station on one of the hills near Gauhati and one at or near Tezpur; this unit might be able to link with Shillong; 120 miles.

The subject of the A.M.P. being called out in aid of the Civil Power has been touched on in the different chapters on the individual Battalions. The first occasion was after the amalgamation of Eastern Bengal with Assam after 1904, which introduced the M.P. to a new, arduous, and exceedingly unpleasant form of duty, which nevertheless was carried out with unquestioned loyalty and thoroughness. With the inception of the new province of Eastern Bengal and Assam unrest showed itself against the separation of the eastern districts from the rest of Bengal, and even affected the Dacca M.P. Thereafter the Swadeshi movement developed, political and revolutionary in character, which while nominally aiming at a boycott of foreign goods, actually took the form of assassination of British officials. Throughout the period 1906 to 1908 large detachments from all Battalions were out on deputation in various places in Eastern Bengal to maintain order and to prevent serious disorder developing. With the handing back of the Eastern Bengal district to their old province, Assam experienced no further trouble of this nature for several years; but in 1917 the A.R. were called on to dispatch 500 men under Major Vickers to Behar and Orissa province, where for two and a half months they were stationed at Arrah and Patna quelling disorder. In 1920 once more serious unrest started in Assam which kept the province, in common with many other parts of India, in a ferment of political agitation. Seditionists working on the minds of the ignorant coolie population fomented disturbances among the tea gardens in Lakhimpur, Sibsagor, and Darrang districts, which spread the following year to Cachar and Sylhet, culminating in the wholesale exodus of all coolies from the estates in the Chargola valley. Immediately on this during 1921 came a serious strike on the Assam Bengal Railway lasting several months and engineered by the same means. Finally, the non-co-operation movement, with its two branches "Khilafat" and "Swadeshi" developing on a very large scale, proved a serious menace to Government, actually subverting all established authority in places for a short time. It was beyond the power of the Civil Police to cope with the situation, and throughout the latter part of 1920, the whole of 1921, until well into 1922, all A.R. Battalions were continuously occupied in furnishing detachments for duty in almost every one of the plains districts to restore order, at one time over half the effective strength of the Force being employed in aid of the Civil Power in addition to a detachment of Manipuri State Police lent by the Maharaja.

Apart from the fact that this work was outside the ordinary sphere of activity for the Assam Rifles, these duties were in the highest degree unpleasant. As servants of the so-called "Satanic" Government, the men were assailed on all sides with insult and obloquy, and subjected also to the strongest pressure, both material and moral, in order to make them desert the Service, but without success. It is indeed the greatest tribute to the discipline and loyalty of the Force that it emerged from such experiences unscathed and with the well-deserved thanks of Government.

We now come to the last bit of active service outside the province in which the Assam Rifles were employed, when towards the end of 1923 the Madras Government, faced with another rebellion following on that of the Moplahs but in no way connected with it, applied to the Assam Government for assistance in quelling the trouble. This was responded to, and in January 1924 a Column from all Battalions of 3 British officers and 400 rifles under Major Goodall, Commandant 2nd A.R., was dispatched to the scene of disturbances in the Rampa State Agency on the east coast and a little inland of Walthair. Later another contingent of 50 rifles from each Battalion followed. The force was sent by steamer, and landing at Narsapatnam proceeded inland. The pursuit of revolutionary gangs was taken up at once, at first in "drives" covering areas of 8 by 12 miles, in which the men got to know the country and gradually drove the enemy out of his usual hiding places. By the middle of April the theatre of operations, covering 5700 square miles, had been divided up into squares each with its movable Column, fixed posts, and Intelligence Staff. This system, following the lines of that which brought the Kuki rebellion to an end, proved most successful; and after many skirmishes in which the rebel leader was killed and all his confederates were either shot or captured in various scraps, by mid June the trouble was stamped out completely after five months' arduous service in an unhealthy climate. In late June the Column returned to Assam, having well earned the thanks of the Madras Government. The A.R. men while engaged in these operations were granted the same higher rates of pay as were enjoyed by the Madras Special Police, and Subadars Jagatsher Limbu, 4th A.R., Kainbir Limbu, 3rd A.R., and Jemadar Surbir Ale, 2nd A.R., earned the King's Police Medal in recognition of their excellent work during the period of operations.

The troublesome "Unadministered Area" lying between the districts of Arrakan, Lushai Hills, Chin Hills, and Lower Burma which has been alluded to earlier as being an "Alsatia," harbouring the bad characters of the surrounding settled districts, was at last (1922) taken over as a Political Control area divided up amongst the older districts, and in which small annual winter military promenades will soon reduce this part of the country to order. It can therefore be said that, at present at least, the Assam borderlands are in a condition of quietude and content. The only portion of the province remaining still unknown is that lying between the Hukong valley, the Saramethi range, western Patkoi range, and the upper Chindwyn river.

This concludes the history of the Assam Rifles after a period of not far short of a century since its first inception as a formed body, ill-equipped and sketchily trained, through various stages of improvement, development, and organisation, into the five fine Battalions of the present day. They have proved their worth in countless frontier expeditions, large and small, in modern warfare, and in loyal suppression of much internal disturbance, which has caused them to be recognised by the Indian Army as worthy of being linked with its Goorkha Regiments. The fighting efficiency of the Force stands high and it is a very independent body, ready to move anywhere at any moment, according to the need of the Governor. Its men can house themselves, not only on service, but also in permanent stations, as has been shown, they have made hundreds of miles of hill roads, and every Battalion can produce numbers of men experts in handling boats, rafts, and in bridging—a most important qualification in a land of big and rapid rivers.

As stated before, the Force has done good service in every one of the many little wars which have taken place since the British first occupied Assam in 1826, in which, if the fighting value of the enemy has not always been very high, the difficulties of country and climate have been really very great; and it can truthfully be said that these difficulties have ever been surmounted with cheerful courage.

Of the future it is not possible to prophesy, but a considerable change in the location of one Battalion would seem within the bounds of future probability. The likelihood of the coming Hukong valley railway linking the Burma with the Assam systems, which would run 150 miles, in parts at less distance, from the Chinese border of Yunnan together with the eventual development of the Lohit valley trade route, may in all probability require protection. As the Lushai hills are now in a happy state of quietude which may well be lasting, it is not unreasonable to forecast that the 1st A.R., no longer needed there, might well find itself moved up to suitable locations on the Patkoi range and in the Hukong valley, filling the gap between the Burma M.P. at Putao and the 2nd A.R. at Sadiya. With the completion of this railway and the move of the 1st A.R., this Battalion would be in direct communication east and west; whereas in the Lushai hills Aijal is eight days' march from the railway at Silchar, and Lung Leh nine days' from Chittagong. Burma has now its Northern Province with its best M.P. Battalions distributed over that area, so with the A.R. and the Burma M.P. holding a continuous frontier line from the Darrang border right round to Kengtung near the Salween river and not far from a French post in Tonking, both our forces would acquire a name and prestige in the east of India, similar to that of the grand old force—the "Piffers" of N.W. Frontier fame.

This, of course, is imagination of far-off happenings, but of one thing the province may be certain, *viz.* that the Assam Rifles will be ever ready when wanted, and will ever maintain their traditions of faithful service, progress, and efficiency.

This work can now fittingly close with a reference to General Sir E. B. Barrow's lectu[illegible] in 1920 at the United

Service Institute, Whitehall, in which he stated he could testify to the admirable work done on the North-east Frontier of India by many officers and local units unknown to fame generally, though locally notable. He added that had this frontier (Assam) had the same limelight thrown upon it as the more dramatic situations on the north-western side have had, much more would have been heard of work and active service there.

CHAPTER XIX

Points of local interest connected with the areas of certain A.R. Battalions.

It may be of use to the officers of the 3rd, 2nd, and 5th Assam Rifles if some brief information is given them relative to ancient history concerning their particular areas, and to ruins of archæological interest, which may possibly lead to enterprising spirits in leisure times taking up further exploration of old-time cities known to have existed in their neighbourhood, and may give them interest beyond that of the daily routine and common tasks.

We will begin with what the "Father of the F.P. Force" (Mr. Grange) saw for the first time in 1840 in the Nambhor Forest at Dimapur (Sketch Map 4), and of which for many years nothing was known as to their origin, the history of the Province not having been then unravelled. During the years 1896–98 when the railway track was being cleared through the forest from Lumding towards Golaghat and construction work followed under Messrs. Thornhill, Buckle, and Venters, they opened up portions of causeways and canals, also turning up a considerable quantity of pottery of various sorts, particularly in the neighbourhood of Rangapahar, 7 miles south of Dimapur, all pointing to this locality having once been well populated and cultivated. About 1905 Mr. Gait, after infinite labour and research, brought out his history of Assam which cleared the mystery surrounding these remains, hitherto known to passers-by but ignorant as to their origin. Gait's work showed that Dimapur had once been the capital of the ancient Cachari kingdom up to 1575, when the conquering

Ruined Monoliths in Dimapur Fort as first seen.

The Same as restored to Original Positions and repaired in Lord Curzon's Time, 1902.

Ahom King Sukmungnung, moving up the Doyang valley, took another Cachari city, Jamaguri, and proceeded against the capital, which he sacked after a desperate defence by Detsing, its king. The Cacharis retreated far to the south and built a new city at Maibong in the North Cachar hills, and the Ahoms took over the whole of the area now covered by the Nambhor forest. As, however, they never really occupied it and it had in the war become depopulated, it gradually relapsed into the densest forest which we now see, and for centuries the only way of crossing it was by a rough track from Doboka to Maibong.

The old fort at Dimapur, one face of it fronting the Dunsiri river, stands just to the south of the present cart road a little beyond the railway station, and is described by Sir James Johnstone when he first saw it in 1874 as " surrounded by solid brick walls in a most ruined condition, bits of it still 12 feet high and 6 in thickness enclosing a space 750 yards square. Only one of the 4 gateways, that on the river front, remains in a fair state of preservation, and inside were found several tanks lined with bricks and with steps leading down to the water, also a certain number of masonry plinths, the entire space being covered with forest not easy to get through." The most astonishing remains inside the old fort are the huge stone monoliths all elaborately carved with representations of birds, animals, spear-heads, etc., which have stood the weathering of many centuries. They stand, these enormous blocks, in 4 rows 16 in each row, those at the ends being 10 to 12 feet, the central ones reaching 17 and 18 feet in height. The two rows to the east are not unlike huge " lingam " stones in shape, the western rows taking the form of a V, and are believed by some *savants* to be evidences of ancient Phallic worship. The tops have deep slots and grooves cut in them as if to receive the supporting timbers of a roof, but whether the roof of a temple, or of a covered approach to a temple long since crumbled away, it is impossible to say. What these monoliths really mean has baffled many a *savant*; Ferguson says they are unique of their kind in Asia, set up by a race long forgotten but still venerated by those who came afterwards, owing perhaps to the mystery surrounding them.

As there is no stone in the Nambhor forest, the nearest places from which such could have been quarried are at Nichuguard in the Diphoo gorge, and the carving must have been done when the blocks were in their final resting places, or it would have suffered in the 10-mile transit. This locality whence the stones were quarried was verified during the road-making operations through the gorge after the Manipur rising in 1891, when marks and holes drilled into rock faces were found showing where the old-time quarrymen worked their blocks out by drilling holes, which then had wooden plugs driven into them and which when wetted and swelling caused the required mass to split away from the parent rock. An engineer official told the writer some years ago, while prospecting for stone some distance below Nichuguard, lying at the side of the river bed he came on one of these rough blocks which had evidently been abandoned in transit for some reason or other. Whether these blocks were floated down the Diphoo stream on rafts to the Dunsiri river, or dragged across the country to Dimapur on sledges by hundreds of men, much in the same way as the Marami Nagas in the present day move their memorial stones, is not known. More likely the river was used when full in the rainy season, which the derelict block seen on the bank might point to.

The writer first saw the old fort and the monoliths in 1897, covered in forest and undergrowth, many broken and fallen through earthquake violence. In Lord Curzon's Viceroyalty, whose interest in ancient remains is well known, these were once more set up in their places, broken portions being securely fixed with

Ruined Gateway in the Ancient Cachari Fort at Dimapur.

One of the Large Excavated Tanks at Dimapur, in the Nambhor Forest.

iron bands, and the surrounding ground was cleared and fenced in for their preservation.

In the vicinity of Dimapur are to be seen several magnificent tanks excavated in far-off times ; on the finest, forming a sheet of clear water 300 by 200 yards, stood the first Rest-house, a commodious timber building only demolished in 1900 on the opening of the railway and the erection of a new Rest-house near it. While on the subject of the Dimapur ruins and the Cacharis, I may mention that about 1919 Major A. Vickers, then Commandant 3rd A.R., at Kohima, was shikaring in the Chatthe valley south-west of the cart road to Nichuguard, and came upon the evidences of an ancient fort of considerable size. It lay about 1½ miles from the present Ghaspani Rest-house and 400 yards beyond a dry river bed. Major Vickers was following up a badly hit tiger which he found lying in a pool in a deep sort of moat. Struck by the straightness of this moat, he later followed its course with great difficulty owing to dense jungle, and found it to average 10 feet in depth and to be in front of an earth rampart 8 feet high, each face being 300 yards long enclosing a large rectangular space. There were signs that the moat, which in places still held water, must have been filled from the river in the rainy season. One entrance only was found facing in the Ghaspani direction, with remains of a roadway approaching it, the moat being filled in at this point to carry it. Evidently from the masses of large stones lying about a wall once topped the parapet, some of these stones being still regularly arranged in courses. The whole locality was covered by forest and dense cane brake, and from the great size and age of the trees growing on and about the parapet, the fort must have been of considerable antiquity. Lying as it does in the low hills 19 miles from Dimapur and 8 miles from the Diphoo gorge, whence the stone monoliths were quarried, this fort may date from the early days of the Cacharis and the old city's prosperity in the

14th century or even earlier, and may have been one of a chain in protection against inroads by savage hill tribes. At first it was thought this fort might have only dated from our early expeditionary days, say 1850, as the old route into the hills lay up a portion of the Chatthe valley, and it might have been a defensive post on the line of communications or for storing supplies in. But we never built permanent military posts, as such would perforce have been, on this scale. Stone defences were not used by our troops anywhere in these hills except the small stone wall enclosure in Piphima village and the present-day stone fort at Kohima built in 1880–81. All other posts were invariably timber stockades which fell to pieces not long after their need had passed and they had been given up. Hence it is safe to conclude the old fort discovered by Major Vickers belonged to the Cachari times, and was probably a defensive post for the old capital.

Some 4 miles up the Doyang river from the railway bridge on the right bank is Jamaguri, the site of another old Cachari town covered by forest, and here have been found more of these curious monoliths though of less size than the Dimapur ones, and also less adorned with carvings. Very little clearing has been done here, which if taken in hand might well reveal more of interest. It is also said a large carved and solitary stone was seen years ago in the forest between Borpathar and Golaghat by men searching for limestone.

While on the subject of monoliths it may be mentioned that the Nagas (Angamis and Maramis) have always been in the habit of setting up huge stones to commemorate events in village life, or celebrated warriors, etc. In early days they set up huge plain blocks, but in the present day content themselves with smaller ones, which they laboriously dig out of ravines and drag up to the required site on wooden sledges, employing scores of men to move them. The Nagas of Maram, 12 miles inside Manipur territory and on the cart road, and

THE "STONEHENGE" AT TOGWEMA.

HUGE MONOLITH AT MARAM.

neighbouring clan villages have in the past set up the largest, and at Togwema (Uilong) (Sketch Map 4) one long march west of Maram near the mouth of the Typhini (Zupvu) valley, is to be seen a most remarkable Stonehenge of gigantic monoliths. So far the only Europeans to have seen this are the writer in 1900, Mr. T. C. Hodson, Assistant Political Officer at Imphal, and Mr. Hutton in 1923. Togwema is well situated at the end of a high spur jutting out into the valley and joined to the main mountain mass by a narrow saddle on which the collection of vast blocks stands, arguing a very large population in the far-off past in order to procure and drag the stones into position, probably a considerable distance, judging from the hillsides. The village nowadays is small, and one is told the Manipuris are responsible for reduction in numbers due to their ruthless methods of subjugating the tribe long generations ago. The erection of this Stonehenge would be impossible now, and from actual practices with stones of lesser size still set up by certain tribes, it is possible to obtain some idea of the expenditure in energy and the resources of the people of the past required for such stupendous undertakings. These Togwema monoliths are arranged 32 in a large and a small oval, from which again start two lines of 14 in each, the height of all varying between 8 and 14 feet with a thickness of 2 and a breadth of 3 to 10 feet. A flight of stone steps leads down to the large oval in which it is the custom of the unmarried men to perform ceremonial dances and wrestling matches at their annual festival for the dead. Mr. Hodson describes these stone monuments as falling into four categories: (1) those which are found either singly or arranged symmetrically in rows, avenues or ovals, (2) cairns or heaps of stones, (3) single smaller stones, (4) large flat stones supported on smaller stones as at Maram, Mao, and Keza Kenoma.

Some are memorials to departed notables, some are associated with luck, as in the case of the large hunting stone at Maram, and others are in memory of village prowess in war. Some of the small ones betoken ancestor worship, and practically all have a sanctity attaching to them and are annually worshipped. A further interest centres round Togwema in that it was below this village that Mr. Grange and his " Cachar Levy " were seriously attacked in 1840, and had to fight their way back up the narrow valley to Paplongmai.

A curious stone roughly carved with a peacock was found by Mr. A. Davis (then Assistant Commissioner at Kohima) about 1887. It stood in jungle on a hill north of the Merema saddle on the old Wokha road, somewhere about the 11th milestone and a good distance from it. The Nagas could not account for it, and it is believed to have marked the halting place of one of the Burmese forces which invaded the Assam valley some years before the war of 1825. Across the Typhini valley westwards one march stands the village of Bakema (Angami) (Sketch Map 6) with a somewhat sinister reputation, on a towering bluff looking down into the deep gorge of the Barak river, which strikes the traveller's eye from the Manipur cart road to the west and 4 miles south of the Maram Rest-house. It is noteworthy as being the refuge of numbers of Khonoma men and those of other villages wanted by the law for murder, robbery, and other crimes, and who have successfully evaded capture by fleeing to this species of Alsatia not easy of access. It is believed to have been visited only by one European, *viz.* the writer, when in May 1900 he trekked across the hills from the Henema post to the cart road at Mao Thana. He arrived there late one evening after a strenuous march from Chakabama across the Barak river, and found the inhabitants at first somewhat aloof and dubious as to the visit, till they found he was a soldier Sahib not bent on hunting up fugitives from the law. They then came round and helped put up his tent and in various other ways, all quite friendly. The following morning a number of cheerful ruffians came to his tent and through an interpreter complained of their bad luck in having to live in this distant spot, also discoursing freely as to their various crimes—robbery, raids, murder, arson, etc.; while one old white-haired man showed a handsome drinking horn mounted in silver with a silver plate inscribed "From Mr. McCabe, Deputy-Commissioner of the Naga Hills to (name forgotten), in memory of his visit with him to the Calcutta Exhibition, 1883." The old fellow had then been one of the head men of Khonoma, but having killed two men as a result of a feud, had fled here.

Turning to the Sadiya area controlled by the 2nd (Lakhimpur Battalion) Assam Rifles (Sketch Map 30), we find again remains of an ancient civilisation in ruined city sites, stone defence works, tanks, etc., now entirely buried in densest forests imaginable, between the Lohit river and the Mishmi hills. These are believed to have belonged to the ancient Chutiya race who owned the country from the Subansiri river eastward round to the Disang river, and were of the same stock as the Cacharis but of older origin; and the Deori Chutiyas, the last small remnant at the present day of a once powerful community, proudly claim to belong to the descendants of the Hindoo Khattrie line of kings who, according to Major Hannay, occupied this part of the country 2000 years and more ago. Nothing, however, is really definitely known as to the builders of these cities such as are evidenced by the ruins at Bishmaknager, Kundina, Payan, and Prithiminagar. Hannay, who served with and commanded the 2nd A.L.I. for years at Sadiya, seems to have made the only real effort at exploration here and of which he wrote accounts in the *Asiatic Quarterly*, 1848. He states the Deori Chutiyas claim is probably correct, in that their language contains a large proportion of Hindoo and Sanscrit words. That this old race was a literate one is shown by the Ahom "buranjis" (records), in which it is stated the Chutiyas were the only possessors of a written language met with at the time of their advent into Assam from Burma in A.D. 1220 and to conquer whom they found was a matter of time and difficulty. These city sites are all found many miles inland, which might point to the fact that when they were occupied by flourishing communities the Lohit river flowed much further north and nearer to the hills, the gradual alteration in its course southwards left the places without easy water supply, and the conquering Ahoms finishing off the inhabitants' discomfort, this area relapsed rapidly into a densely jungle-covered tract similar to the Nambhòr forest.

With interest stirred by stories told by Mishmis as to what these forests held, Hannay and some friends set out, being guided to a spot some 16 miles north of Sadiya near the foot of the hills between the Dikrang and Dibong rivers. The track led for 6 miles on the level, thence up the bed of the Dikrang, on leaving which the only onward track was that beaten down by wild elephants, and frequently this had to be cleared by cutting a way. The party then reached a fine piece of table land covered with splendid timber trees, where they came on the first traces of a bygone people, in a high earthwork rampart facing the plains. A little further on was found the remains of a strong parapet, its lower portion formed of solid hewn granite blocks topped by a wall of well-made bricks apparently loop-holed for spears and arrows. There were signs of gateways and many cross walls, but all had crumbled into the heap of bricks littering the locality. From what was seen these defences surrounded an immense area, while in the bed of the Dikrang were found numerous debris of earthen vessels closely resembling the earthenware of Gangetic India, and different from what was used in Assam.

Another ancient site explored by Hannay and friends was called Prithiminagar, also not far from the Dikrang river. Here they found an 18-feet high rampart with ditch circling round north and north-west for several miles. Inside this rampart, now supporting enormous forest trees, they came on several large tanks, one measuring 280 by 90 yards with ruined bathing ghats of hewn stone. A brick gateway was seen and a raised roadway to the river, where large stone slabs lying about suggested there might have been a bridge, and all pointed to the presence here once of a very large town. On the Kundil river Hannay also found traces of another place spoken of as Kundina, also as Bishmaknagar from the name of its legendary founder.

There are the remains of two shrines once famous in the far-off past to which Hannay found his way, *viz.* those of "Tamasari Mai" or the Copper Temple, from its copper roofing, and of "Bhora Boori." The former lies 8 miles up the Dalpani stream from Sonpura and was dedicated to Kamakhya and the Yoni, but Shiva and the Lingam were also worshipped with barbarous rites and human sacrifices. In ancient times this shrine, the sites just mentioned, and the once populous lands around were undoubtedly connected with the western end of Assam by the great raised roadway from Kamatipur in Cooch Behar through Narainpur to this extreme eastern corner. Long stretches of this road known as the Gosain Komla Ali are even nowadays in use, but very many generations have passed since the votaries at these shrines were numerous enough to keep open the roads leading to them. As late as the opening of the 19th century human sacrifice was still practised here, but ceased naturally on the British taking Assam in 1825. Hannay states that in 1850 there were still families living near Sadiya who for generations past had been set aside specially to provide the unpleasant honour of becoming victims to the dread Goddess, and who acquainted him with the gruesome details of the fatal ceremony. He gives a detailed description of "Tamasari Mai" as to size and shape of the well-hewn granite blocks forming the walls, and from signs in regard to bricks and a thin layer of mortar between them in the upper parts conjectures it may have been added to about the time of the Brahminical revival, *i.e.* in the latter part of the 11th century. When he saw it there were still some portions of the famous copper roofing to be seen but which have vanished now. The temple doorway was elaborately carved, and in front stood an elephant carved out of a block of porphyritic granite of a hardness requiring well-tempered tools to work with, and tradition says the tusks, no longer existent, were of silver.

The "Bhora Boori" temple visited by Hannay, lying some 15 miles from Sadiya across the Lohit river, is generally stated to be the most ancient as well as the most sacred shrine in Assam. Hindoos consider it as dedicated to Mahadeo, but Hannay is certain as to its Buddhist origin. A large hexagonal altar stands in a well-flagged courtyard, in front of which is a stone terrace on which offerings were placed, and a raised roadway led from the western face of it. Both temples are in a ruinous state and overgrown with jungle round and upon them, which growth, of course, displaces stones, while the general dilapidation is probably increased by the numerous wild elephants tearing down shrubs from the highest reachable points and rubbing themselves against the walls. In 1919 and 1920, when at Sadiya, the writer in company with Major Cloete (Commandant) and Mr. Jackman, American missionary, did a little exploring in these forests. When returning from inspecting the Denning post on the Lohit valley road inquiry of Digaru Mishmis as to any ancient remains led to the information of piles of bricks having been seen in the jungle near the foot of the hills and to north of Payan, the 3rd stage out of Sadiya, which they could take us to. About a mile or so below Payan Rest-house we turned north off the cart road and were soon swallowed up in the thickest jungle imaginable, through which our Mishmi guides cut and hacked, t we came on a narrow track used by the Chulikatta clan from the Dibong side, which further on crossed a jungle-covered raised roadway. After 4 miles of this and across two broad stony river beds our way was again cut into the jungle to the west, and soon we found ourselves crossing a high earthwork rampart with ditch in front, and which from the masses of bricks lying about showed a wall must have topped the rampart which enclosed, as far as we could get along it, a vast space. Inside this we found traces of tanks now choked with earth and jungle growths, many plinths and stone platforms, while a good way into this space was the brick plinth with in places 3 to 5 feet of walls standing, of what must have been an extensive building. The bricks were large and thick, nearly square, reminding one rather of those found in Mesopotamia at ruined Ur of the Chaldees, but without marks or ornamentation.

On another occasion the same party with elephants explored up the right bank of the Deopani river from where the Nizamghat road crosses it, and after hours of forcing our way through the forest came on to two fine sheets of water the sides of which were revetted with large bricks going well down to the bottom, all being laid endways. We also uncovered the stone-flagged descents to the water's edge made of large slabs, some being grooved to fit together. Evident signs of canals from the straightness of their courses were come across. Not very far from the road and river crossing our party found a long block of stone lying on the ground, one end just visible amongst the jungle. Dismounting from the elephants we began clearing it of surrounding growths when a broken column was revealed, well carved with a serpent twisted round, its head semi-human resting on the top. Later this pillar was transported into Sadiya, where, cleaned and with the two broken portions cemented together, it was set up on the golf course opposite the Political Officer's house. Round the base of it is an inscription worn with age and weathering, but apparently nothing could be made out of it. Enough, however, has been written to show that this locality has a history, and that those whose interests and activities tend towards exploration and diving into the remote past have a large field of operations ready to their hands.

Round about Sibsagor (Sketch Map 3) are also to be seen evidences of the old Ahom kings in the height of their power—the fine temples on the big lake, an old fort, the palace at Gargaon, and several magnificent tanks, all of which repay a visit and are best reached from Nazira station on the Assam Bengal Railway. In the same neighbourhood but near the foot of the Naga hills east of the Dikkoo river lies Charaideo, the early capital of the Ahom rulers, a number of whom were buried here. It was their custom also to bury here the heads of notables killed in battle, these tombs being covered by large mounds, some of which have been dug into, and human bones, ancient gold ornaments, etc., have been unearthed from them. One authority supposes Charaideo to have been the point at which the first Ahom force from Burma entered the Assam valley, but it is far more likely their route lay up the easier Hukong valley and over one of the low passes in the western Patkoi range, whence they would have entered Assam in the vicinity of where Margherita now stands. As their first conquests were over the Morans of Mattak and the Chutiyas across the Lohit, the latter route for their advance and entry into the valley is the more probable.

Maibong in the North Cachar hills (Sketch Map 4), the 4th station south from Lumding Junction, also possesses historical interest. Here the Cacharis in the 16th century, having had their capital, at Dimapur sacked by the Ahoms, retreated and built another city through which the Mahur river flows and which they occupied for 250 years. The construction of the hills section of the railway through the valley revealed the city's remains in forest-covered plinths, walls, roadways, etc. Further exploration, chiefly at the hands of Messrs.

Stevenson and Nolan (railway engineers), and in which during 1912 the writer took a small share, laid bare some stone statues, one or two inscribed stones clear enough to be deciphered, and a gigantic boulder 18 to 20 feet high and over 90 feet round at the base, the upper half of which is carved into the shape of a temple with an inscription showing it to have been fashioned in the beginning of the 17th century. It stands on the edge of the Mahur river close to and visible from the railway bridge, as the jungle has been cleared around it. Most of the statues and ornamented stones found here have been set up in the compound of the railway bungalow at Haflong.

In the locality watched over by the new 5th A.R. (raised in 1920) along the foot of the Aka and Daphla hills in the Darrang and North Lakhimpur districts are said to be the remains of bygone fortified towns of the Kocch days prior to those of the Cacharis and Ahoms, some of which were seen by Mr. Jackman in the neighbourhood of the Subansiri river (Sketch Map 3) and further west, but which locality the writer had no opportunity of visiting. Tezpur, the centre of civil administration of the Darrang district, shows likewise evidences of much bygone importance and grandeur in the massive granite temples and ruins in its vicinity. Copper-plate inscriptions unearthed here as well as carved pillars, etc., show that in early days Bana Raja's palace and fortress stood on the ground now occupied by the Deputy-Commissioner's office, and all goes to show that Tezpur at one time must have been the seat of powerful civilised princes; it is thought to be those of the Pal dynasty of A.D. 900. During 1920, while clearing a site for a house a little up stream of Tezpur, the workers uncovered what must have been a stonemason's workshop in ancient times, blocks of squared stone, some finished with grooves cut for fitting together and holes drilled to take iron clamps, others again in an unfinished state, portions of must completed carvings, etc., lying under a considerable amount of earth and jungle. Probably war caused the mason's labours to be closed down.

Gauhati (Sketch Map 1) nowadays has but little to show of its strength and importance of former days, and of which Captain Welsh, in a report on his expedition of 1792, writes he " found it a populous and large city on both banks of the Brahmaputra river with extensive commerce. A rampart along the river front mounted 113 cannon, while in the centre is a citadel—a large oblong enclosure with brick walls and surrounded by a wet ditch. The city entrances are through fine masonry gateways while the fortifications at Pandoo 3 miles off guard the river approach from the west." The map accompanying his report of the operations shows Gauhati to have been defended by many strong-works, the gap in the hills near the present Kamakhya railway station being particularly well fortified. The citadel mentioned, with its outworks, stood some 1200 yards from the foot of the Nilachal hills slightly west of the present Civil station. It also shows Korrye hill above Amingaon on the opposite bank to have been fortified. All these evidences of power and of thriving state have vanished. A hundred years later Mr. MacDonald, in his book on Kamrup, writes thus of the same place: " Of the former glories of Gauhati, whether under Hindoo, Ahom, or Burmese rule, the only relics which remain are the mounds and extensive lines of once brick fortifications, which lie scattered about the neighbourhood and the Brahmaputra bank. Gateways existing at the end of the 18th century have now entirely vanished. A large proportion of the soil in the surrounding cultivated fields is composed of brick dust, mortar, and broken pottery; while carved stones and beautifully finished slabs, the remains of once noble temples, are often found beneath the surface. The numerous large tanks attesting the command of unlimited labour possessed by ancient rulers, are now choked up with weeds and jungle." It is difficult to understand how in so comparatively short a

Inscribed Stones unearthed at Maibong.

Statue dug up at Maibong.

THE SERPENT PILLAR AT SADIYA.

Statues dug up at Maibong, in the North Cachar Hills.

Huge Boulder at Maibong, the Upper Part of which is cut into the Shape of a Temple.

ANCIENT HINDOO TEMPLES AT SIBSAGOR.

RUINS OF THE PALACE OF THE EARLY AHOM KINGS, AT GARHGAON, NEAR SIBSAGOR.

space of time as only a century all such evidences of greatness and power should so utterly have disappeared, to be replaced by a few pleasant bungalows along the river bank and a mildewed, dilapidated bazaar with an air of decay hanging over it.

Looking down on Gauhati is the beautifully wooded hill of Nilachal, well worth the climb up the steep path, stepped with heavy stones worn smooth by the feet of the myriads of worshippers at the famous temples which crown the hill top. These are mostly of great antiquity, the principal one being that dedicated to Kamakhya, the dread Goddess of the Tantric form of Hindooism, for centuries undisturbed and the dominant religion throughout Assam in olden days. It was a debased style of original Hindooism, and on the annual festival of Kamakhya human sacrifices were offered, certain girls out of the large numbers dedicated to the services of the temples being selected for the dubious honour, and of which Mr. Risley has written interestingly though with gruesome details. The extensive view from the topmost temple overlooking the noble river and surrounding ranges rising in tiers away to the Shillong Peak is alone well worth the climb.

Of our occupation of Goalpara (Sketch Map 1) and its early military importance there is little left beyond a few old masonry buildings, plinths of barracks and roads, on and around the conical hill above the steamer ghat; or of the once important fort of Jogighopa on the opposite bank near the mouth of the Manas river, the last officers to garrison which in 1824 are recorded as Lieuts. Crump and Lennon with two companies of English Infantry. Still Goalpara is worth a short visit if only, when standing on the hill mentioned overlooking the broad river, one can conjure up in mind the amazing spectacle which the Mahommedan general Mir Jumla's advance into Assam in 1662 must have presented, when old records state he collected a force of 12,000 horse and 90,000 foot at Dhubri a little below Goalpara, and moved up river. The account states he divided this army into two wings, one marching up each bank with a fleet of over 300 boats on the river between them. Many of these boats were of great size, were styled "Gharabs" (from the Persian word "ghorab," a raven), due to the sombre appearance of their sails and hulls, each carrying 12 to 14 cannon and 70 to 100 soldiers. The whole was the most formidable array of force which has ever entered the province, and to a watcher on Goalpara hill must have presented an exceedingly impressive spectacle. Eventual defeat a year and a half later was its portion, in spite of numbers and a capable leader who, struck down by illness, died on the retreat back to Bengal.

Throughout the Assam valley is still to be seen a series of raised roadways connecting old-time centres of population and industry, which was made by the very early rulers. Perhaps the most remarkable of these is the Gosain Komla Ali (Sketch Map 3), which was made in very ancient times by either the first Hindoo conquerors or their Kooch successors, according to Major Hannay, about the 4th century B.C., to connect the old capital Kamatipura (Cooch Behar) with the Chutiya cities and venerable shrines in the eastern corner of Assam. This was further raised and improved by Nar Narain, the Kooch ruler, in 1332 into a fine causeway for 340 miles of its length as far as Narainpur, which place he fortified. Up to this point it is in use even now for long stretches, but beyond Narainpur it is lost sight of in densest forests, save where a few clearings have revealed its presence.

On the Brahmaputra south side are several more of these great raised roadways each retaining its old time name, and in many parts still used. These were mostly made by old Cachari rulers from about 1040 A.D. on, and all attest the unlimited labour commanded by them, for Assam then was thickly populated, till later wars reducing the numbers, made it impossible to keep back the encroaching forests which now cover such large areas of once fertile cultivated lands. The best known of these roadways on the south side of the river are: the Dhodur Ali running from Nagura near Golaghat on the Dunsiri river through Titabar, Charaideo, and Borhat, ending at Tipam on the Bori Dihing river; Garh Ali and its continuation in the Seoni and Bogota Alis, which, starting from about the junction of the Kolliani and Dunsiri rivers, runs more or less parallel with and north of the Dhodur Ali through Jorhat, Rungpore near Sibsagor, Garhgaon, to the Bori Dihing river at Rangarora (Sketch Map 3).

To the writer this ancient life and its history had always been of deepest interest, but unfortunately it is not always possible to follow out such interests to the desired extent. A verse of the old Persian poet Abu il Illa illustrates feelings that must come to all thoughtful men when confronted with evidences of unknown ancient peoples, their labour, and war, etc. It runs:—

> "I never look upon the placid plain
> But I must think of those who lived before
> And gave their quantities of sweat and gore
> And went—and will not travel back again."

This, I trust, will be accepted as my excuse for having embarked on this chapter.

APPENDIX A.

LIST OF COMMANDANTS OF THE ASSAM RIFLES FROM 1882.

1st A.R. (*Lushai Hills Battalion*).

The old Surma Valley Frontier Police, later Military Police Battalion, were commanded by Mr. Daly (Civil Police) for many years. He was followed in 1882 by Lieut. Plowden, Capt. Bromhead, and Capt. Broughton. In 1890 the major portion of the S.V.M.P. was sent up to Aijal, where it became a separate unit, known from then on as the North Lushai Hills M.P. Battalion. As such from that year to the present time its Commandants have been:—

Lieut. H. W. G. Cole, 2nd Goorkhas, 1890 to 1892.
Captain (later Lieut.-Colonel) G. H. Loch, C.I.E., 3rd Goorkhas, 1892 to 1914.
Major H. C. Nicolay, 2nd Goorkhas, January to November, 1914.
Captain Hensley, Guide Corps, 1915 to 1917.
Captain Falkland, 13th Rajputs, 1917 to 1920.
Captain W. A. Gardner, 4th G.R., 1920 to 1921.
Major W. Lowry Corry, Bengal Cavalry, 1921 to 1924.
Major J. D. Scale, D.S.O., O.B.E., 1924.

2nd A.R. (*Lakhimpur Battalion*).

In the early days of the Lakhimpur Frontier Police they were commanded by Civil Police officers whose names are not recorded, as details of the unit's life prior to 1882 do not appear to have been kept, but the whole Frontier Police had only seven District Superintendents of Police with six Assistant D.S.P.'s to officer it. Mr.

Cawley's (Civil Police) name only appears as the last to command the unit before the reorganisation of the Frontier Police Force in 1882. He held command for the first year under the new organisation as a Military Police Battalion until an officer was appointed from the Indian Army. Thereafter the Commandants were successively :—

Captain E. H. Molesworth, 44th Goorkha Rifles, 1883.
Lieut. A. M. Maxwell, 6th Jat Light Infantry, 1888.
Captain G. Row, 44th Goorkha Rifles, 1894.
Captain J. B. Chatterton, 42nd Goorkha Rifles, 1899.
Captain A. T. Strange, 6th Goorkha Rifles, 1905.
Captain Sir G. Sutherland Dunbar, 1909.
Captain A. L. M. Molesworth, 8th Goorkha Rifles (temporary), 1914.
Captain H. R. C. Lane, 5th Goorkha Rifles, 1914.
Captain H. D. Cloete, M.C., 90th Punjabis (murdered at Sadiya, 1920), 1917.
Lieut. W. Bryce (temporary), 1920.
Captain G. B. Davies, 48th Pioneers (temporary), 1920.
Major W. Lowry Corry, Bengal Cavalry (transferred to 1st A.R.), 1920.
Captain W. A. Gardner, 4th Goorkha Rifles (died at Sadiya), 1921.
Captain J. M. Stapleton, Skinner's Horse (temporary), 1922.
Captain C. W. Thorpe (temporary), 1922.
Major M. Goodall, M.B.E., 9th Goorkha Rifles (transferred 4th A.R.), 1922.
Captain J. D. Sainter, 1925.

3rd A.R. (Naga Hills Battalion).

As with the 2nd A.R., there are no lists of Civil Police Commandants available during the years 1834 to about 1875, but from old books on the province one finds a few names that stand out, *viz.* Mr. Grange, who raised the Cachar Levy in 1834, the first formed body for border defence and forbear of the 3rd A.R.; Lieut. Gregory, in Civil employ 1866; Major John Butler in Civil employ and followed later by his son Captain Butler; Messrs. Broderick, Cawley, and Savi of the Civil Police up to 1881. Thereafter under reorganisation as the Naga Hills Military Police Battalion the Commandants are :—

Captain C. Plowden, 5th Bengal Cavalry, 1883.
Lieut. D. Macintyre, 2nd Goorkhas, 1888.
Captain Little, 21st Punjab Infantry, 1892.
Captain L. W. Shakespear, 2nd Goorkhas, 1897.
Captain H. Thompson, 1st Goorkhas, 1902.
Captain E. S. Gale, 2nd Goorkhas, 1905.
Captain C. Bliss, 8th Goorkha Rifles, 1908.
Captain A. M. Graham, 5th Goorkha Rifles, 1913.
Captain F. K. Hensley, Corps of Guides (temporary), 1914.
Major A. Arbuthnot, 7th Goorkha Rifles (temporary), 1914.
Major E. L. D. Fordyce, 87th Punjabis (died at Kohima), 1915.
Major A. Vickers, 48th Pioneers, 1917.
Captain W. S. Shakespear, 2nd Goorkhas (temporary), 1920.
Major A. Vickers, 48th Pioneers, 1921.
Major J. B. Gordon, 52nd Sikhs, 1922.

4th A.R.

This Battalion was raised at Dibrugarh in August 1913 by Major C. Bliss, 8th Goorkha Rifles, who commanded it for a year, thereafter followed by :—

Major Croslegh, 32nd Pioneers, 1914.
Colonel G. Row, late 8th G.R., who had retired but joined up in the War, 1916.
Captain P. B. Hebbert, M.C., 39th Garhwalis (temporary), 1920.

Major A. Dallas Smith, M.C., 2nd Goorkhas, 1921.
Major M. Goodall, M.B.E., 9th Goorkha Rifles (transferred from 2nd A.R.), 1925.

5th A.R.

Raised in June 1920 at Lokra in the Tezpur district:

Lieut. E. J. Hooper, I.A.R. (temporary), 1920.
Captain Ogilvie, 1st Goorkhas, 1920.
Captain R. Wright, Bengal Cavalry, for a short period.
Captain Abbott, 8th G.R., 1925.

APPENDIX B.

213. AFFILIATION OF THE ASSAM RIFLES WITH THE GURKHA INFANTRY GROUPS OF THE INDIAN ARMY

It has been decided, on the recommendation of the Government of Assam, that the Battalions of the Assam Rifles shall be affiliated to Gurkha Groups of the Indian Army. The affiliation will not in any respect affect the status of the Assam Rifles as a Military Police force under the control of the Government of Assam.

2. In pursuance of the arrangement above described, it has been decided that:—

(I) The battalions of the Assam Rifles shall be affiliated to the Gurkha Groups as detailed in the appendix to this Instruction.

(II) The British Officers of the battalions of the Assam Rifles shall be selected, as far as possible, from the Gurkha groups to which the battalions are affiliated, subject to the approval of the General Officer Commanding-in-Chief concerned, and of Army Head Quarters India.

(III) A party consisting of 1 Indian Officer, 2 Havildars, and 4 Naiks from each battalion of the Assam Rifles shall be attached for training annually to one of the four battalions of the parent Group; such attachment not to exceed a period of six months in any one year.

(IV) The Commandant and the Subadar-Major of the Gurkha battalion to which the party referred to in III above is attached for training may, subject to the sanction of the local military authorities, visit the affiliated battalion of the Assam Rifles during the year in which the training takes place, the cost involved by the visit being borne by the Government of Assam.

3. All other expenditure in connection with the scheme for the affiliation of the Assam Rifles to Gurkha Groups of the Indian Army will also be debitable to the Government of Assam.

Appendix to Army Instruction (India), No. 213 *of* 1925.

Details of the affiliation of battalions of the Assam Rifles with Gurkha Infantry groups of the Indian Army.

1st. (Lushai Hills) Battalion to the 2nd Gurkha Group (2nd and 9th Gurkha Rifles).
2nd. (Lakhimpur) Battalion to the 5th Gurkha Group (7th and 10th Gurkha Rifles).
3rd. (Naga Hills) Battalions to the 1st Gurkha Group (1st and 4th Gurkha Rifles).
4th. Battalion to the 4th Gurkha Group (5th and 6th Gurkha Rifles).
5th Battalion to the 3rd Gurkha Group (3rd and 8th Gurkha Rifles).

APPENDIX C.

COPIES of some of the letters from various Commanding Officers of Goorkha Regiments to whom the Assam Rifles sent reinforcements during the Great War between January 1915 and the end of 1918, and which show the value of their services during that period.

Copy of letter, No. 123/108/A, of 9th August, 1921, from the O.C. 1st K.G.O. Goorkha Rifles to the I.G.P. Shillong.

"I am very glad to take this opportunity of expressing on behalf of this Regt its high appreciation of the services of the men of the Assam Military Police who served with it from January 1915 to October 1918 in three theatres of war—*viz*. France, Mesopotamia, and Palestine, and who helped to maintain and enhance the reputation of the 1st K.G.O. Goorkha Rifles. I can assure you that their services were at all times of the most willing, their bravery and devotion to duty of the highest order, and to give them high compliment they fell at once into the order and discipline of this Regt as if to the manner born. We would have been disappointed with anything else from Goorkhas among their brother Goorkhas.

"In all, 1 Jemadar, 2 N.C.O.'s, and 156 Riflemen of the Assam Military Police served with us, of whom 14 were killed and 44 wounded. There were several promotions for gallantry and for deserving work, and they have themselves largely to thank for the fact that while with this Regt they were treated and regarded as 1st Goorkhas.

"I would be grateful if the men of the A.M.P. (especially those of the 2nd A.R.) still serving may be informed of our high appreciation of their work, and also that if at any future time of great stress their services be again lent, the reputation secured by their relations in the Great War will ensure them a hearty welcome with us."

Copy of a letter, No. 2639/47/E, of August 9th, 1921, from the O.C. 2nd K.E.O. Goorkhas to the I.G.P. Shillong.

" Two drafts of the Assam Military Police joined this Regt in France early in 1915. The first was a party of 1 Indian Officer (Subadar Mansur Rai) and 90 other ranks of the Aijal Battn (1st A.R.). They arrived at the Depot in Dehra Doon as early as November 1914. A second draft under Jemadar Bakhatman Gurung joined us in April 1915 in France after training with the 1/7th G.R. at Quetta, and consisted mainly of men from the Naga Hills and Lakhimpur Battn. A small party of these under Havildar Sasikarn Rai was attached to the 1/4th G.R. and proceeded with them to Gallipoli in August 1915. The remainder of these drafts left us in Egypt to join our other Battn in Mesopotamia.

" It is difficult adequately to express the gallantry, keenness and willing cheerful spirit displayed by the men of the A.M.P. whilst serving with us. They quickly settled down to trench warfare and conditions utterly unlike any they had formerly experienced, and rapidly identified themselves with the interests and spirit of the Regt.

" At Neuve Chapelle, Richebourg 9th May and Aubers Ridge 25th September, 1915, they took part in the attacks, showing the utmost gallantry. On the 9th May only two men of the assaulting Brigade reached the German line, both belonged to this Regt and one of them was from the Sadiya Battn. (2nd A.R.). It was on this occasion that Jemadar Bakhatman Gurung was killed while leading his platoon in the assault, while Capt. Mathew, who had been several years with the Garo and the Naga Hills M.P., was mortally wounded.

" Subadar Mansur Rai (Aijal Battn) was awarded the Indian Order of Merit for the following act of gallantry :—

" On the 25th September, 1915, this Officer led his Company across the parapet in the most gallant manner though exposed to a very heavy fire of rifles and machine guns. Later in the day when the attack was stopped he succeeded in getting his Company back with a number of casualties, and again went out in front of the parapet and was instrumental in bringing in several wounded under the most trying circumstances. Ever since this Officer joined us he has proved himself a capable and gallant leader of men. Awards of the Meritorious Service Medal were subsequently made to the following :

" No. 1443 Havildar Singbir Lama (Lakhimpur Battn).

" No. 1213 Havildar Sasikarn Rai (Lushai Hills Battn).

" The total casualties amongst the men of the A.M.P. while with this Regt were :—

" Killed—Jemadar Bakhatman Gurung and 9 other ranks.

" Wounded—18 other ranks.

" Missing—1 " "

" It is hoped that such survivors may be as proud of their record while serving with us, as this Regt is proud of its association with such a fine body of men, and for whose willing help and support in such strenuous times this Regt will ever be grateful."

Copy of a letter, No. 4219/V.M.P., of 8.8.21 from the O.C. 1/3rd Q.A.O. Goorkha Rifles to the I.G.P. Shillong.

" I beg to give you shortly what my experiences were in connection with the men of the Assam Military Police who joined our 3rd Battn when it was first raised in Palestine, February 1917, and who served with me. The preliminary organisation was made by Major G.R. Channer, D.S.O., and on my arrival in March I arranged so that all A.M.P. men were kept in their own platoons under their own Officers and N.C.O.'s. All were contented and worked with zeal and keenness, being especially noticeable for their eagerness to learn so that they could the quicker be ready to meet the Hun or the Turk. During the period February to June 1917 some 250 men of the A.M.P. joined us. For the distinctions they won I would refer you to this Regiment's records which at present are with the 2/3rd Goorkha Rifles at Dardoni on the N.W. Frontier.

"I regret I cannot give you further details, but I can assure you that the services rendered by men of the A.M.P. were worthy of their fine traditions and of the parent Regular Battn of the Goorkha Brigade with which they served."

Copy of letter, No. 97/9/110, of 5.8.21, from the O.C. 1/5th Royal Goorkha Rifles to the I.G.P. Shillong.

"Reference your letter No. 44/54 of 27/7/21, I have the honour to reply as follows:—

"Not very many men of the Assam Rifles served with this Battn during the war and then only in Mesopotamia, where they never really had a chance of proving their fighting powers. They were however extremely useful in every way, were excellent signallers, and owing to their initiative and resourcefulness were much used by this Battn.

"They identified themselves with us from the beginning, were easy to deal with, and never gave any trouble. Considering the circumstances under which they offered their services and the difficulties (impossible to avoid) which they had to contend with, I think their work can only be considered invaluable.

"I tried in 1916 or 1917, in conjunction with Major Molesworth, who had just come from duty with the Assam Military Police, to draw attention to a scheme which I considered useful, by which that Force would be affiliated permanently to the various Goorkha Regts so that in the event of war on a large scale again and the possibility of their services being lent, they might know which units they would be attached to.

"It was hoped that both sides would take more

interest in each other during peace, and that in the event of any Assam Riflemen joining their affiliated Battns they would feel they were going amongst friends. But I never heard more of the matter and did not like to press it.

"Personally, I consider the Assam Rifles helped the Army greatly in the war, that they would help it again, and I think the desire to effect liaison with them shows perhaps better than anything that their services were really appreciated throughout."

Copy of a letter, No. 1806/D.C./A.T., of 23.8.21, from the O.C. 2/7th Goorkha Rifles to the I.G.P. Shillong.

"Reference your No. 7344–54 of 27.7.21. I would like to address you on the subject of the most excellent work performed by men of the Assam Rifles who were attached to us during the Great War. Drafts from all A.R. units served with us. The first one of 200 rifles joined this Battn when it was in process of reforming in Mesopotamia after the fall of Kut in April 1916, and you may be pleased to learn that out of nothing we made a Battn again in 5 months, were sent up to join the 3rd Division, and one month later were in action, being the first of the reforming units to go up to the front line again. In December 1916 volunteers were called for to swim the Tigris at night and reconnoitre the Turkish position, 2 men of ours and 2 of the A.R. being chosen. These gallant four set off in the dead of the night in bitterly cold weather, but unfortunately the two Assam Riflemen were drowned in their courageous attempt. I could tell many tales of their bravery and devotion to duty at all times and of their exceptional cheeriness when circumstances were most trying and uncomfortable.

"It was with great regret that I parted with these men on our return to India from Palestine. For four years they had served with my Battn on active service in Mesopotamia and Palestine, and their loyalty, devotion to duty, and gallantry, was beyond praise."

Copy of letter, No. 7/1/219/A of 31/1/22, from the O.C. 1/8th Goorkha Rifles to the I.G.P. Shillong.

" I have asked several of my officers with whom men of the Assam Rifles served during the Great War and who state that the first draft which joined this Battn at Umballa in the spring of 1916 were an exceptionally fine lot and well trained. On service they were at all times willing to take on anything that turned up. The Jaruas amongst them were as willing as any to volunteer for any particular work involving risk. That their services were appreciated by us can be realised from the fact that of all the Indian Orders of Merit granted to us during the War, actually more than half were obtained by men of the Assam or the Burma Military Police.

" To mention individually, one of the most prominent was Motiram Mech, who gallantly captured a party of Turks single-handed at the battle of Istabulat, 21st April 1917, hunting them out of their trench at the point of his bayonet. The Jaruas were fine athletes and helped us a lot in sports and football, chief amongst them being Subadar Raimat Cachari and Havildar Maniram, both wonderful sprinters and the latter very good at football. In making things cheery during bad times the Jaruas were better than the Goorkhas as singers, dancers, and actors; prominent in this line was one Manmohan Rajbangshi of the 4th A.R.

" To conclude, the old reports of officers on men of the Assam Rifles contain the following terms:—smart and soldierly—keen and intelligent—good leader—keen and good Lewis gunner—and so on."

Copy of a letter, No. 27/3/44, of 6.8.21, from the O.C. 1/9th Goorkha Rifles to the I.G.P. Shillong.

" I have the honour to state that a draft from the 1st (Lushai Battn) A.R. joined us in early November 1914, and remained with us till our return from active service in Mesopotamia in 1917. During 1914–15 in France, although they were in no big actions they were almost continuously in the trenches, and were in 6 small battles This continued till March 1915, when the 1/9th G.R took part in the battle of Neuve Chapelle.

"The Battalion was in France till November 1915 and then sailed for Mesopotamia, being twice shelled by submarines during the voyage.

"The 1/9th G.R. returned to India in January 1917, having been continuously on active service for 30 months, and the A.R. draft which was with us throughout lost 7 men killed and 17 wounded. Jemadar Gajman Rai (A.R.) was awarded the I.D.S.M. for gallantry. I have made enquiries from many officers who knew your men well and all agree in saying that they were extremely good material, their standard of training was high, and above all, they were always a credit to this Battn during their stay with it."

Copy of letter, No. A.F./2/13 of 29.3.22, from the O.C. 1/10th Goorkha Rifles to the I.G.P. Shillong.

"A draft of A.R. volunteers under Subadar Nain Sing Sahi joined this Battn in Mesopotamia in September 1916 and remained with it until return to India in March 1920.

"The draft of the A.R. did splendid work throughout the whole of the four years they served in Mesopotamia with the unit under my command. Two of the draft obtained the I.D.S.M. for bravery in the field—*viz.* No. 734 Havildar Chandra Sing Chettrie for gallantry in action during the Arab Rebellion of 1920, and No. 1067 Rifleman Karnabahadar Chettrie for gallantry at the battle of Kala Shergat in 1918. The timely arrival of these A.R. volunteers filled a much needed want of trained men in Goorkha Regts when recruiting was strained to its utmost limits."

Copy of memo., No. 1468/27 of 5.8.21, from the O.C. 1/11th Goorkha Rifles to the I.G.P. Shillong.

"Only a few men from the Assam Rifles were transferred to this unit on its formation in Mesopotamia during

1918. All these had previously been serving with the 5th or the 6th Goorkha Rifles. They were re-transferred to Assam very shortly after this unit arrived in India in 1918, so very little was seen of them, but they were excellent men in every way."

APPENDIX D.

About the year 1900 Annual Police "Weeks" were instituted which were held at different Headquarter Stations in Assam, at which teams and individuals from the Civil Police, the Military Police, and the Volunteers competed for various athletic and sporting events. The Military Police also held their inter-Battalion competitions at these gatherings, which often, what with races and dances, came to be looked forward to and largely attended. These "Weeks" had to be discontinued about 1911, as several expeditions, followed by the Great War, precluded the possibility of holding them. With 1922 they were renewed but became an Assam Rifle week, and it is only from then that any records of winning teams have been kept. Prior to this the only notices of these events as concerned the A.M.P. are :—

1902 week held at Dibrugarh, when the Lakhimpur Battalion won the inter-Battalion Hockey Cup and the Musketry Shield.

1904 week held at Dibrugarh, when the Lakhimpur Battalion again won the same events, and the Naga Hills Battalion won the Shooting Cup.

1905 week held at Dibrugarh, when the Lakhimpur Battalion won the inter-Battalion Hockey Cup for the third time, and retained it.

1906 week held at Dibrugarh, when the Lakhimpur Battalion won the Musketry Shield, Tug of War Cup, and the Athletic Sports Cup, while the Naga Hills Battalion won the Hockey Cup.

1908 week held at Dacca, the Naga Hills Battalion won the Hockey and Tug of War Cups, and the Shooting Shield.

1909 week held at Dibrugarh, Lakhimpur Battalion won the Athletic Sports Cup and the Hockey Cup.

1922 week held at Jorhat, when the Naga Hills Battalion won the Athletic Sports and the Hockey Cups.

1923 week held at Dibrugarh, 2nd A.R. The Burma M.P. Musketry Shield, Daly Memorial Cup, Hockey and Sports Cups. 3rd A.R. The Football Cup. 1st A.R. The Fuller Cup.

1924 week held at Tezpur, 3rd A.R. Tug of War and Relay Race Cups. 2nd A.R. Football Cup. 4th A.R. Prize for best "turn-out." 5th A.R. Athletic Sports Cup.

1925 week held at Imphal, 4th A.R. Tug of War Cup. Fuller Musketry Shield. Burma M.P. Shield (Rifle Matches). Best "turn-out" prize. Daly Memorial Cup for best all-round Battalion. 3rd A.R. Putting the Shot prize. 2nd A.R. Football Cup. 5th A.R. Hockey Cup.

APPENDIX E.

CHANGES AND DEVELOPMENT OF A.R. UNITS SINCE EARLIEST FORMATION.

1st Assam Rifles.

1863 The Surma Valley or Cachar Frontier Police, formed from the old North Cachar Hills F.P., together with a Kuki Levy.

1891 The major portion of the Surma Valley Military Police moved up to Aijal and became the North Lushai Hills M.P. Battalion.

1860 A special body of Bengal armed Civil Police were formed for protecting and controlling the Chittagong Hill Tracts.

1866 This body became the Chittagong Hill Tracts Frontier Police.

1891 It became the South Lushai Hills Military Police Battalion.

1896 On Assam taking over the South Lushai Hills, this unit then was amalgamated with the North Lushai Hills M.P., which became known as the Lushai Hills M.P. Battalion.

1917 The 1st Assam Rifles (Lushai Hills Battalion).

2nd Assam Rifles.

1864 Previous to this year a body of armed Civil Police assisted the troops in border control and protection. In this winter they were formed into the Lakhimpur Frontier Police.

1882–83 Under reorganisation became the Lakhimpur Military Police. Battalion.

1917 The 2nd Assam Rifles (Lakhimpur Battalion).

3rd Assam Rifles.

1834–35 Previous to this the eastern border was guarded by armed Civil Police who assisted the Regular troops, and who in this year were made into the first specially formed body—the " Cachar Levy " for border duty.

1840 The Jorhat Militia was raised and later amalgamated with the Cachar Levy.

1851 The Cachar Levy's frontier line being too extensive for control from Nowgong, its Headquarters, the Levy was split in two portions, the major portion becoming known as the Nowgong Frontier Police, the lesser one as the North Cachar Hills F.P. Later this last-named unit became merged in the new Surma Valley F.P.

1868 The Nowgong F.P. became known as the Naga Hills F.P.

1883 On reorganisation it became the Naga Hills Military Police Battalion.

1917 The 3rd Assam Rifles (Naga Hills Battalion).

4th Assam Rifles.

1913 Raised this year as the Darrang M.P. Battalion.

1915 Sent to Manipur permanently and Darrang title dropped.

1917 Became the 4th Assam Rifles.

5th Assam Rifles.

1920 Raised this year for duty on the Darrang and Kamrup borders.

APPENDIX F.

Honours and Rewards gained by the Assam Rifles since 1891.

Year	Name	Honour
1891	Subadar Sangram Sing	Indian Order of Merit. South Lushai Hills rising.
	Havildar Chandra Sing Thapa	
1894	Havildar Major Bakshi Ram	Order of Merit—Abor Expedition.
	Havildar Bhuta Sing	
1897	Subadar Major Jitman Gurung.	Title of " Rai Bahadur."
1907	Subadar Major Arjan Rai	Title of " Sirdar Bahadur," also awarded the I.D.S.M. and King's Police Medal, and later Order of British India, 2nd Class.
1912	Jemadar Harka Sing Rai	I.D.S.M., Chinlong Expedition.
1912	Captain G. S. Dunbar, Sergt. Dorward, Subadar Jangbir Lama, and Jemadar Sarahjit Thapa were mentioned in despatches	Abor Expedition.
	Subadar Jangbir Lama	I.D.S.M. (Abor Expedition.)
	Havildar Dalbahadar Thapa	
1913	Captain A. Graham	K.P.M., Daphla Expedition.
	Subadar Sanjai Subha	Order of British India, 2nd Class, and later the title of " Bahadur."
1914	Major C. Bliss	C.I.E., K.P.M.
	Subadar Major Jamaluddin	K.P.M.
	Subadar Hari Ram	
1915	Subadar Major Jamaluddin	Order of British India, 2nd Class, and later the title of " Khan Bahadur."
	Captain Montifiore	O.B.E., Chin Hills rising.
1917 to 1919	Subadar Hari Ram	I.D.S.M. Kuki operations.
	Subadar Nain Sing Mal	
	Jemadar Hanspal Limbu	
	Rifleman Kishenbahadur Chettrie	
	Havildar Jangbir Gurung.	
	Rifleman Bhabajit Rai	
	Subadar Pokul Thapa	K.P.M., Kuki operations.

Also 6 Riflemen specially promoted in the field, numerous " mentions " in despatches and a number of Jangi Inams were granted for these operations. Ten Indian officers and 22 other ranks also received various honours for the Kuki operations.

1915 to 1920	Eleven Indian officers and 131 other ranks were specially promoted on the field, and 7 Indian officers and 69 other ranks were awarded various honours, including 7 I.O.M., 5 I.D.S.M., 12 M.S.M. . . .	The Great War.
1920	Subadar Major Hetman Rai .	The title of " Rai Bahadur."
	Subadar Birman Thapa . Jemadar Satal Sing Cachari .	I.D.S.M.
1921	Colonel L. W. Shakespear, C.B., C.I.E., Kuki Operations.	
1924	Subadar Major Jangbir Lama .	The title of " Sirdar Bahadur."
	Jemadar Surbir Ale . Subadar Jagatsher Limbu . Subadar Kainbir Limbu .	K.M.P., Rampa State Rebellion.
	Subadar Major Mansur Rai .	I.O.M.

INDEX

Abors :
Origin and locality, 37
Early troubles with tribe, 38
Lowther's expedition, 1858, 41, 42
Hannay's expedition, 1859, 42–45

Affiliation Scheme :
Assam Rifle units with Goorkha Regts., and details of same, 245, 246

Aijal :
Started as a small station, 1890, 95
Improved and rebuilt by Col. Loch, 99, 100

Akas :
Early troubles with tribe, 36
Graham's expedition, 1914, 194–96

Appendices :
A. Lists of Commandants, 274–77
B. The Affiliation Scheme, 278, 279
C. Letters from C.O.s of Goorkha Regts. *re* War Drafts, 280–87
D. Sports Weeks, 288, 289
E. Development of A.R. units since early days, 290, 291
F. Honours and Rewards, 292, 293

Armament :
Muzzle-loading muskets, 1835, 23
Enfield rifles, 1871 and 1877, 72, 142
Snider rifles, 1881 and 1891, 97, 158
Martinis, 1901, 187
Lee-Enfield, ·303, long, magazine, 1918, 230

Asaloo :
Post established, 1844, 20
Becomes a civil station, 1852, 29
Given up in favour of Gunjong, 1868, 52

Assam :
Early history, 1–7
Defence of, 5–7
Assam Gorkha Regts., 6–7
Protection of Province, 53–57
Assam becomes a Province, 2, 142

Bhutan :
First contact with Bhutanese, 1826, 33
Pemberton's mission, 1837, 34
Hon. A. Eden's mission, 1863, 34, 35
War with Bhutan, 1864, 35, 36

Blockades of tribes :
Akas, 36
Daphlas, 37
Abors, 38
Eastern Nagas, 47
Naga Hills clans, 29, 51, 154

Bogchand (*Daroga*) :
In charge of Samaguting, 1849, 23
Visits Mozema, and disaster at Piphima, 24

Brigg's Trace :
First road from Sylhet to Gauhati, 1828, 12

British officers (with Frontier Police):
Prior to 1882 and after, 243
Since 1904, 244

Butler (Major J.) :
Commands the Cachar Levy, 1845, 20, 22, 51
His son commands Naga Hills F.P., 1868, 52, 112, 141
Placed in charge of Naga Hills, 142
Action at Wokha, 1874, 143
Killed at Pangti, 1875, 144

Cachar :
Brought under British control, 1826, 10
Becomes a Regulation District, 1830, 11
The Cachar Levy formed, 1835, 7, 8, 9
Its duties and defensive posts, 12, 13
Its uniform, 1850, 23
Jorhat Militia added to it, 1852, 30
Cachar Levy split in two—Nowgong and N. Cachar F.P., 1852, 29
New Cachar Frontier Police Battn. raised, 1863, 50

Camp of Exercise :
Mayankhong, 1901, 187

Cherrapunji :
Civil and military station started, 1829, 12
Given up for Shillong, 1866, 50

Chittagong and the Hill Tracts :
Chittagong taken over by British, 1761, 60
Mr. Verelst first Chief of, 10, 60, 61
First recorded expedition (Ellester's), 1777, 61
Early border line, 1795, 61
Troubles with Arrakan and border extended, 61
Rennell first to visit South Lushai border, 1800, 61
Naaf River Expedition, 1823, and first Burma War, 61, 62
Disaster to Noton's force at Ramu, 62
Hodgkinson's exploration, 1848, 62, 63
Forlong's road through Arrakan hills to Burma, 1850, 63
Mutiny at Chittagong, 1857, 63, 64
Raban's expedition, 1861, 64
First body of Special Police formed, 1862, 65
Hill tracts definitely taken over, 1862, 65
Armed Civil Police becomes Bengal Frontier Police Battn., 1867, 66
Major Lewin first Superintendent, 1864, 65

Civil Power (aid to) :
In 1917 and succeeding years, 137, 139, 197–99, 205, 207, 250–52

Communications :
Early days in Assam, 3, 4
Nowgong to Dimapur, 1846, 22
Silchar to Upper Assam, 1849, 22, 23
Shillong and vicinity, 1866, 50
Sylhet to Gauhati, 1829, 12
First reconnaisance Hukong valley route, 1835, 40, 41
South Lushai hills, 1889, 87
Lung Leh to Haka, 1890, 93
Lung Leh to Aijal, 1896, 105
River route to Aijal improved, 107
Proposed railway routes to Burma 1890, 121
Wokha to Golaghat, 1876, 145
Naga Hills roads, 1892, 170
Dimapur cartroad to Manipur, 1892, 181
A.B. railway construction, 1898, 183, 184
Roads opened in Manipur hills, 1920, 237
Ancient roadways in the Assam Valley, 272, 273

Daphlas :
Early troubles with tribe, 36
Corrie's and Stafford's expeditions, 1871, 36, 37

Deputy Inspector-General :
First appointed to the Assam Rifles, 1917, 209, 247
Abolished in late 1921, 247

Dimapur :
Ruins first discovered, 1840, 17, 256–58
Its destruction by the Ahoms, 17, 257
Old fort and monoliths, 257, 258

Expeditions :
Earliest ones, 3, 5, 9, 10, 38–40
Lister's (Khasi hills), 1829, 12
Ellester's (S. Lushais), 1777, 61
Burma War, 1824, 10, 11, 61, 62
Brodie's (Eastern Nagas), 1840, 47
Blackwood's and Lister's (Lushais), 1844, 21, 22
Grange's (Nagas), 1840, 16–19
Eld's and Wood's (Nagas), 1846, 20
Vincent's and Foquett's (Nagas), 1850, 25–29
Eden's (Mishmis), 1855, 46
Lowther's (Abors), 1858, 41, 42
Hannay's (Abors), 1859, 42–44
Mutiny at Chittagong, 1857, 63, 64
Synteng Rebellion (Khasias), 1860, 49, 50
Raban's (S. Lushais), 1861, 64, 65
Bhutan War, 1864, 35, 36
Lewin's (S. Lushais), 1865, 65
Garstin's (Abors), 1865, 111
Gregory's (Nagas), 1866, 52
Nuthall's (N. Lushais), 1868, 59
Bourchier's and Brownlow's (Lushais), 1871, 67–76
Corrie's and Stafford's (Daphlas), 1871, 36, 37
Holcombe's disaster (E. Nagas), 1875, 112–14
Butler's (Rengma and Lhota Nagas), 1874, 143, 144
Williamson's (Nagas), 1875, 145
Siege of Kohima (Nagas), 1879, 148, 149
Nation's campaign (Nagas), 1879–80, 151–56
Sambudhan's Rebellion (N. Cachar hills), 1882, 80, 81
Sale Hill's (Akas), 1883, 115, 116
Tiernan's (Ao Nagas), 1884, 161
Macintyre's (Sema Nagas), 1887 and 1889, 165, 166
Maxwell's (Masungjami), 1888, 167–69
Tregear's first (S. Lushais), 1889, 86–88
Tregear's second (S. Lushais), 1890, 89–93
Rising in N. Lushai hills, 1890, 95, 96
Trouble in S. Lushai hills, 1891, 96–98
Rebellion in Lushai hills, 1892, 100–106
Maxwell's (Abors), 1894, 117–20
Row's (Aoa Tanangs), 1894, 120
Porteous' Somra tour, 1890, 173, 174
Manipur Rebellion, 1891, 176–81
L. W. Shakespear's (Yachumi), 1900, 184–87
Bliss' (Makware and Somra), 1910, 189, 190
Bower's (Abors), 1911, 125–33
Mishmi and Lohit Valley reconnaisance, 1912, 134, 135, 191–93
Loch's and Wilson's (Trans-Dikkoo Nagas), 1913, 192, 193
Graham's (Akas), 1914, 194–96
Goodall's (Daphlas), 1918, 137, 138
Kuki and S. Chin hills rising, 1917–19, 209–38
The Great War, 1914–20, 109, 136, 196, 244, 245
Vickers' (Trans-Lanier Nagas), 1920, 199
W. B. Shakespear's (E. Nagas), 1923, 199
Rampur State Rebellion (Madras), 1924, 139, 200, 252

Forests :
Density, 37, 38, 68, 79, 88
Nambhor, 160, 161, 257, 263, 264

Frontier Police Battalions :
Raised, 1835, 8
Early uniform and equipment, 7, 8, 23
Changes in same, 52, 53
Reorganisation recommended, 1875, 53–57
Carried out as Military Police Battns., 1882, 158

Frontiers :
Earliest eastern, 1830, 5
Frontier drawn back, 1852, 29
Forward policy with tribes renewed, 1865, 51

Garos :
Their country, origin, and subjugation, 30–32

Grange (Mr.) :
Raises first Frontier Police unit (1835), 8, 13
His early expeditions into the Naga hills, 16–19

Gregory (Mr.) :
At Samaguting, 1866, 52

Gunboats :
Indian Marine gunboats on Brahmaputra, 1826–60, 39, 42

Gunpowder :
Local make, 78, 79

Historical interests :
The Dimapur ruins, 256–59
Jamaguri ruins, 260
Monolithic remains, 260, 261
Bakema village, 262, 263
Ruins in Sadiya area, 263–67
Ruins in Sibsagor area, 268
North Cachar hills (Maibong), 268, 269
Tezpur area, 269
Gauhati area, 270, 271
Goalpara, 271, 272
Ancient highways, 272, 273

Hukong Valley :
First proposals for route to Burma, 1835, 40
Bennett's reconnaisance, 1836, 40, 41
Surveys for railway, 1895 and 1919, 121

Inspections :
Annual inspections by G.O.C.'s began, 1887, 171
General Mitchell's, 1898, 171, 172
General Keary's Report, 1919, 238
Sir John Kerr's, 1925, 206

Jamaluddin :
Subadar Major, Naga Hills M.P. Battn., 1924, 200

Jitman Gurung :
Subadar Major, S. Lushai M.P. Battn., 1895, 89

Jorhat :
Militia unit raised, 1838, 8
Amalgamated with Nowgong F.P. 1852, 30

Kekrima :
Vincent's fight at, 1851, 27–29

Khasias :
Origin, 11
First Khasia rising, 1829, 12
Second Khasia rising, 1863, 49
Dunsford's expedition, 1863, 49, 50

Khonoma :
Major Foquett's assault of, 1850, 26, 27
General Nation's ditto, 1879, 151–54

Kohima :
Military and Frontier Police post established, 1877, 146
Besieged by Nagas, and Damant's disaster, 1879, 147–49

Kuki Levy :
First formed in Cachar, 1850, 22, 51, 58
Habits of Kukis and autocratic rule, 30
Mr. Edgar's adverse remarks on them, 1872, 71

Kuki Rebellion :
Kuki and S. Chin hills rising, 1917, 209–38

Lakhimpur F.P. Battn. :
Raised 1864, and its early posts, 111, 112
H.Q. moved from Dibrughar to Sadiya, 1913, 136
Becomes 2nd Battn. Assam Rifles, 1917, 137

Lewin (Major T.) :
Appointed first Superintendent Chittagong Hill tracts, 1864, 65
Boundary settlement with Arrakan, 65
Early border posts, 66
Serious Lushai raids, 1871, 67
Lewin with General Brownlow's force, 1871, 72–75
Rangamatti becomes Civil H.Q. station, 1867, 66
Border posts on new frontier line, 1872, 76
Revision of posts and their strengths, 76
Retirement of Lewin and his monument, 77

Lung Leh :
Post established, 1889, 89, 94

Lushais (or Kukis) :
Origin, 64
Early expeditions, 21, 22
First visit of Lushai notables to Silchar, 22
Lushais under autocratic rulers, 30
Nuthall's and Stevenson's expeditions, 1868, 59
Establishment of F.P. posts and their reduction, 76, 89, 93, 107, 108

Manipur State :
Origin of tribe, 15
First visited by Jenkins and Pemberton, 1826, 5
Butler and Brown settle boundaries, 1868, 52
Johnstone with Manipur troops at Kohima, 1879, 149, 150
Manipur State forces, 175, 176
The Rebellion, 1891, 176–80
State's aid to Civil power in Assam, 1921, 251

Mishmis :
Dr. Griffiths first visits the tribe, 1836, 45
Murder of French missionaries, 1855, 46
Eden's punitive exploit, 1855, 46, 47
Molesworth's expedition, 1899, 122
Mishmi and Lohit Valley Exploration and survey, 1912, 134
Abigail's punitive expedition, 1920, 138, 139

Missionaries :
Drs. Bronson and Clarke, 1852, 47, 48
Messrs. Lorraine and Savidge, 1891, 109

Naga Hills :
Wokha held as a post 1875 to 1902, 143, 187
Kohima established as H.Q. station, 1877, 146
Military Police posts, 1884, 159
Ao Naga country taken over, 1889, 170

Nagas (Eastern) :
Brodie's early visits to, 1840–44, 47
Holcombe's disaster, 1874, 112–14
Loch's and Wilson's expedition, 1913, 192, 193

North Cachar hills :
Asaloo post established, 1845, 8, 20
Frontier Police Battn. formed, 1852, 29
Gunjong becomes H.Q. station, 1869, 52
Ancient remains (Maibong), 268, 269

Nowgong :
Military and Civil station, 1826, 5
Special Police Force formed, 1835, 8
"Cachar Levy" divided into Nowgong and North Cachar hills F.P. Battns., 1852, 29, 30
Frontier Police moved from Nowgong to Naga hills, 1872, 141

Patkoi Range (Hukong) :
Early expeditions and posts, 1826 to 1850, 9, 39

Pay, etc. :
As Cachar Levy, 1835, 239
As Military Police, 1882, 239, 240
As Assam Rifles, 1918, 241, 242

Police :
Civil, 5
Armed Civil, 7

Railways :
First line and extensions, 1883, 4
Further railway proposals, 1850 and 1895, 63, 121
Assam–Bengal Railway begun, 1897, 184, 256

Rampur State Rebellion :
Details of A.R. units sent and their work, 1923, 252

Recruiting :
Civil Police, 1830, 7
Shan Militia (Jorhat), 1838, 8
Nepalese, Cacharis, and Jaruas enlisted, 51, 66, 133, 243
Depots opened at Sylhet, 1865, Purneah, 1891, 51, 242, 243
Sikhs and Dogras tried, 1882, 57
Finally only Goorkhas and Jaruas enlisted, 57

Sadiya :
First occupied, 1826, 9
Col. White's disaster, 1839, 9
Bruce's first visit to Rima, 1828, 40
Neufville's and Charlton's expeditions, 1835–43, 39, 40
Early description of, 40
Becomes Military Police H.Q., 1913, 136
Present Lines completed, 1920, 138
Ancient remains, 263–67

Samaguting :
Establishment of first post at, 1848, 22, 23
Abandoned and frontier withdrawn, 1852, 29
Frontier again advanced, 1865, 51
Post moved to Kohima, 1877, 145, 146

Sambudhan's Rebellion :
In North Cachar hills, 1882, 80, 81

Scott (*Mr. David*) :
First Agent in Assam to the Governor-General, 1826, 4, 5, 11, 12

Shillong :
Station decided on and started, 1866, 50
The Happy Valley detachment, 1920, 207

Signalling :
Introduced in M.P. Battns., 1892, 248
Communications by, 249, 250

Somra area :
Porteous' first visit, 1889, 173

Surma Valley F.P. Battn. :
Protection of Cachar and Sylhet borders revised, 1862, 58
New F.P. Battn. formed at Silchar, 1863, 58
Moved up to Aijal and becomes N. Lushai Hills Mil. Pol. Battn., 1891, 99, 100
Sedition and strikes, 1920, 251

Sylhet :
First taken over by British, 1765, 10
Sylhet Light Infantry, 1824, 7
Frontier Police recruiting depot opened, 1865, 51
Sedition and strikes, 1921, 251

Tea Industry :
First garden started in Upper Assam, 1832, 3
Ditto in Cachar, 1855, 3

Tregear (*Fort*) :
Built, 1890, 93
Destroyed by fire and abolished, 1898, 108

Tribes :
Origin of Nagas, Kukis, Lushais, 14, 15
Origin of Manipuris, Abors, etc., 15, 37
Naga village " Khels," 25

Tularam's Rebellion :
In N. Cachar, 1841, 20

Unadministered area :
Between Arrakan and S. Lushai hills, 107
Taken into Political control, 1922, 253

Uniforms :
Cachar Levy's, 1835 to 1864, 7, 8, 23, 239
As Frontier Police Battns., 1868, 52, 53, 141
Khaki adopted, 1885, 56, 158, 164, 171
Chittagong F.P. Battn., 1871 and 1894, 72, 97, 106
Assam Rifles, 1917, 241, 242, 247

Value of Force :
Its efficiency, 253, 254

War Drafts :
Naga Hills M.P. (3rd A.R.), 196, 245
Lakhimpur M.P. (2nd A.R.), 130, 245
Darrang M.P. (4th A.R.), 202, 203, 245
Lushai Hills M.P. (1st A.R.), 245

Welsh (Capt.) :
His first expedition into Assam, 1792, 3, 270

Weapons (tribal) :
Angami Nagas, 1841, 19, 27, 29, 112, 153
Kukis and Lushais, 1852, 30, 77, 205, 216, 220, 225
Abors, 1859, 43, 120, 129
Burmese, 1824, 62
Trans-Dikkoo Nagas, 1887, 166
Manipuri, 175

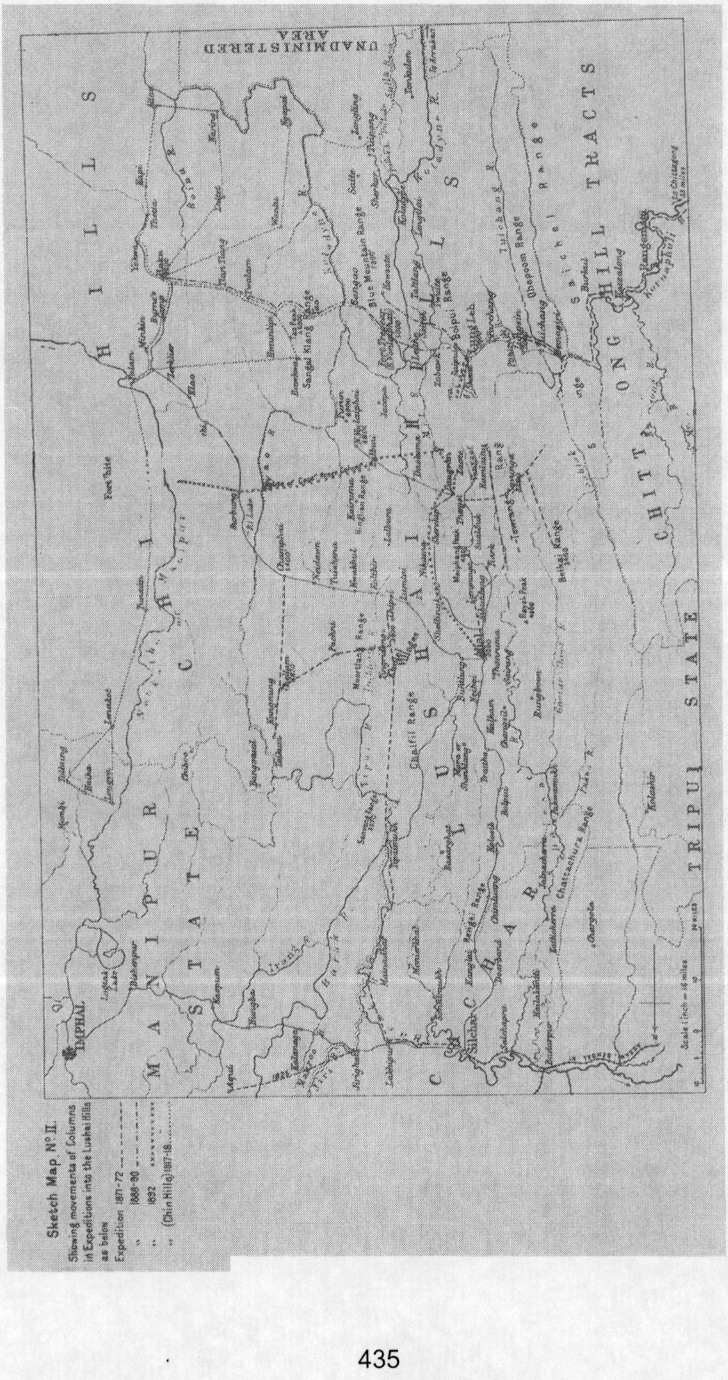
Sketch Map No. II
Showing movements of Columns in Expeditions into the Lushai Hills as below
Expedition 1871-72
" 1888-90
" 1892
" (Chin Hills) 1917-18

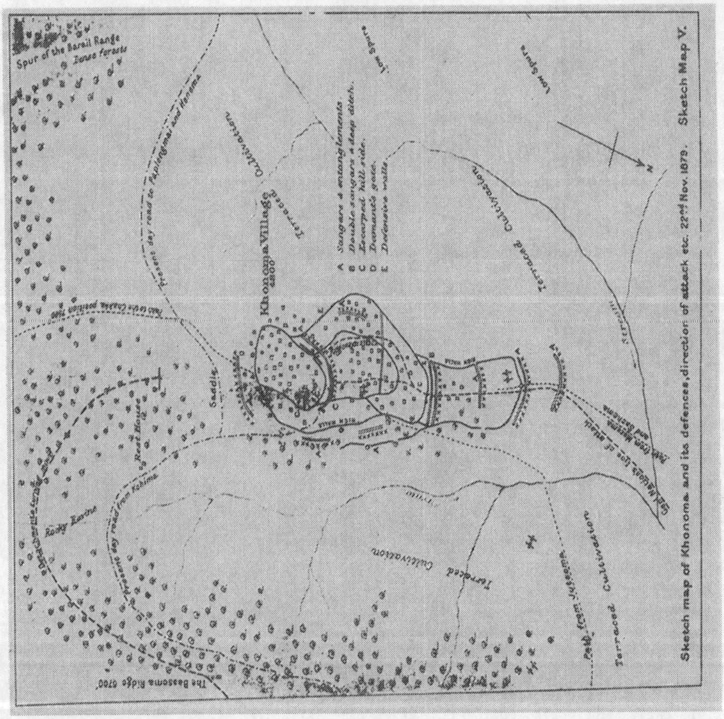

Sketch map of Khonoma and its defences, direction of attack etc. 22nd Nov. 1879. Sketch Map V.

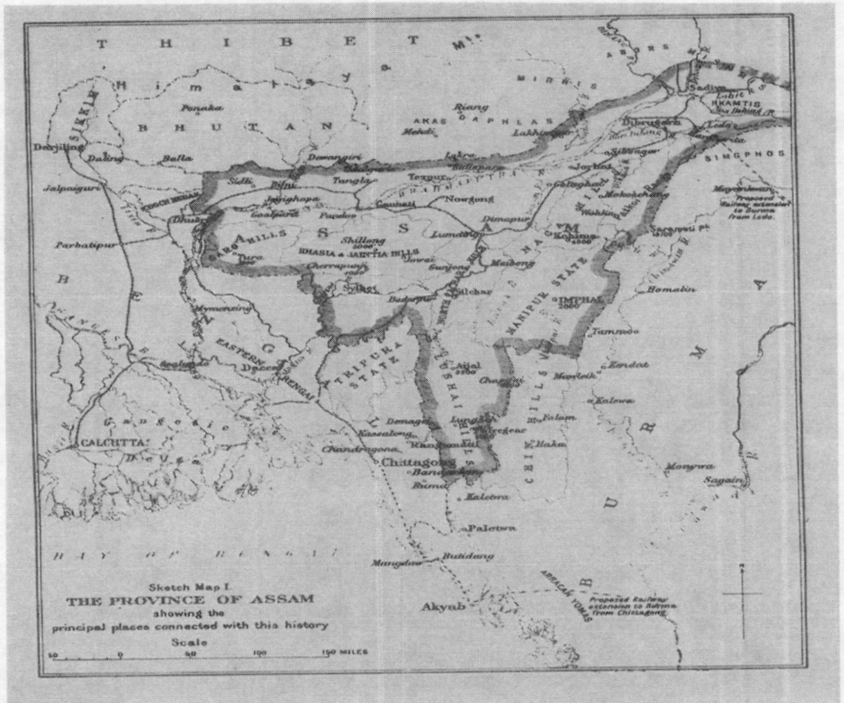

Sketch Map I.
THE PROVINCE OF ASSAM
showing the
principal places connected with this history

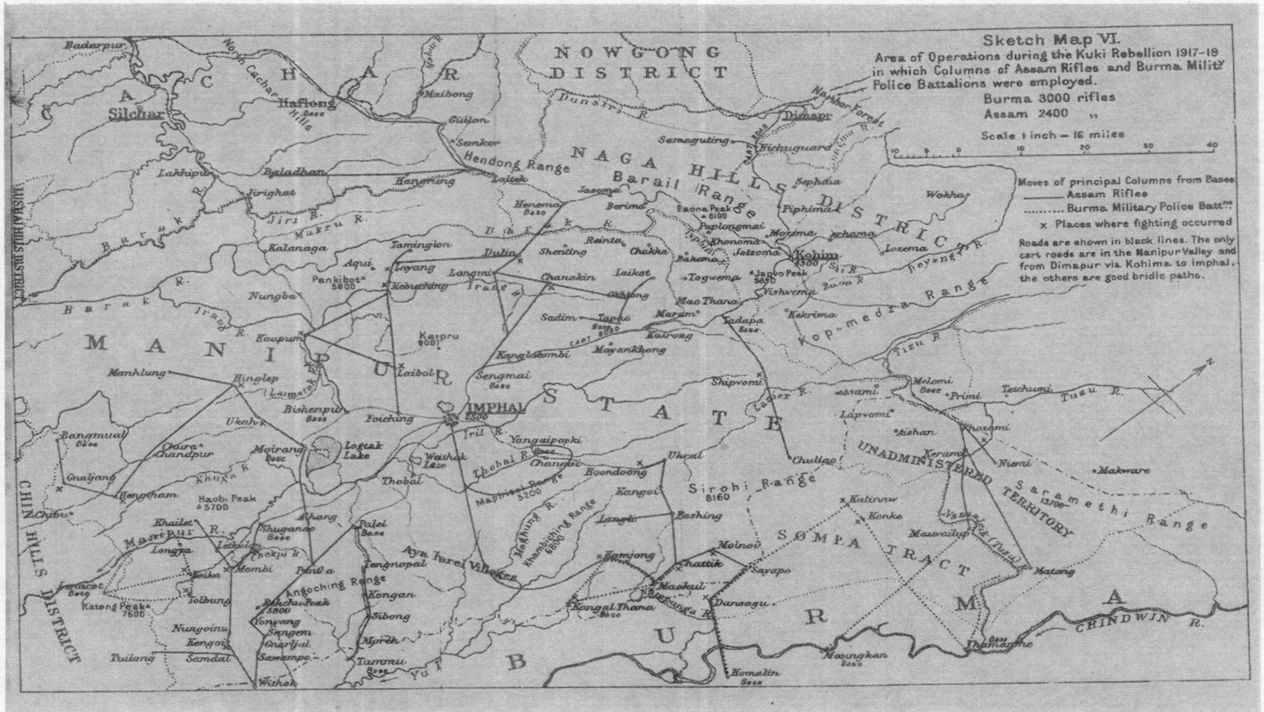
Sketch Map VI.
Area of Operations during the Kuki Rebellion 1917–19 in which Columns of Assam Rifles and Burma Milit'y Police Battalions were employed.
Burma 3000 rifles
Assam 2400 "
Scale 1 inch — 16 miles
Moves of principal Columns from Bases
Assam Rifles
Burma Military Police Batt'ns
x Places where fighting occurred
Roads are shown in black lines. The only cart roads are in the Manipur Valley and from Dimapur via Kohima to Imphal, the others are good bridle paths.
NOWGONG DISTRICT
NAGA HILLS DISTRICT
CACHAR
MANIPUR STATE
BURMA
UNADMINISTERED TERRITORY
SOMPA TRACT
LUSHAI HILLS DISTRICT
CHIN HILLS DISTRICT
Barail Range
Hendong Range
Sirohi Range
Angoching Range
Kop-medza Range
Saramethi Range
Silchar
Haflong
Dimapur
Kohima
IMPHAL
Logtak Lake
CHINDWIN R.

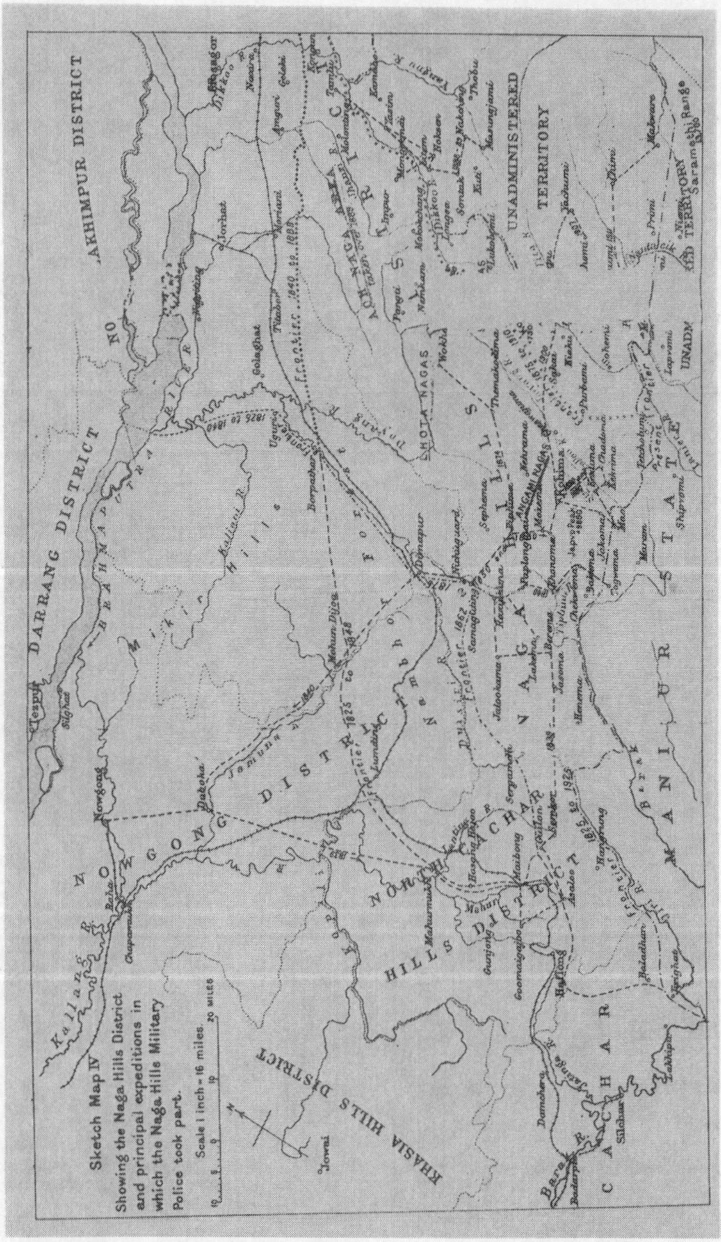
Sketch Map IV
Showing the Naga Hills District and principal expeditions in which the Naga Hills Military Police took part.
Scale 1 inch = 16 miles.
20 MILES
AKHIMPUR DISTRICT
DARRANG DISTRICT
NOWGONG DISTRICT
NORTH CACHAR HILLS DISTRICT
KHASIA HILLS DISTRICT
CACHAR
MANIPUR STATE
UNADMINISTERED TERRITORY
CHOTA NAGAS
ANGAMI NAGAS
Kohima
Dimapur
Jorhat
Golaghat
Nowgong
Tezpur
Silchar
Jowai
Saramethi Range

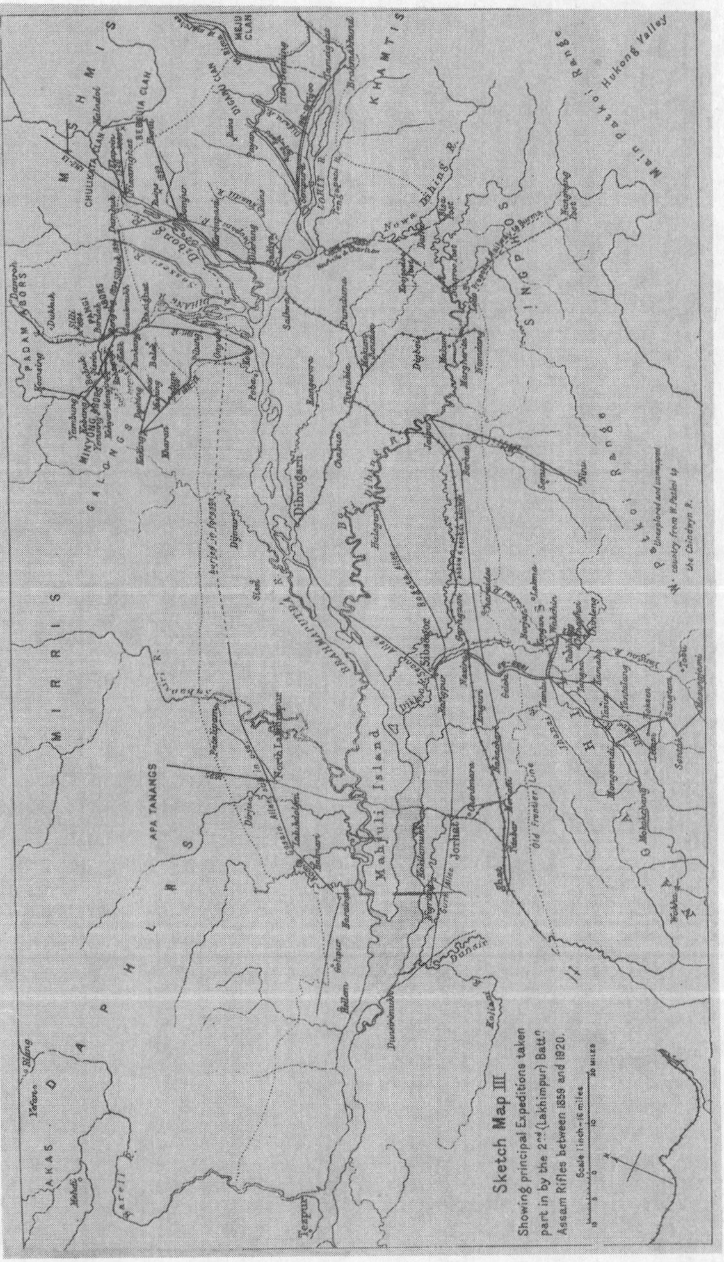

Sketch Map III
Showing principal Expeditions taken part in by the 2nd (Lakhimpur) Battn Assam Rifles between 1859 and 1920.